CIVIC PURPOSE:
URBAN DESIGN IN PRIVATE PRACTICE

JOHNSON FAIN

CIVIC PURPOSE: URBAN DESIGN IN PRIVATE PRACTICE

JOHNSON FAIN

Cont

CIVIC PURPOSE:
URBAN DESIGN IN PRIVATE PRACTICE

As urban design and planning practitioners who engage both public and private clients on projects of significant scale, the Johnson Fain team has naturally been at the center of issues regarding the public realm and the environment. Our predecessor firm, William L. Pereira & Associates, historically had dealt with projects requiring an interface between public and private interests. Much of the work done then seemed appropriate for its time given each project's political and economic context, but today, matters have become more complex, requiring greater reliance on research and user engagement to achieve the highest level of public good. In 1987, when the Johnson Fain office was launched, we felt comfortable working on complex projects, yet recognized that success with projects of scale going forward would require ever-greater attention to public issues and mitigations. This is especially true for clients who initiate projects through public entrepreneurial agencies and public-private partnerships, and for private developers seeking entitlements. In the interest of achieving a successful project for the client, acquiring their entitlements and the requisite community support, we believe it is vitally important to establish a collaborative process of engagement. Listening to the voices of increasingly sophisticated communities allows us to gain clearer understanding about how the community and the client can mutually benefit. In other words, an axiom for Johnson Fain going forward has been that all our projects should achieve some level of *civic purpose*, so that both our private and public clients and the end users share in the benefits. Our urban designers and planners embrace this outlook, front and center. We consider it to be a priority of the highest order, no matter what the nature of the client or project.

One consequence of Johnson Fain's quest for shared benefit that underlies civic purpose is a commitment to intensive preparatory research at the broad scale of environmental, programmatic, and contextual data pertaining to urban design and planning. Indeed, a significant part of an urban design project's budget is devoted to informing ourselves through research to understand the nature of the problem

GLOBAL PRACTICE

LONDON
PARIS
ROME
BADALING
BEIJING
DANDONG
YINCHUAN
TIANJIN
CHANGLI
XI'AN
QINGDAO
TOKYO
MIANYANG
OSAKA
CHENGDU
SHANGHAI
LUZHOU
GULIN
NEOM
AL KHOBAR
DOHA
YANBU
HENGYANG
XICHANG
TAICHONG
GUANGZHOU
MUMBAI
HAINAN
SAIPAN
BANGKOK
GUAM
COLOMBO
JAKARTA
GOLD COAST

to be addressed and the challenges it poses. For public clients, this often entails broadly inclusive interviews with decision-makers and end users alike, public site walks, and hands-on workshops. In approaching a corporate client's master plan, for example, the team might look internally at the company's core values by identifying and analyzing corporate goals, principles, and growth strategies, or documenting their market interests, and externally at public policy and regional plans, all fundamental to understanding the regulatory context for any given scheme.

Many projects entail intensive research on both programmatic and structural levels which determines the project's ultimate outcome. This is a process of involving a whole cast of characters in a project's conceptualization, not the projection of a single designer. Team members with broad experiences are essential to the process, whether in landscape, real estate development, public policy, building design, planning, or any number of other disciplines. The process is open-ended from the outset, and many questions may be asked as a result. We like to say, "No stone is left unturned." In the collaborative urban design process, everyone involved is searching, reaching for answers, and sharing ideas to arrive at an innovative and imaginative outcome.

One of Johnson Fain's unique strengths has always been effective collaboration among a tenured senior team of professional architects and urban designers and planners, each with individual talents and complementary strengths, all trained and experienced with broad interests and views of the profession. The technical strengths of the team, as important as they are, nonetheless need to be considered in the context of planning and decision-making given the dynamics of the public forum. For example, an urban design that offers flexibility and choice ultimately may seem antithetical to "top down" public decision-making. Plan-making needs to start with the question "whose plan is this?" In a democratic society, is a "top-down" urban plan — conceived by an urban designer for others and presented to them as a *fait accompli* — an acceptable interpretation of civic purpose? Or is a plan developed through a "bottom up" process — entailing *engagement* and community discourse about what is important for the users themselves — a better expression of civic purpose? While the latter approach is increasingly common today, the most viable solutions really come from a thoughtful combination of the two, where collaboration among the design team, the client, and the client's constituents allows for the most balanced process and equitable outcomes.

Urban designers in private practice have a special responsibility — and a unique opportunity — to interpret public policy, facilitate public expression, and account for private development constraints, but also to mediate among these factors in order to guide a process toward achieving shared benefit. Fundamental to that mediation is the application of a multivalent set of ten principles of urban design and planning — diverse in nature and touching on a broad range of social equity and environmental issues — which exemplify the practice of good urban design and are the subject of the present monograph:[1] *Urban Design as Public Policy; Systems for Collective Benefit; Deference to Others; Space as Object; Time-Form; Past and Future; Stepping into a Fluid Context; Balancing the Big and the Small; Sustainability: Conservation and Resilience; Not Formulaic*. As work on any given project progresses through the Johnson Fain office, the team draws upon these principles, each of which may be applied with different weight or priority depending on circumstances and conditions unique to the situation.

1 The ten principles were first formulated and published in tandem with a series of texts by William H. Fain, Jr., in *If Cars Could Talk: Essays on Urbanism* (Los Angeles: Balcony Press, 2012). Over a decade later, they remain relevant and ultimately central to the practice of urban design and planning in the Johnson Fain office. Not surprisingly, two shifts occurred as we began preparing this manuscript for publication. One of the original principles, "Timeless Systems" (like the "age-old street grid system"), was logically absorbed into a more comprehensive one, "Past and Future." On the other hand, what had always seemed to be an implicit and underlying theme in our work, "Sustainability: Conservation and Resilience," has by now gained such urgency that we reframed it as a principle in its own right.

Taken together, they provide the conceptual framework for an urban design and planning practice committed to achieving civic purpose in the broadest sense.

URBAN DESIGN AS PUBLIC POLICY *Create public policy frameworks to bring certainty to development decision-making. Such frameworks are anticipatory, allowing for incremental change while providing flexibility according to market conditions.*

There is a clear relationship between the physicality of urban design and the policy orientation of urban planning. Johnson Fain's work has always had a strong physical design basis, and yet, as explored here, physical plans of scale are achieved through well-defined policy provisions. In his 1974 book on urban design,[2] Jonathan Barnett carefully framed urban design measures as belonging to the realm of public policy, and it is useful to borrow that term here. Land planning in the United States is typically about resolving conflicts between public and private interests. Johnson Fain's urban design and planning projects are no different, offering what economists call "Pareto optimal" solutions, the goal being to achieve a sustainable balance among disparate or competing interests.

Zoning codes are becoming more and more form-based, which provides a broad legislative platform for urban design. In the 1970s, New York City pioneered the use of "special purpose districts" to stipulate zoning requirements and incentives addressing the needs of particular neighborhoods by prescribing vital land uses, for instance, or the conservation of noteworthy buildings for development in targeted areas in the city. A broad range of urban design provisions in these new ordinances were required along with setbacks, lot coverage, and floor area ratio (FAR). Elective improvements were encouraged by offering developers FAR bonuses in exchange for specific public improvements. With the Fifth Avenue Special Purpose District, for example, additional commercial office space was offered in exchange for providing residential and vital pedestrian-generating retail. For a project in the Fifth Avenue District, bonus incentives were reviewed by the Office of Midtown Planning and Development (OMPD) and the Planning Commission to assure they were consistent with the Fifth Avenue District Plan. The plan anticipated the needs for the area and implemented an "as-of-right" zoning approval process with baseline entitlements and elective and mandatory provisions that minimize overly prescriptive discretionary review. Since market conditions and values change over time, the elective provisions in these ordinances needed regular updating in order to be effective.

In California, during the same period, urban design began to be regulated largely through the environmental review process. The California Environmental Quality Act (CEQA) of 1970 required detailed analysis and justification for projects of scale with Environmental Impact Reports required in all jurisdictions, subject to review and approval by the public. Whether through as-of-right zoning or environmental review, urban design requirements imposed on a private development often get mixed with programmatic considerations and costs related to the underlying land transaction. Large building projects under single ownership and their economic success may favor a more "internalized" project when instead the neighborhood and community would benefit from a project more open and 'externalized' to its surroundings. Johnson Fain's redevelopment plan for *Mission Bay* in San Francisco and our master plan for *Westfield Promenade* at Warner Center in Los Angeles — both developed under single ownership — externalize benefits for their surroundings.

Like the special purpose district in New York, the State of California introduced the local "specific plan" framework as a zoning instrument to address the special needs of large districts or individual neighborhoods. Through the designation of a specific plan, urban design provisions for these districts and neighborhoods were tailored to the needs of multiple property owners in order to structure

2 Jonathan Barnett, *Urban Design as Public Policy* (New York: Architectural Record Books, 1974).

decision-making. This is the impetus for Johnson Fain's master plan for *LA Rivertown*, a twenty-seven-acre site straddling the Los Angeles River in a largely industrial and commercial zone under increasing market pressure to convert to residential. Concerned that residential market forces were displacing jobs, the City of Los Angeles embarked on preparing a specific plan for a district spanning both sides of the LA River and thus connecting the east and west sides of the city. Their objective was to incentivize property owners to retain job-generating uses and also allow residential development. Since our clients were among the two largest property owners in the district and were supportive of a program that established a good jobs-housing balance, they requested that we collaborate with the City in developing the specific plan. Consequently, our *LA Rivertown* project proposes a process for providing jobs and housing with urban design conditions applied to each.

The redevelopment of Mission Bay was a source of civic controversy for nearly forty years. Many of San Francisco's most prominent environmental and planning groups were formed in opposition to development on its site. Four previous master plans had all failed for environmental, political, or economic reasons, in spite of some receiving national recognition for thoughtful planning and design. Johnson Fain's plan became the fifth. It was approved and built partly because the team had the benefit of learning from the experience of others. The success of our plan was also due to the fortuitous alignment of government under Mayor Willie Brown, private development under Nelson Rising of the Catellus Development Corporation, and the University of California San Francisco (UCSF) under Senior Vice Chancellor Bruce Spalding, all of whom were committed to seeing the plan built. Importantly, many community group members who had weathered storms during the development of the first four plans were much more receptive to one that took into account their opinions about the public realm, especially with respect to public open space, and also demonstrated a significant commitment to affordable housing. The Standards and Guidelines developed in our office with community input "externalized" individual projects by emphasizing the streetscape, including public parks designed by Laurie Olin and several local landscape firms. The San Francisco Redevelopment Agency in charge of implementing the Johnson Fain plan was also instrumental in ensuring a consistent application of our Standards and Guidelines and thus spatial unity for the neighborhood over the years. Design for Development, the Redevelopment Agency's instrument for establishing development requirements, responded to the plan that divided the acreage into multiple parcels so that commercial developers could build housing, office, or hotel projects over time, depending upon economic conditions.

The urban design guidelines for *Playa Vista Phase II* on the Westside of LA were not unlike those Johnson Fain developed for Mission Bay, although they were executed under a City of LA specific plan and administered by the developer, Playa Capital. Detailed design guidelines were prepared by the developer for approval by the City, and then served as an addendum to the specific plan allowing projects conforming to the guidelines to proceed without further protracted review. Our Playa Vista Town Center was designed and built under these guidelines, as were over 2,600 units of housing by other developers and design firms.

SYSTEMS FOR COLLECTIVE BENEFIT *Establish urban design frameworks that ensure collective benefits, including the environment and respect for nature, providing an essential bridge between private gain and public benefit. Such frameworks can prevent projects from internalizing development benefits at the expense of the community, the city, and the environment.*

Systems for collective benefit can be both programmatic and structural: innovative plans can arise from both. Programmatic benefits are conveyed through a plan's program, often by the types and mix of land uses. For instance, Johnson Fain's plan for the *West LA Veterans Administration* introduces a much broader range of land uses and services than originally envisioned by the VA, which was primarily focused on permanent supportive housing for the broader homeless veteran population. The plan proposes amenities and services that address the needs of the region's greater veteran population, including a veterans Town Hall or meeting center, a recreation building with a gym and bowling alley, a digital media library, art labs and galleries, and an outdoor café, all organized around a central plaza that acts as the center for the entire property. The plan also proposes a district for education and job training for all veterans as they transition from military service back into civilian life.

Our San Francisco *YMCA Piers* has similar programmatic benefits. Although the idea of including a YMCA facility within a maritime retail project was considered unusual, it was enthusiastically supported by the public during Port Authority hearings. An overwhelming majority of stakeholders from all corners of San Francisco turned out to support the project and argued how the new YMCA would provide access to the waterfront for residents from all neighborhoods of the city. The Port Authority approved the project, recognizing the civic purposes it served and the collective benefits it offered.

Structural benefits are physical and more tangible than programmatic ones. Our *LA Greenways* regional open space and development plan, for example, adds a new structural system to the fabric of Metropolitan LA based upon a framework using many of the region's ubiquitous utility corridors, including abandoned rail lines, power easements, the new Metro rail system, and reclaimed streets, as well as the LA River and its tributaries. Like the street system, freeways, and transit system, *LA Greenways* provides an open space armature that connects the region's neighborhoods with much needed public-accessible open space. Where the open space framework crosses public transit and there is available land, the intersection marks a location for intensification of the region. The structure of the plan is physical and transformative and offers new collective benefits in common open space and sensible development as a vision for the future of the city. Our *LA Rivertown* project was effectively a case study to test the provisions of a much larger City of LA initiative in the works at the time, the Cornfield Arroyo Seco Specific Plan, which looked at the entire district and was far-reaching beyond the scope of the *LA Rivertown* development per se. Similarly, Johnson Fain's master plan for the 3.5-mile *Highway 111 Corridor* has been transformative for the city of Indian Wells, adding a structural landscape armature to the image of the city. The City Council voted to change zoning of this section of Highway 111 from "Highway Commercial Use" to "Landscape and Residential Use", thus establishing the programmatic premise of no commercial uses along the corridor. This triggered a lawsuit against the City by commercial property owners who had expected to develop their properties as "strip" retail. The City and its homeowners prevailed, and the landscape corridor was built as planned, reinforcing the city's distinct identity as a collective benefit for the entire community.

Johnson Fain's winning submittal for an international urban design competition to master plan the *Beijing Central Business District* incorporated and adapted the structural framework of the old city's grid of *hutongs*, narrow pedestrian and cart paths first laid out in the late thirteenth century. This traditional grid structure remains important in offering predictability for the rising class of entrepreneurs experimenting with private enterprise and democratic reforms in China: effectively, the grid provides equal access. Weiming Lu, who chaired the jury that selected our plan, noted that it was chosen because it "had a clear and comprehensible structure that could be easily implemented."[3] From our point of view, the plan facilitated the aggressive new development sought by the City of Beijing, but it also retained for residents the character and utility of the historic city through its structural organization.

3 Weiming Lu, personal communication with William H. Fain, Jr., 1999.

DEFERENCE TO OTHERS *Establish frameworks that allow others to act. Instead of viewing pluralism as mega-buildings with a variety of expressions, pluralism should be seen as an inclusive decision-making and development process, wherein many individuals are enabled to act. By means of deferential frameworks, urban designers can design cities without designing buildings. The success of an urban design plan should be measured by how well others can act.*

Urban designers must establish an appropriate balance between creating a plan that meets the general standards of public policy and professional practice and enabling developers and users to engage meaningfully in determining the outcome. This balancing act at times requires the urban designer to guide rather than direct the process and to listen carefully to stakeholders at every level. In a democracy, designing cities requires a process of engagement that is often as important as the outcome. Engagement gives people the opportunity to express opinions and to see how they are translated into action through the plan. Not only is the success of an urban design plan measured by how well citizens and key constituents are able to claim ownership of it, but also, once it is adopted, how well it defines a future image of the city that enables future actors to infill their projects within the structure of the plan. Indeed, the success of an urban design plan can be measured by how well it enables developers and users to act over time.

Johnson Fain's *Hemisfair Park Redevelopment* master plan for the City of San Antonio, Texas, was largely conceptualized with local citizen participation in deference to over 2,000 local households displaced and disenfranchised when their neighborhood was razed to make way for the 1968 World's Fair. Over decades, the loss of housing and public amenities remained unaddressed, as opportunistic incremental development was allowed to go forward. To engage the community in the process, we initiated and facilitated a series of seven public workshops and listened to residents' responses to questions like, "What makes San Antonio a great place to live?" "What would make it better?". Each workshop built upon the previous one, with participants generating 28 alternative concepts that break-out group leaders presented to the community. Successive workshop sessions reduced the number to seven, and eventually winnowed it to a single scheme that served the interests of the city's residents with a focus on housing and the introduction of a central park and a system of pocket parks throughout the city. Ultimately, the plan was submitted to the San Antonio City Council with no community objections, and the vote in favor was unanimous.

Like San Antonio in Texas, Culver City on the Westside of LA has a well-informed and very active citizenry. With a new light rail metro station at its center, the City sought to plan the properties bordering the station and to find solutions to a historically difficult nexus of heavy traffic congestion in the surrounding streets which prevents residents from navigating their own local neighborhoods at peak hours. Johnson Fain's *Culver City Transit Oriented Development Plan* was based on priorities established by the citizens through an extensive series of nine public workshops, sorting out the vehicular congestion and introducing new infrastructure, incorporating many of the ideas and solutions proposed by members of the community themselves.

SPACE AS OBJECT *Reverse our obsession with building form, so that urban space is the predominant form to be measured, analyzed, and designed, with buildings evaluated on how well they create and support urban spaces and their activities.*

For urban design, spaces between buildings are as important as the buildings themselves. In fact, buildings should be evaluated for their support of urban spaces, their contribution to urban activity in those spaces, and their ability to connect and hold a city together. Well-conceived urban spaces literally form a city's connective tissue. They are containers that become places for acting out civic life, for pursuing commerce, and for making connections between here and there. As Tao philosopher Lao Tzu put it over 2,000 years ago,

> *With a wall all around*
> *A clay bowl is molded*
> *But the use of the bowl*
> *Will depend on the part*
> *Of the bowl that is void.*[4]

The form of buildings is inseparable from the spaces between them that they create, and both are equally important in the context of a city. All too often in suburban settings, roads and buildings are spread out and separated, blurring spatial clarity and meaning. Indeed, the two become antithetical. Urban spaces need activity to have meaning. Like Lao Tzu's bowl, they need to fill the "void" with activity so the city comes alive, fostering civic life. The term "sense of place" refers to the shape and activities in space that appeal to one's perception of the place.

While working on the General Plan Update for the University of California Irvine (UCI), the Johnson Fain team realized that the existing campus lacked spatial clarity. When viewed from above, William Pereira's original circular plan was bold and clear. Yet when the viewpoint was moved to a pedestrian's eye level, orientation and sense of direction was lost. Moreover, the earlier plan located the University Village far from the center of campus. To address both issues, our *UC Irvine Main Street* plan moves the commercial land uses of University Village to a newly formed street tangent to the circle that organizes the academic areas. Not only does the proposed street challenge the traditional "town and gown" relationship, but it also challenges the suburban notion of spatial separation by creating an urban main street populated with commercial retail and services that densifies and brings life and spatial clarity to the suburban UCI campus.

The importance of clearly defined urban space and what it means to a campus plan also informed Johnson Fain's master plan for the *Amgen* biotech campus in Thousand Oaks, California. When we began our work there, the client told us, "the culture of Amgen will happen in the open spaces between buildings, those outdoor spaces where scientists, technicians, businesspeople, and visitors can gather for the exchange of ideas, not only about business but also casual conversation and socializing about life in general."[5] Implicit in this statement is the importance of company identity and the sense of place that results from spaces being created by building arrangements, the landscape that surrounds them, and very importantly, the activities that take place in them. Similarly, Johnson Fain's state-funded master plan for the *University of California Berkeley College of Engineering* was designed hand in hand with our "collaborative science building", Sutardja Dai Hall, which houses the new interdisciplinary California Institute for Technology Research in the Interest of Society (CITRIS). The building and the outdoor spaces are closely related and designed to support collaboration between traditionally separate disciplines. The plan combines science laboratories and classrooms with café-like spaces facing outdoor terraces that are oriented southerly, basking in the sun's warmth, promoting casual conversation along with academic discourse.

4 Lao Tzu, *The Way of Life, A New Translation of the Tao Te Ching*, XI, trans. Raymond Bernard Blakney (New York: The New American Library, A Mentor Book, 1955).

5 Kevin W. Sharer, Amgen president and COO (1992–99), chairman and CEO (2000–12), personal communication with William H. Fain, Jr., 1995.

Johnson Fain's master plan for *Dreamworks SKG Studio* in Playa Vista, LA, responded to Steven Spielberg's concept for his twenty-first-century studio, a significant departure from the classic Hollywood studios built in the 1920s and 1930s. His idea was to turn the "backlot" into the "front lot." At the center of the plan, a new lake in a lush landscape with inlets and walkways amounts to a procession of views akin to tracking shots in a film — and indeed, the site could be used as a set for filming. The lake is surrounded by buildings for producers and collaborators. Whether at *Amgen*, *UC Berkeley*, or *Dreamworks*, the character and identity of the institution is synonymous with the space around the architecture that defines a place: the space is the object.

TIME-FORM *Treat urban environments as figure-ground fields that incrementally form and re-form over time based on the movement of people, capital, infrastructure, and resources.*

All urban design plans operate with time as a factor to evolve into one *form* or another. Cities form and reform over time based upon the movement and activities of people as well as the movement of capital and (especially today) the evolution of information-based technologies, whose impact on the spatial order of urban environments is still being understood. Urban form affects time, in that urban structure will affect movement within and around a city, creating flows or congestion; conversely, open-ended structures such as grids provide multiple opportunities for redundancy, flexibility, and phasing to change over time. Like space-as-object, time has form: activities in urban places require time, and in cities, movement is a manifestation of time. Urban design is thus constantly in motion, and to recognize that time affects form and form affects time is a way of understanding cities.

Jet Propulsion Laboratory (JPL) in Pasadena, California, may appear to be old and static, but in fact, the site is extremely dynamic and constantly in flux. The campus emerges and withdraws over time as projects arrive and depart, its activities pulsing by nimble expansion and contraction within the structures that comprise it, enabling advanced research and technology to flourish unfettered. While the open space armature provides clarity, hierarchy, orientation, and sense of place, the plan is flexible enough with its older warehouses, informal outdoor spaces, and large interior assembly buildings to adapt to changing programs over time.

Culver City's desire to manage movement of people and services within the city core to prioritize local movement over regional through-traffic lies at the heart of our *Culver City Transit Oriented Development* project discussed above. By sorting out local movement systems and deflecting the commuter through-traffic that disrupts daily life within the city, time is altered for residents and commuters. The plan's structural elements — roadways, bikeways, bus lanes, and pedestrian pathways — become conduits of time-form.

Similarly, as one drives along the *Highway 111* — the primary corridor running through the Coachella Valley in Southern California — a cacophony of roadside signs and attractions subsides as one enters Indian Wells on the western end through the symbolic "Grove Gate", where the natural desert landscape dominates. Exiting at the eastern gate, motorists pass through a "cut" in the large rocky extension of the mountain range into La Quinta, where one re-engages with a plethora of signs beckoning attention. The journey through Indian Wells over time gives form and identity to the city in stark contrast to other cities along the same highway.

One of the central ideas behind Johnson Fain's master plan for *Knowledge City* on the Interstate 10 corridor west of Houston, Texas, is to bring urban living to an exurban location. Since the owner is also the sponsor of Sampoerna University in Jakarta, education is the catalyst for the urban development of a 15,000-acre site. In the plan's higher-density mixed-use center, knowledge-based employment becomes a catalyst for growth. Education at all levels — elementary and secondary programs and a university campus based on collaborative degree programs that engage faculty from multiple universities — is tailored to those working and living on the site. In the master plan, educational buildings are mixed with municipal services and supportive land uses, including housing and retail. Combining urban and educational land uses, the time-form shifts from the typical single-family residential tracts to a very different pedestrian-oriented place where urbanity and education go hand in hand.

PAST AND FUTURE *Urban design solutions should draw upon what came before, but also anticipate the future. Projects are placed in a continuum somewhere between being and becoming. Testing future scenarios, phasing, and flexibility become important elements of project design.*

Research is a basic part of the process of developing an urban design plan — research on the market, environmental conditions, users and their characteristics, comparisons or benchmarks, history, and cultural phenomena. Uncovering history makes the planner and urban designer aware of the context within which a project exists and helps avoid the prospect of repeating bad acts. Urban design should represent the emergence of creative ideas arising from new ways of viewing the city, which are informed by the past in order to make progress.

Literally copying the past is questionable progress when there is not good reason to do so; however, sometimes reinterpreting conditions of the past provides good principles for imagining the future. Decoding the DNA of a place and then using that DNA in future planning locates the place appropriately within its context. For instance, most people regard San Francisco as a walkable city where pedestrians can move about the downtown easily because the city block dimensions are small and convenient. The DNA of our *Mission Bay* master plan was derived from the "vara" block, named for the unit of measure used by Jean-Jacques Vioget, the Swiss surveyor who laid out the first twelve blocks of San Francisco at Montgomery Street in 1839. At 275 x 412.5 feet, vara blocks are highly walkable, yet also large enough to enable developments of scale. Other factors, including the orientation of streets with view corridors toward the bay and the hills, publicly accessible open space, and public access to the water's edge, are all drawn from the nature of the city and its history and incorporated into the plan as it was adopted by the City of San Francisco.

Johnson Fain's master plan for the *JinJiang River Corridor* in Sichuan Province draws upon the natural and cultural character of the river corridor through the heart of Chengdu's agricultural region, where for centuries some of China's finest produce has been grown and harvested. The master plan redirects the City's plan for urbanization to the west, away from the valley, conserving many of its agricultural and agritourism resources, essential elements of its history.

Johnson Fain's urban design and planning project for the *First Americans Museum* in Oklahoma City began with in-depth research into Native American cultures and beliefs. Listening to and guided by the wise counsel of Don L. Fixico, Regents and Distinguished Foundation Professor of History at Arizona State University, we translated our findings into conceptual site plans aimed at understanding the past in order to project the future. "Circularity" became a major form determinant for the site plan as well as the museum building that followed, commemorating seasonal changes, natural forces, and Native and settler histories. Approaching this highly sensitive site through the spiritual lens of Native American cultures, the design team embedded in the plan a fundamental distinction between the concept of "Earth" and exploitative approaches to "land," effectively returning a despoiled oil drilling site to a natural condition that brings together the three ecologies in which Oklahoma's tribes originated: woodlands, river, and plains.

STEPPING INTO A FLUID CONTEXT *Understand the implications and influence of building projects within their contexts. Context is not a static setting for a project, but rather a dynamic situation reflecting ever-changing social and economic conditions at local, regional, and global scales. As such, an urban design intervention influences the situation it enters, becoming a context maker as well as a context-responder.*

Central to any urban design process are conditions that enable cities to change over time while also providing stability and security. The overall framework of a plan provides for choices within it; these are constrained by community values already in place which limit, but also inform the designer's options. Plans need to account for conflicting objectives: to minimize congestion but assure movement; to allow for growth and expansion but maintain local neighborhood character; to encourage social interaction but provide intimate, contemplative spaces.

Our master plan for *Jiangwan New Town* in Shanghai, a 2,600-acre site on the Huangpu River not far from the Bund, was the result of an international design competition. Four teams were invited to participate in a twelve-week charrette. The planning department of the city had no idea of what to do with the site other than to put it in the hands of the contestants. The Johnson Fain team was presented with a "fluid context" and had to adjust the process to arrive at an appropriate scheme, so elected to provide the authorities with options to engage them in the decision-making. Surprisingly, much of what was proposed has been built and can be seen there today.

Realizing that the city of Beijing never had a central business district, government officials in China decided they needed one to attract private business from abroad and to compete in the international marketplace. By transforming a dilapidated former industrial area, Johnson Fain's master plan for *Beijing's Central Business District* provides the context necessary for real estate development by using a gridded road system that enables incremental development to occur over time, much in the way business districts have evolved in the West. The irony, of course, is that other business districts in democratic nations with free markets depend upon sensitive shifts in supply and demand that can delay or accelerate development. China's greater emphasis on supply-side economics has led to many buildings being left vacant or underutilized. In contrast, commercial developments in the United States rely on demand-side economics and absorption rates that help to slow overbuilding conditions. Each context is different, and the planning and designing of a project must be fluid enough to respond to the differences.

American developments are also subject to entitlement processes that are sometimes prolonged and cumbersome. Although frustrating due to the time and resources these processes consume, engaging citizens and considering environmental reviews provide important checks and balances in determining what is an appropriate development for a given location. For example, at the outset of our planning process for *Mission Bay*, it was understood that the previous master plan had become "un-economic" because the low-density development was insufficient to support tax revenues necessary to retire the bonds earmarked for building the infrastructure. The Johnson Fain team drafted the master plan over a nine-month period, so that basic plan parameters could be determined beforehand to arrive at development costs and revenues to ensure that the project would be economically feasible. The twelve-month public workshop process that followed was very important in terms of refining and confirming the plan, but the project economics were solid going into that process, and they remained intact.

Our redevelopment plan for *Hemisfair* in San Antonio was organized by a publicly funded authority of the City, which meant that the plan could be broad in scope and less dependent upon a return on investment, unlike Mission Bay. It became evident early in the process that the citizens could themselves be entrusted with a substantial role in planning the property. Although opinions differed at times, the public showed a willingness to discuss and work toward consensus in the workshop setting. For both *Mission Bay* and *Hemisfair*, our team had to adjust the urban design approach to the fluid context of each project setting in order to arrive at a master plan that was appropriate for each respective city.

BALANCING THE BIG AND THE SMALL *Good urban design balances a city's need for both big ideas and opportunities for countless small actions. For example, New York has benefitted from the work of Robert Moses and the advocacy of Jane Jacobs in becoming a great city.*

Having said this, large development projects in parts of low-scale cities with vital neighborhoods can be inappropriate and disruptive. Yet neighborhoods need to be connected and regions need to be accessible as cities change and grow. In a market-driven democracy, small action changes happen continually and enabling and fostering them is essential for the vitality of the city. Urban design is most effective when it is a part of this. Designing cities, unlike designing a building, is more akin to designing decision-making frameworks within which others can participate in evolving urban places and form. "Bigness" arises from a desired need to control. Indeed, authoritarian regimes similarly see bigness as a way of exerting power and control of civic action. Large capital investments for the financing of large projects also often seek to monopolize potential market benefits, often by internalizing them. A suburban shopping mall is an example of this, as are some urban developments like the Sony Center in Berlin, Hudson Yards in New York, or the older Renaissance Center in Detroit. Such projects can benefit city revenues, but if walled-off and separated from the city, they become detractors rather than contributors. Government can also cause bigness in their development of large-scale civic infrastructure projects in the name of benefiting the greater population. But without mitigations, they can also challenge local neighborhoods. This ceases to be good urban design.

To achieve a master plan flexible enough to accommodate both big and small development projects, several of Johnson Fain's plans use a grid street system to divide the land. In the design for *Beijing's Central Business District*, the plan's grid network of *hutongs* provides pedestrian through-block connections, while the larger grid of roadways divides the land into parcels to provide developers with flexibility in locating their projects. The grid provides the overall structure, and the intent is for this to be the basis for government development policies that are applied consistently and equitability. That said, the government broke the grid by closing some roads to allow CCTV to assemble a large parcel and build ten million square feet in a highly secured building that turns its back on the rest of the CBD. Other developments have worked within the structure of the plan and there have been attempts to build the plan's publicly accessible open spaces. As one American tenant commented, "it's one of the only places in Beijing that you can walk to places in the neighborhood."[6]

Our design for the *Westfield Promenade*, Warner Center, LA, also uses a grid to divide its 34-acre site into small blocks, since the previous development was one contiguous parcel with a shopping center at its center, surrounded by parking. The grid allows for small block developments with higher density while enabling ease of pedestrian movement with a broad mix of uses to support an active environment. As the property has undergone a recent change of ownership, it remains to be seen whether the city and the owner will use the plan as a guide for future development.

Our master plan for *Mission Bay* is also based on a grid that functions to divide 303 acres into small *vara* block sized parcels that establish a great degree of porosity within the scope of the development. When *Mission Bay* was selected over two other potential sites as the location for a new UCSF Bio-Tech campus, the Johnson Fain team worked with Nelson Rising of Catellus and Bruce Spaulding of UCSF to

6 Jack Rodman, personal communication with William H. Fain, Jr., 2010.

identify a site. A design competition for a campus plan within our Mission Bay master plan was recommended and sponsored by the nonprofit BALSA.[7] The winning scheme by architects Machado Silvetti with landscape architect Laurie Olin embraced the pedestrian-friendly *vara* block, so that instead of the campus becoming an enclave and deepening the traditional separation of town and gown, the streets of *Mission Bay* run through the campus to scale down its size, and more importantly, structurally integrate it into the urban fabric of *Mission Bay*, with unobstructed view corridors toward the bay and downtown San Francisco.

SUSTAINABILITY: CONSERVATION AND RESILIENCE *Designing with nature is fundamental to designing sustainable environments. It is foremost in how architects design for the future.*

Underlying all projects is the need to conserve earth's resources, an awareness that has become increasingly central over the years as we see the extent to which environmental dynamics change due to human causes. Environmental sustainability in urban design takes many forms, sometimes as an explicit program theme, and sometimes understood as one of a set of goals. Johnson Fain's *Chinese Whiskey Valley* project for a 790,000-acre site in the southern Sichuan county of Gulin (Luzhou) confronted a conflict between two major Chinese industries over critical water resources. With the uniquely pristine water essential to whiskey production under threat of contamination from coal-mining activity along significant stretches of the Gulin and Chishui Rivers, Johnson Fain's strategic master plan achieves a balance among competing interests by restricting land uses in the watershed and concentrating development where water supplies can be sustainably used.

The Johnson Fain master plan for the *"Seven Mile Sea" Tianjin Ancient Wetland Restoration*, a 400-square-mile site east of Beijing near the East China Sea, provided an environmental overlay on derelict farmland by restoring the wetland adjoining the sea. By accommodating modest development, farming, and river estuary restoration, the region establishes a sustainable balance between human activity and natural processes for water and habitat reclamation.

Conservation calls for the protection of natural resources, and although urbanization is so often seen as the enemy, thoughtful urban development can be a positive contributor to environmental quality. Architect Thom Mayne invited Johnson Fain to join the Morphosis team and take the lead in developing a regional conservation plan for a 6.5-million-acre site in Saudi Arabia that has been opportunistically exploited as farmland for centuries at the expense of environmental degradation.[8] The Morphosis proposal concentrated urban development on four percent of the site, with an urban corridor 2 km wide and 170 km long — with zero spread — accessed by a high-speed rail system with episodic development in and around metro stops. This enabled the remaining 96 percent of the land to be restored and rewilded. The comprehensive land- and water-use zoning strategy fundamental to our conservation plan, currently being implemented, is envisioned to enable a symbiotic relationship between intensified urban development and the conservation and rewilding of the natural setting. Future-use metrics for tourism, agriculture, and other potential impacts are determined by a transect analysis of seven categories relating to the natural phenomena of the site and sensitivity classifications established by the International Union for Conservation of Nature (IUCN).

7 BALSA, the Bay Area Life Science Alliance, was founded by biochemist William J. Rutter, chairman of the UCSF Department of Biochemistry and Biophysics and a co-founder of the Chiron Corporation, in an effort to support the development of the new UCSF Mission Bay campus.

8 A fuller profile of NEOM has not been included in the present monograph owing to confidentiality constraints still in place at the time of publication.

Resilience, as a planning concept, is essential today for surviving tomorrow. It is a somewhat different environmental strategy implying defensive positions to prepare for a rapidly changing world. Planning for major droughts, floods, hurricanes, extreme heat, rising sea levels, and wildfires, to mention just a few of the consequences of climate change, must be anticipated. For example, much of the 15,000-acre site for Johnson Fain's *Knowledge City* in Houston lies within the floodplain of the Brazos River. Anticipating inevitable flood conditions in the future, the plan distributed development on elevated "islands" in the plain, with restored wetlands and more resilient agricultural uses in between. More broadly, regional strategies for resilience in this master plan involve the sale of wetland credits to compensate with new wetlands on the site for the loss of wetlands elsewhere in the greater watershed region.

NOT FORMULAIC *Good urban design offers creative conflict resolution, a process leading to customized solutions that cater to specific local needs. For public agencies, local market conditions determine methods for implementation, which may require different types and degrees of public intervention. This determines the appropriate urban design framework for a local site.*

In developing alternatives for our *Jiangwan New Town* in Shanghai, three diverse ideas were presented projecting three different futures for the projected addition to the city. There was nothing formulaic about them, and features from all three were incorporated into the "Good Life City" scheme selected by public officials. The *First Americans Museum* project, on the other hand, incorporates Native American iconography that is culturally distinct, with its references to circularity, the Earth and nature, and the history of Indigenous peoples; here again, nothing formulaic. The vast project for a *Chinese Whiskey Valley*, a uniquely tailored master plan for a vast 7,800-acre watershed, addresses a broad range of regional issues, including making one of the most rural areas of southern China accessible by high-speed rail, protecting rural family farming by limiting the expansion of nearby small towns, and promoting the expansion of the 1,000-year-old Chinese whiskey industry by protecting water sources that are threatened by the mining of coal. None of this is formulaic.

Approaches to the design of cities and regions will vary according to the given array of differing conditions, economic, social, political, historical, topographical, cultural, and environmental, such that relentless research and data analysis are required to understand the nature of each urban problem and how to address it in the context of a particular place. In addition, urban design and planning processes often become a matter of enabling community involvement in the setting of goals and visioning, as well as the physical planning through active stakeholder engagement. Given the complexity of the urban design process, the time necessary to create and implement plans of major scale, and the uncertainty of the outcome, one wonders how many challenging urban design projects are achievable within the lifetime of an urban designer.

* * *

The pages that follow present more detailed narratives and illustrations of the principles laid out above as they have been applied in the development of Johnson Fain's urban design and planning projects since the office was founded. They document more than thirty-five years of effort and include projects that in some cases span entire careers, from inception to fruition. Time is the ultimate fermenter of good urban design.

William H. Fain, Jr.
David Alpaugh
Juan Carlos Begazo

CITY CULTURE KNOWLEDGE REGION

Development of the 300-acre Mission Bay district of San Francisco — the largest addition in the city's history — presented an opportunity to marshal the physical, social, political and market forces of urban growth all at once, in contrast to typical conditions that unfold incrementally over time. Originally a marshland and later the dump for debris from the 1906 earthquake and fire, Mission Bay was repeatedly planned for redevelopment four separate times over a twenty-year period, consistently failing to garner support and, in the process, hardening the surrounding communities into opposition of real estate development throughout the city. In a bold move, the site's owners terminated the fourth plan because it lacked economic viability with its low densities and high costs. The new, fifth plan had to achieve greater densities and, critically, gain community support by being attentive to their concerns and unquestionably "San Francisco" in its character.

The master plan drew from historic research seeking the "DNA of the city" and found the "vara block" (*vara* being a Spanish unit of measure) used by surveyor Jean-Jacques Vioget in laying out the original twelve blocks of the city in 1839. The block dimensions are an efficient size for today's development types and yield walkable streets. The plan also adopted the layout of San Francisco's street grid, nearly always perpendicular to the Bayfront, enabling views of

MISSION BAY
SAN FRANCISCO, CALIFORNIA

Award

- AIA National, Honor Award for Regional and Urban Design

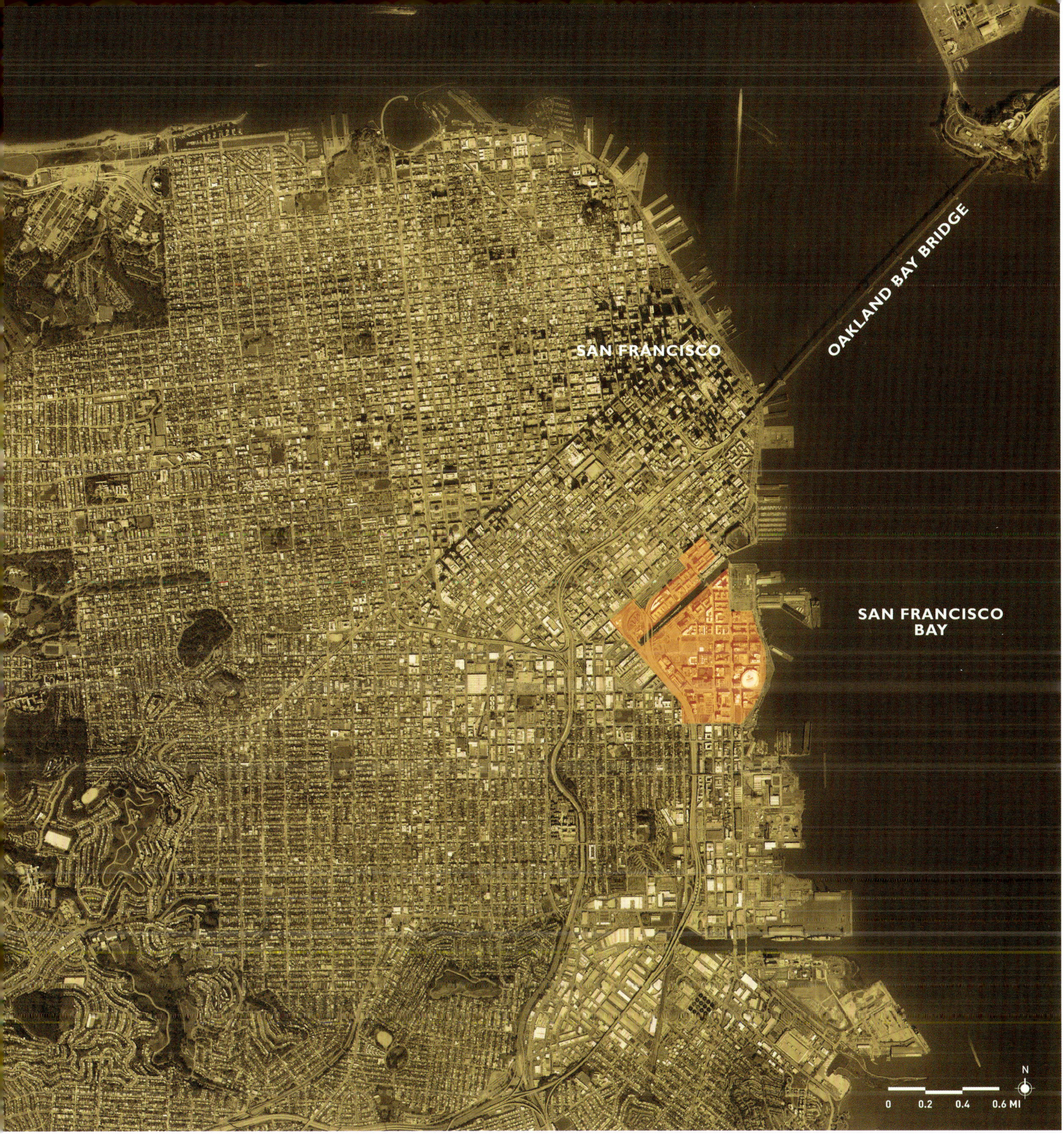

SAN FRANCISCO
OAKLAND BAY BRIDGE
SAN FRANCISCO BAY
N
0 0.2 0.4 0.6 MI

the water. A public open space network helped to organize the neighborhoods and facilitate public access to the waterfront. These formal elements of the plan aimed to provide authenticity to the new neighborhood's character.

The plan also addresses social and political elements in deference to community interests. Its public access and usable open space reflect public requests to support community use and civic life. A high percentage of affordable residential units mitigates the high cost of housing in San Francisco. Extension of light rail into the site makes the project a Transit First development. Mixed use development throughout the project ensures a walkable city. Finally, the city's mayor made it very clear that he wanted the UCSF Biotech campus in the Mission Bay project, and that's where it is. All other urban uses surrounding the university are integrated with the campus so there is no distinction spatially between campus and city. Mission Bay subsequently has become one of the most prominent biotech innovation districts in the country.

1993

2022

N
0
300
600 FT

CHASE
CENTER

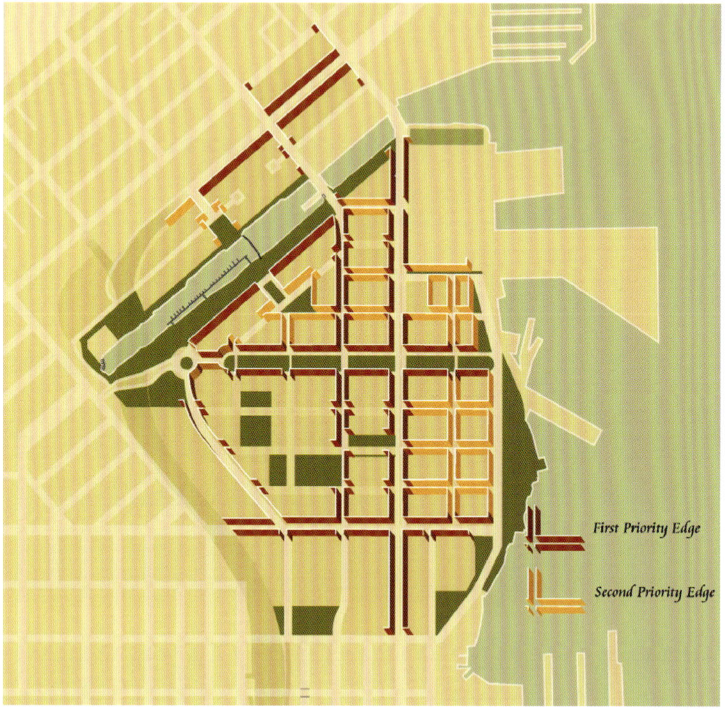

Streetwalls

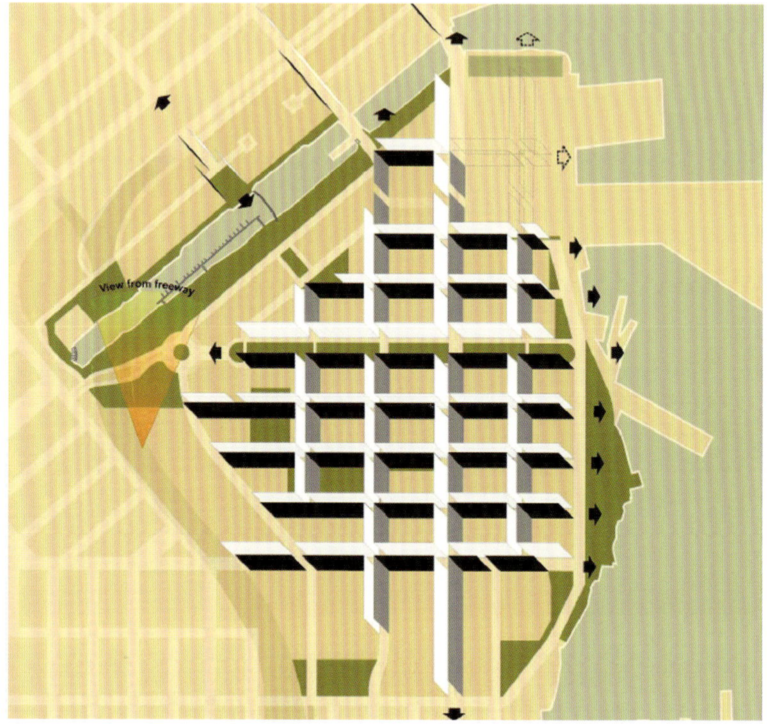

Streetwalls and view corridors

Walking distance to parks

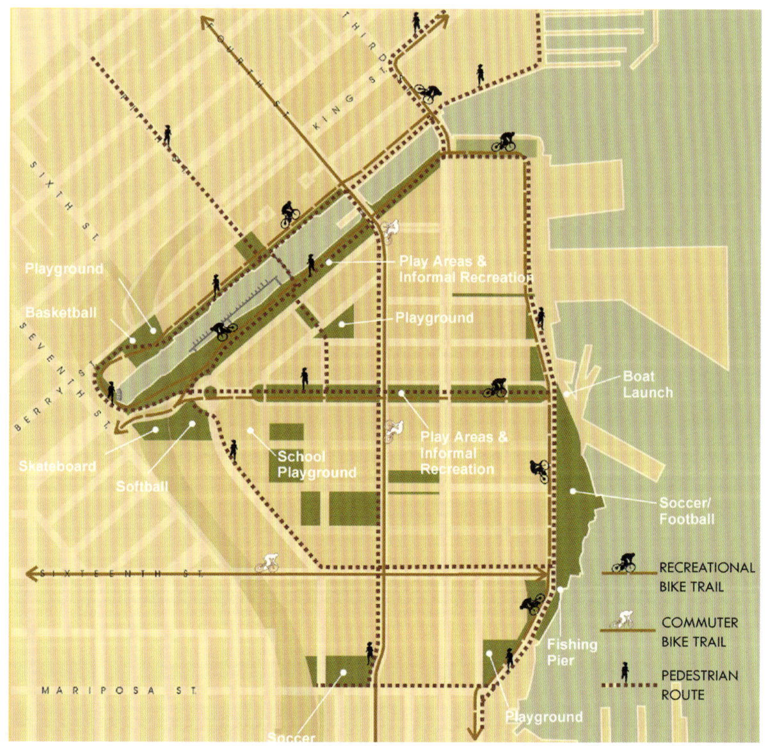

Open space

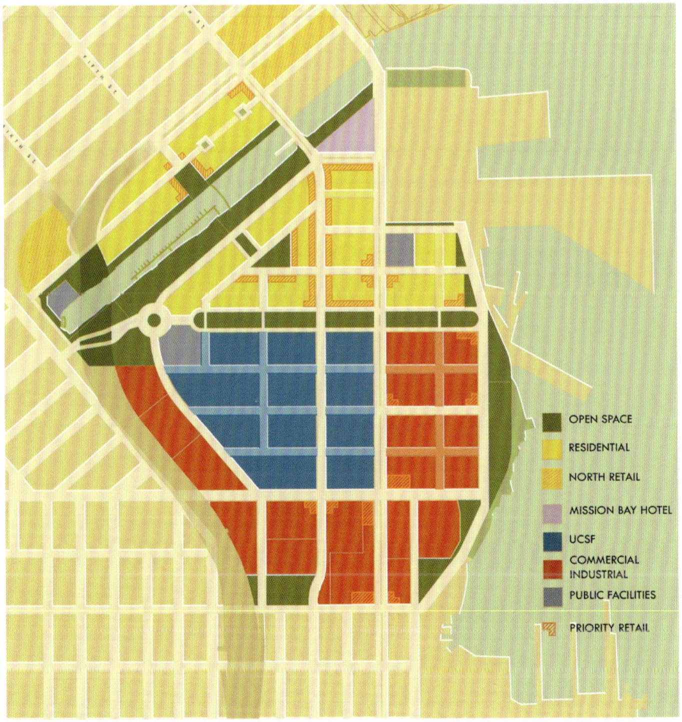

Land use

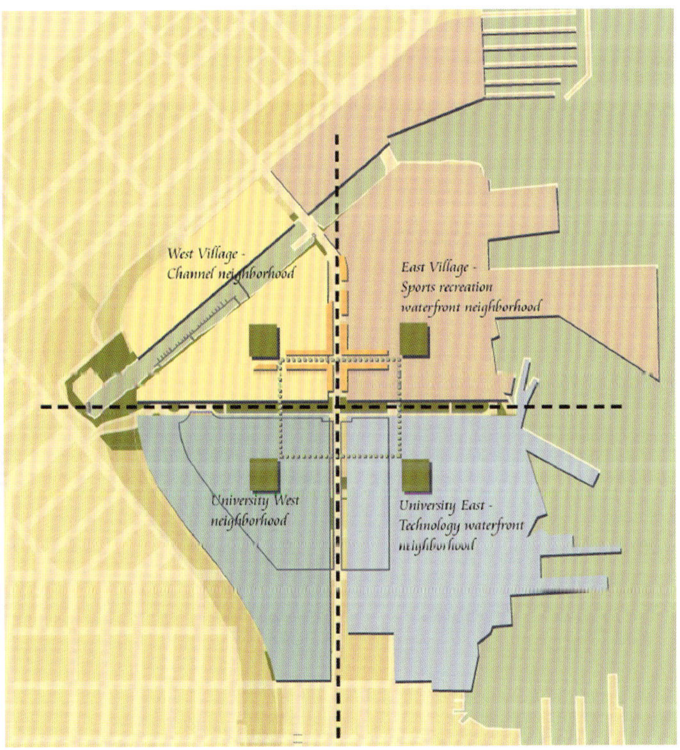

Mixed-use

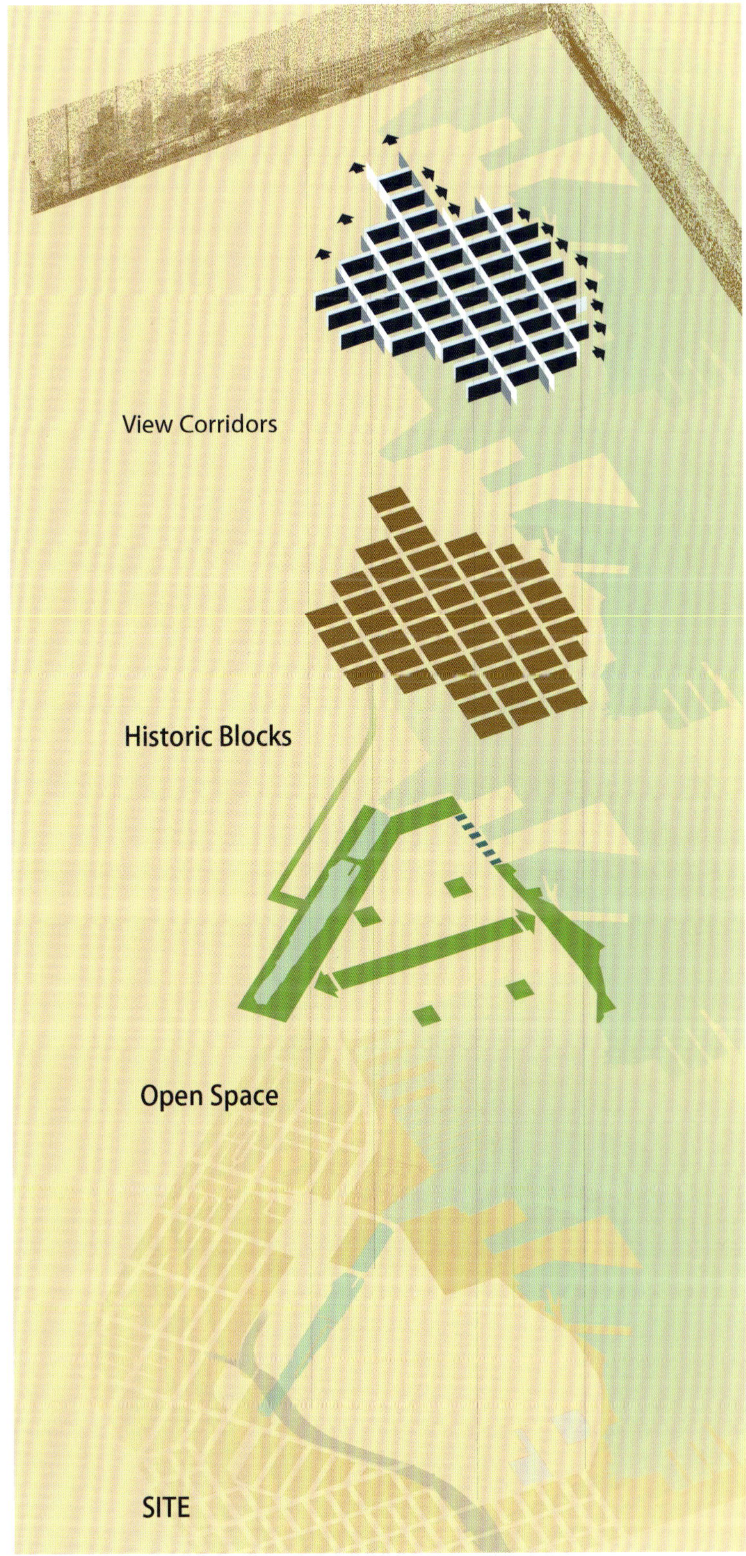

Urban design framework

Project exhibit

Public workshop

Public workshop — breakout session

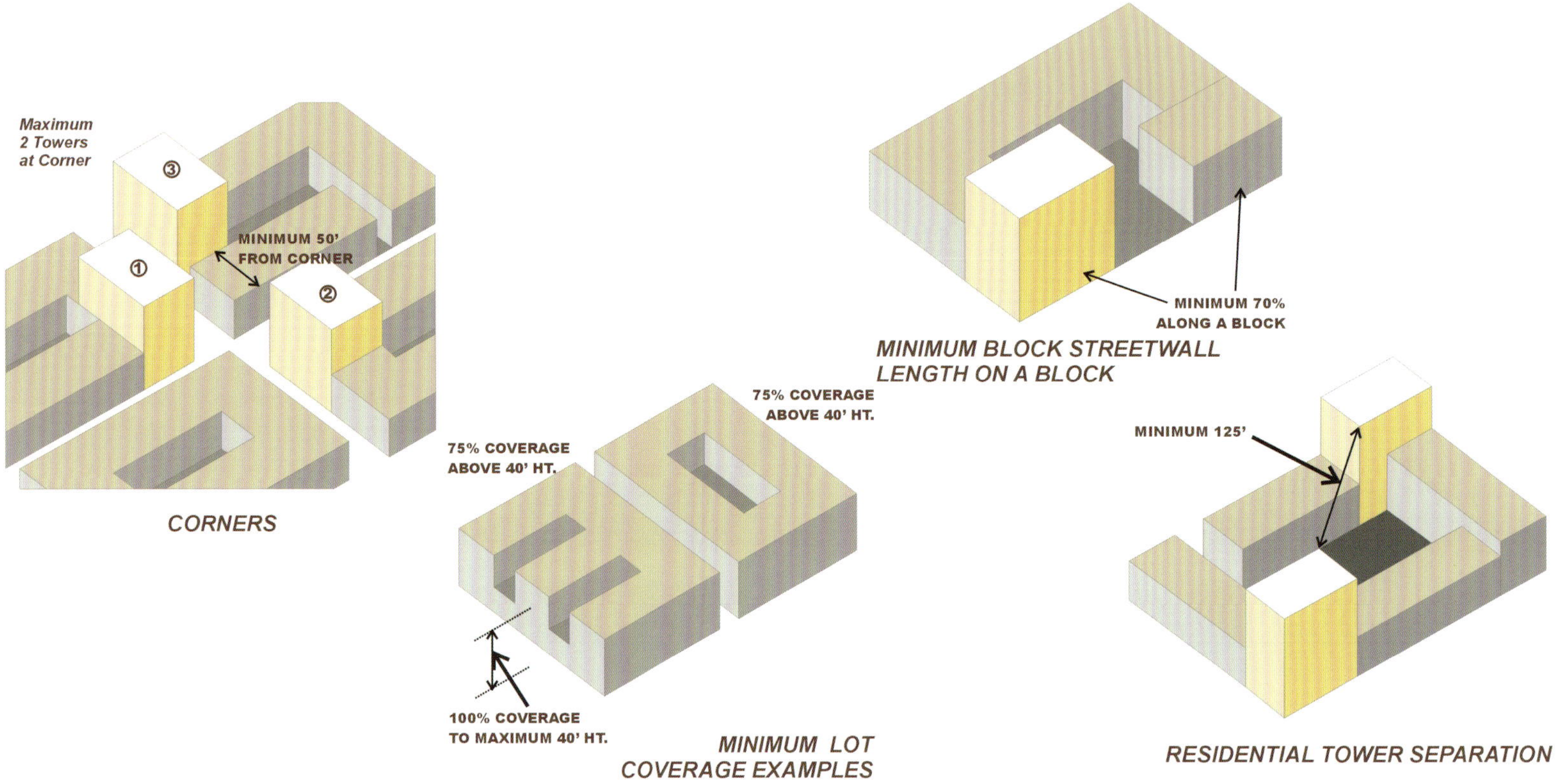

Urban design guidelines

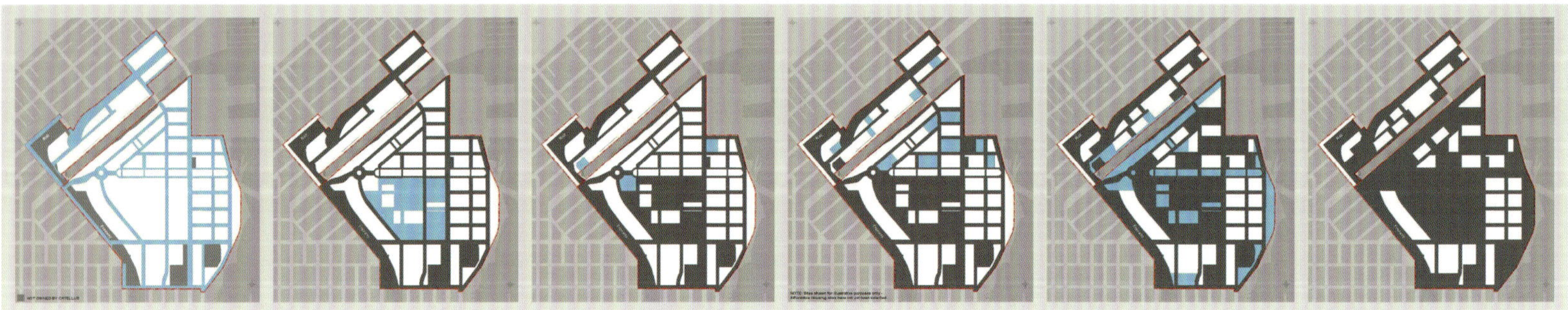

Streets 32% (82 ac)

UCSF 12% (32 ac)

Community Facilities 2% (5 ac)

Affordable Housing 6% (16 ac)

Open Space 17% (47 ac)

Development Parcels 31% (85 ac)

Land utilization

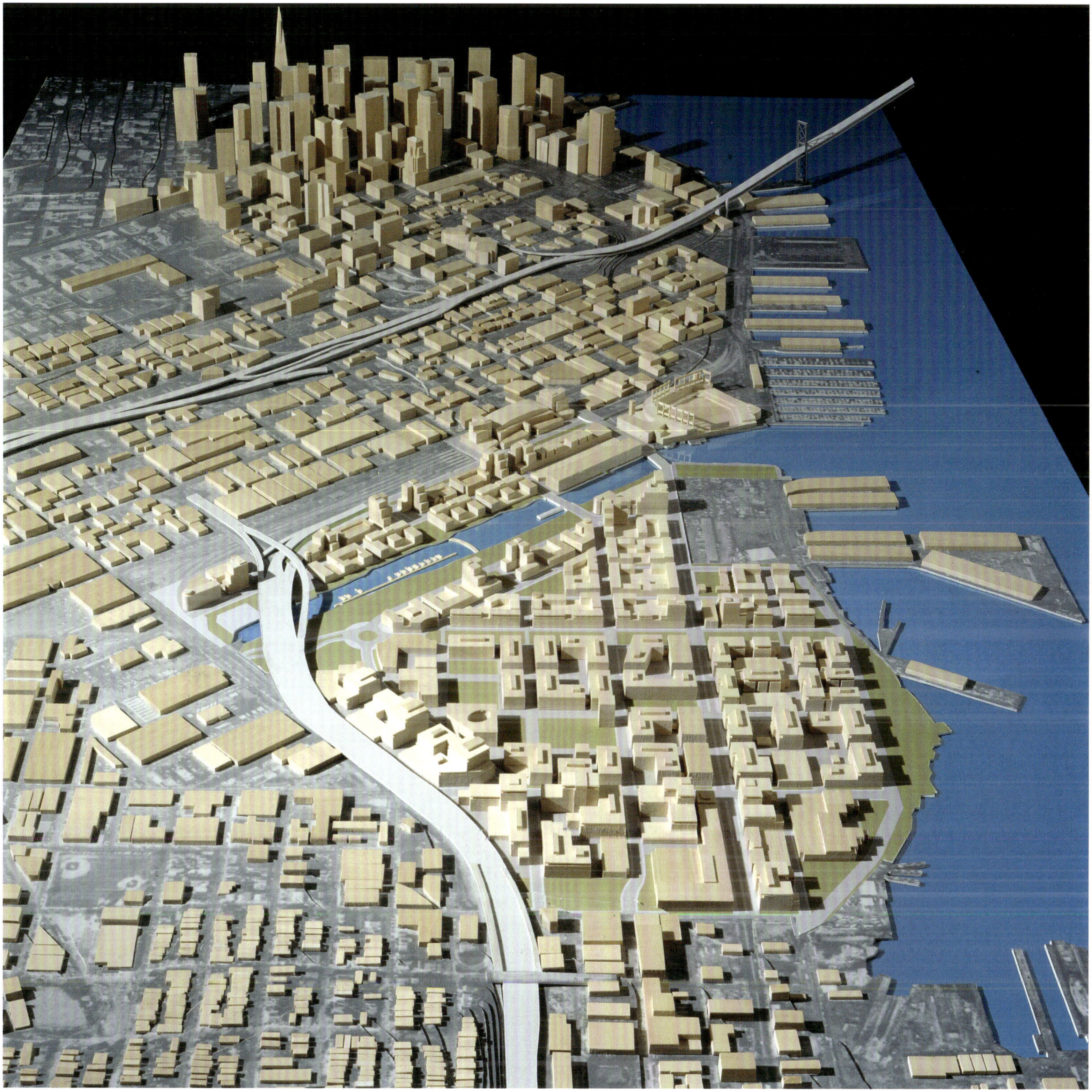

Study model

COME,
TAKE A SEAT

Mission Bay [illegible]

Mission Bay Kid's Park

King Street promenade

Mission Creek

azure
AZUREAPARTMENTS.COM

The economic reforms initiated by Deng Xiaoping in 1978 brought major change to China following thirty years of Mao Zedong's free market shutdown. The reforms focused new attention on Beijing, which never had a Central Business District (CBD). The government intended for China's capital to compete with world commercial centers and planned for a new Beijing CBD at the outset of the new millennium, with the goal of attracting new global enterprises. Civic leaders commissioned a plan for a four-square kilometer industrial site east of Tiananmen Square at the intersection of the Third Ring Road and Jianguomen Outer Avenue, an intersection known as the "Golden Cross." One objective was to protect the city's historic core from demolition or other compromise by locating the new district away from it.

Drawing from traditional Chinese city planning, the master plan divides the site into four distinct districts, each centered around a prominent public park. Each of these parks is connected to the others by four additional linear parks, forming an overall open space network. The four districts have a mix of land uses linked by canals and distinct rights-of-way for pedestrians and vehicles in the parks. The park network contains a "necklace" of premier cultural institutions. The plan draws from historic organizing principles that contribute to Beijing's distinct identity: lakes linked by canals; a strong plan geometry with axial views; large "super-block"

CENTRAL BUSINESS DISTRICT
BEIJING, CHINA

AWARD

- First Place, International Design Competition

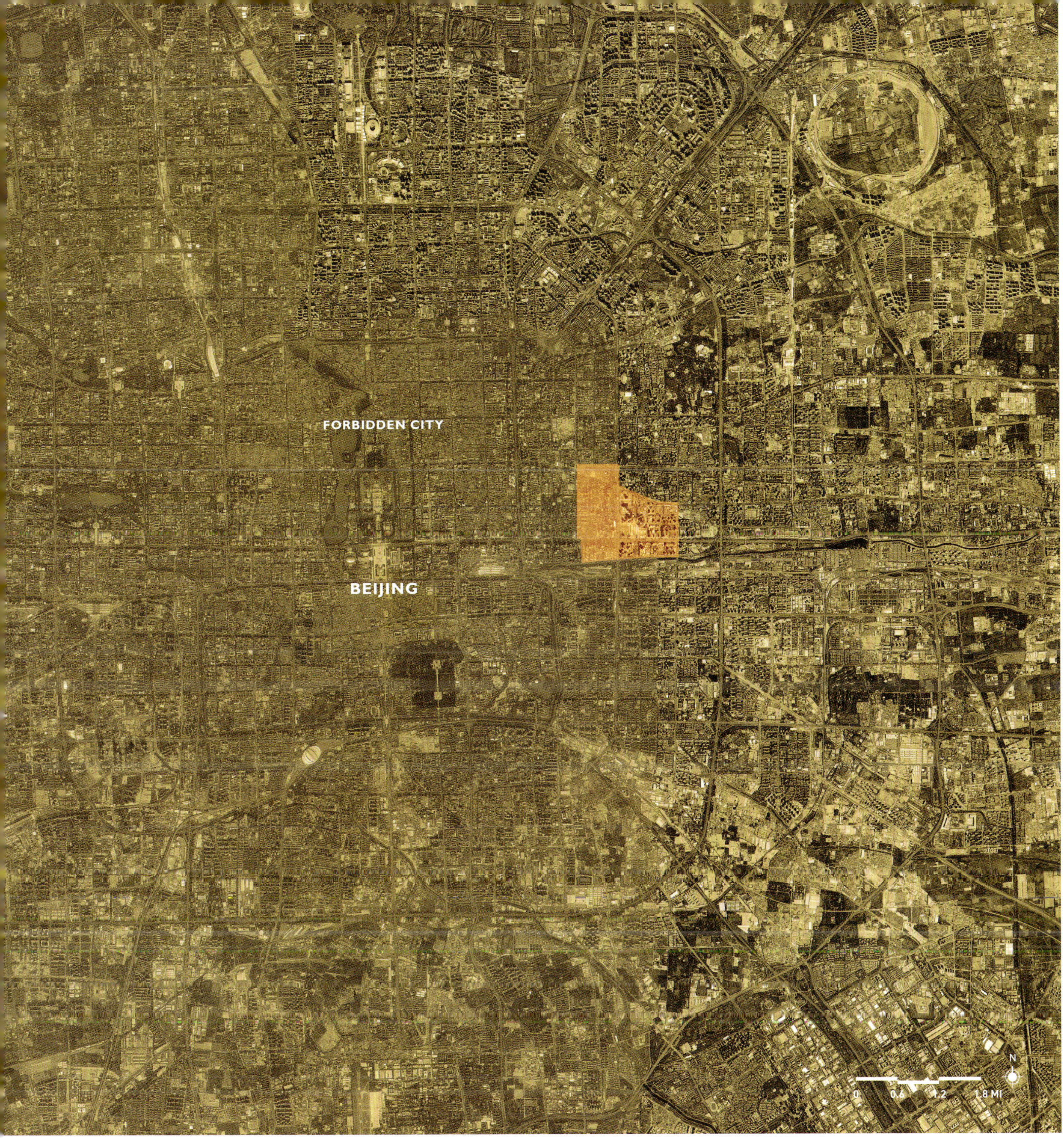
FORBIDDEN CITY
BEIJING
0
0.6
1.2
1.8 MI
N

development areas with through-block walking streets (*hutongs*); distinct gateway entrances; sun access that helps to provide heat for housing units during cold weather; and thematic open space. Respectful of its urban context, the plan also establishes a unique skyline for the CBD while fully integrating it with its surroundings. Since 2001, Beijing's CBD has emerged as China's primary global business address, drawing more than 117 Fortune 500 businesses in the financial, media, information technology, and consulting service industries. The plan proposed 150 million square feet of development and is nearly built out today.

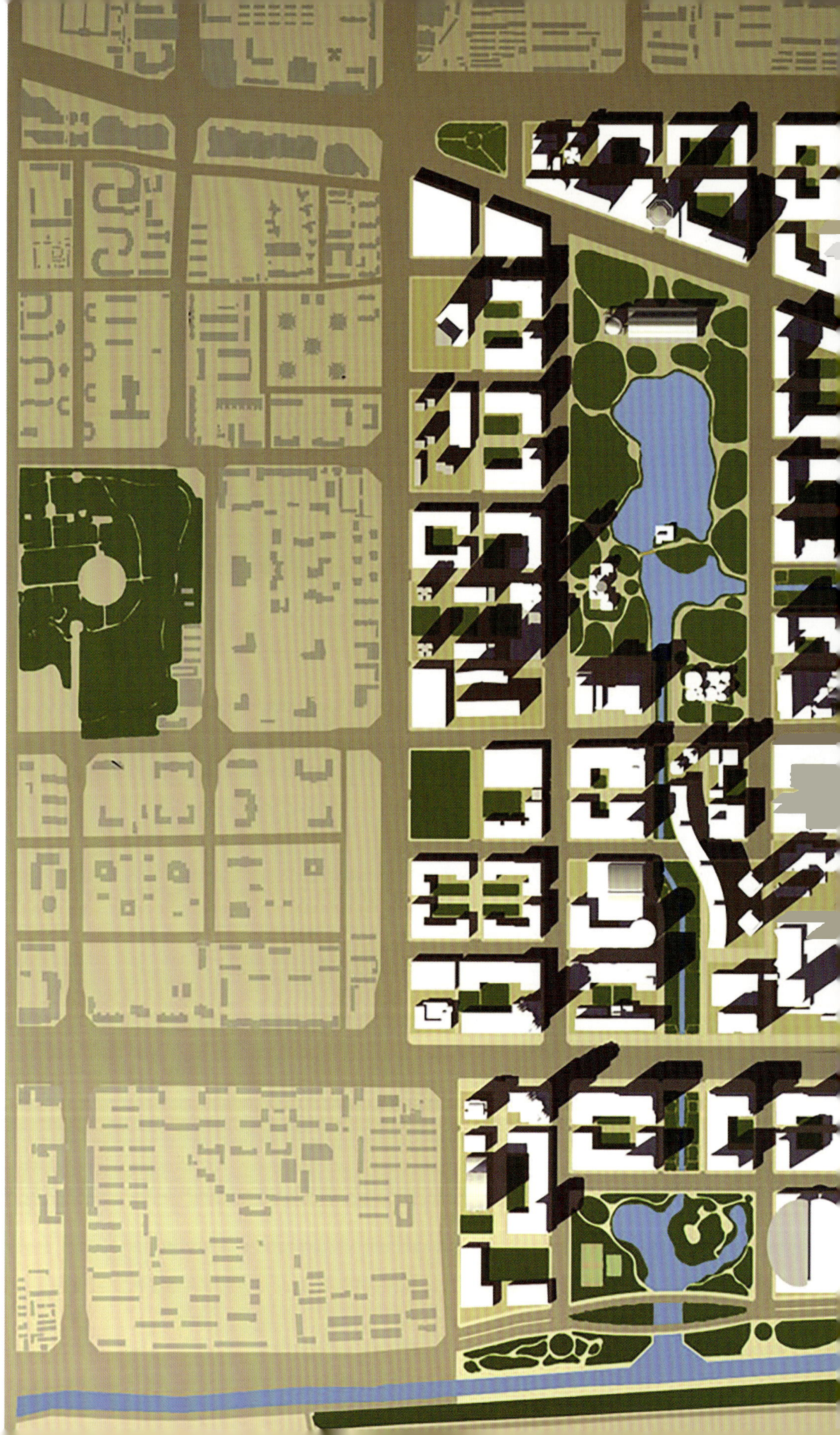

N
0
500
1,000 FT

YINTAI
PICC

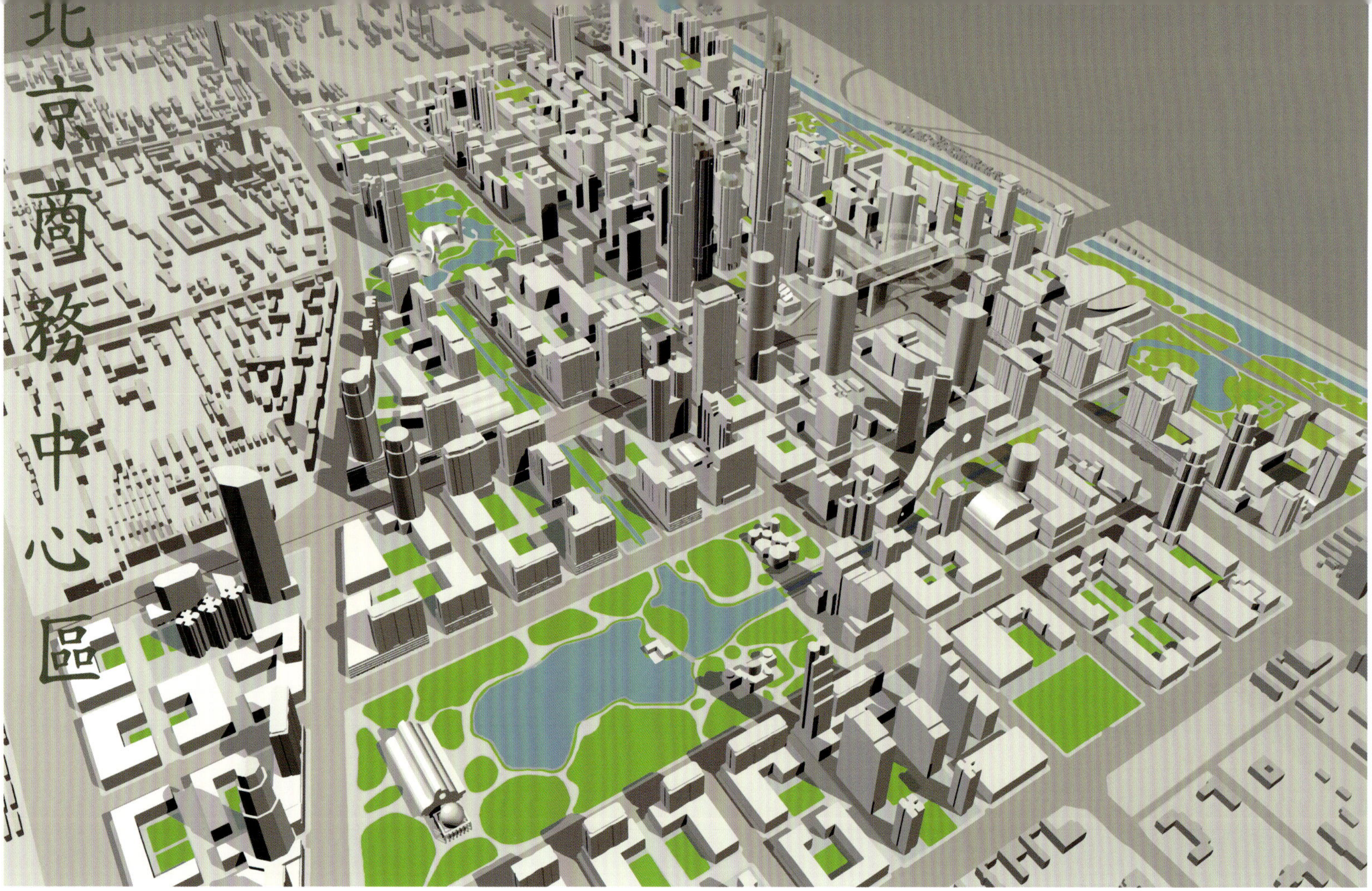

Model showing major open space system

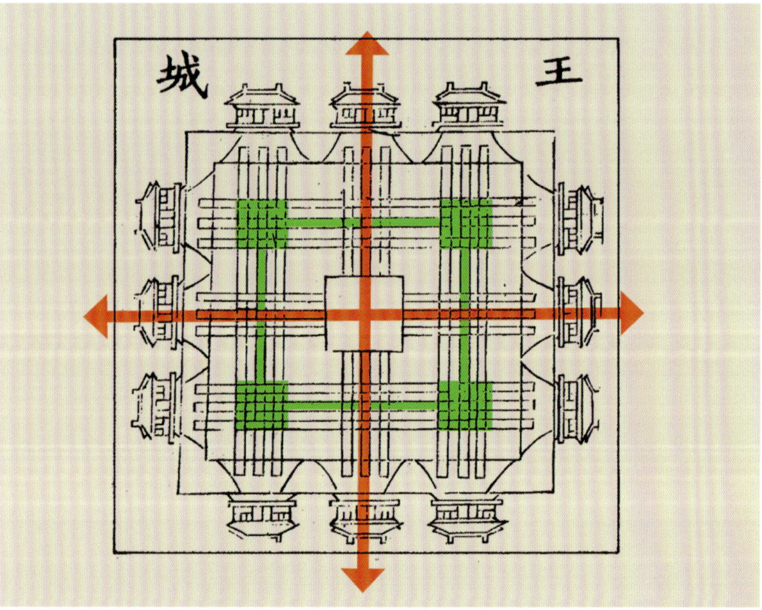

Historic organizing principles

“The Golden Cross”

Model showing skyline

Open space necklace with cultural activities

Landmarks

The City of Shanghai sponsored an international design competition, in which Johnson Fain was the only US participant, to repurpose a formerly separate and secured site and incorporate it into the day-to-day life of the city. To replan the site, a 1,000-hectare decommissioned Naval Air Station just north of the Bund along the Huangpu River, the government's competition brief required a presentation to city officials in Shanghai midway through a twelve-week schedule. However, the organizers did not give the planners a development program. The idea was that Chinese engineers would evaluate progress and make suggestions concerning site issues involving hydrology and mobility. Faced with no program, the team elected to develop three schemes with different programs and spatial frameworks for the midway presentation. With three concepts the hope was to ascertain the sponsors' aspirations and expectations for the site.

Each of the three schemes was built around a different organizing theme. *The Knowledge City* built upon the idea that education was a prerequisite to a prosperous future and included the expansion of a nearby university and two additional universities, and housing areas surrounded by small parks with "lighthouses of learning" (a form of high-tech library) in each park. *The Green City* built upon concepts of resilient environmental planning, focused especially on China's historic building code requirements for energy conservation and solar access for living space, providing for restored wetlands and water

JIANGWAN NEW TOWN
SHANGHAI, CHINA

AWARD

- First Place, International Design Competition

YANGTZE RIVER
HUANG PU RIVER
SHANGHAI
PUDONG INTERNATIONAL AIRPORT
N
0
1
2
3 MI

conservation measures. *The Good Life City* built on the idea that with increased prosperity the Chinese would have more time for a broad range of leisure activities having to do with wellness, recreation, and entertainment. We asked the officials to select a scheme and its corresponding program. After three weeks, the planning director of Shanghai sent a fax stating, "We like *The Good Life City*." This was the scheme that was developed further and submitted, incorporating some of the elements of the other schemes such as the universities, restoration of the wetlands and other features. Today, more than twenty years later, much of the plan has been built out.

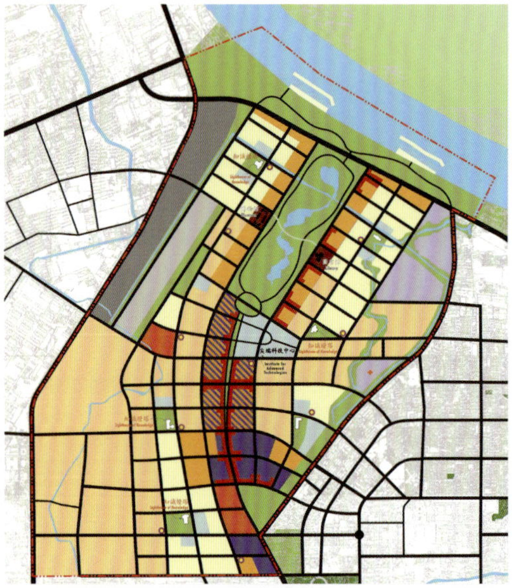

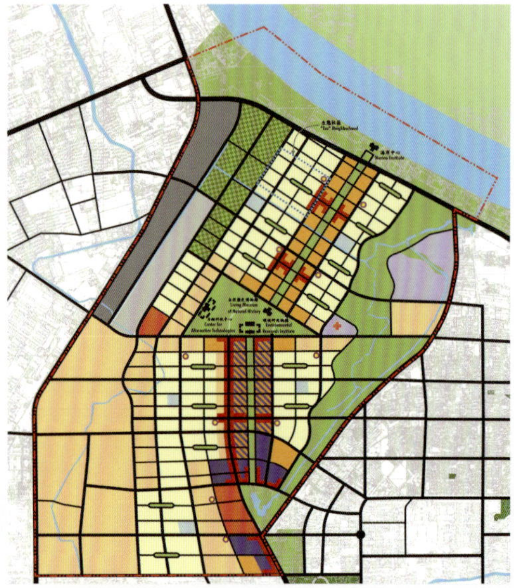

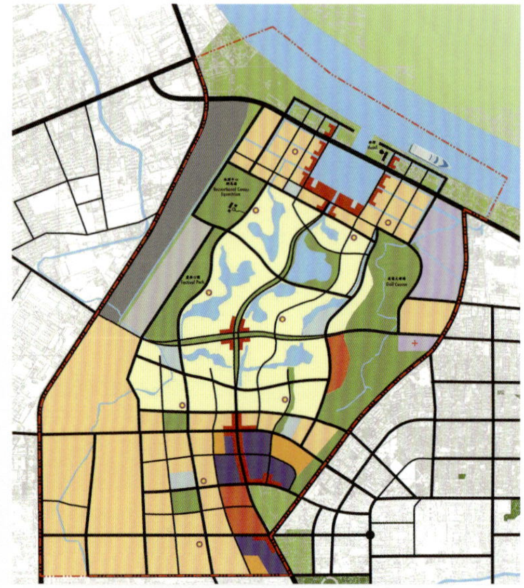

Alternative 1: Knowledge City

Alternative 2: Green City

Alternative 3: Good Life City

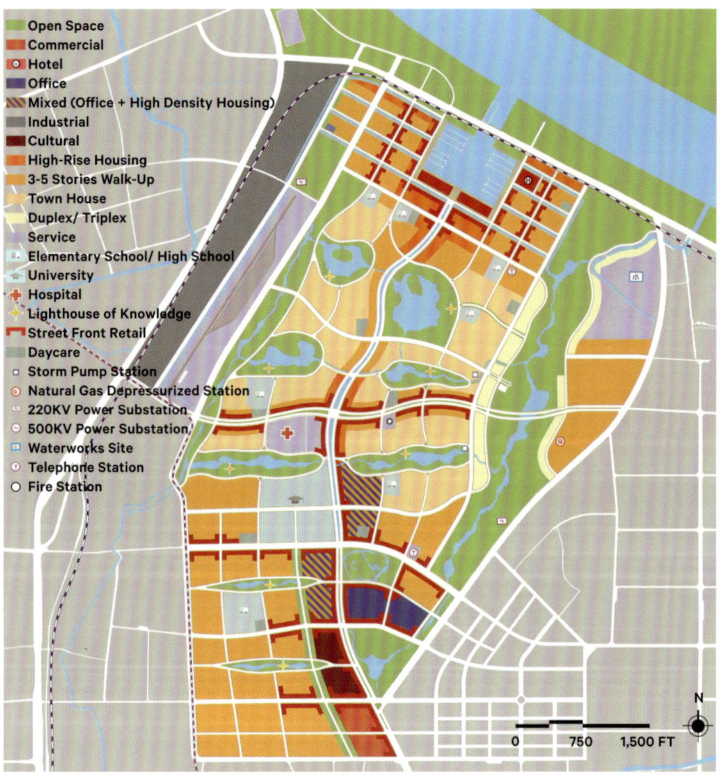

Land use

View corridors and streetwalls

0
1,000
2,000 FT
N

JIADING
OLD TOWN
SHANGHAI AUDI
INTERNATIONAL CIRCUIT

Urbanization and redevelopment of city-adjacent areas presents the challenge of transforming farmland and low density industrial areas into high intensity development suitable for the new economy. The Shanghai regional plan called for a satellite new town in Jiading, northwest of Shanghai and historically an economic pillar in the automobile manufacturing industry in China. Seeking to attract international companies to locate their Chinese headquarters there, as well as domestic businesses from the Yangtze River Delta region, Jiading New Town is envisioned to be "an international headquarters office campus" with a mixed-use town center. Assuming the Shanghai region will continue to expand, the Jiading New Town will be expected to absorb "back-of-the-house" corporate users as well as headquarters for small multinational companies.

The plan for the headquarters campus proposes an "Informational City," a dense urban core for a knowledge-based economy. The Informational City can be described as a "space of flows," electronic communication that is predominantly non-spatial. But it is, in addition, a "space of place" that draws upon social, cultural, and political references. The Informational City is planned to accommodate both with a 24/7 dense urban center with mixed land uses and building design to provide a vibrant amenity-rich and hyper-

JIADING NEW TOWN
SHANGHAI, CHINA

active streetscape. An active public pedestrian environment helps to facilitate communication and frequent encounters. Informal and formal discourse helps to encourage collaborative work environments that promote entrepreneurship and creativity. The plan emphasizes the importance of establishing world class educational institutions for all educational levels, and requires that urban infrastructure, buildings, and the extensive open space system be designed and developed under the most rigorous principles of environmental sustainability.

Land use

OFFICE / RESIDENTIAL/ HOTEL
COMMERCIAL
EDUCATION
OPEN SPACE
EDUCATION RESEARCH
CONVENTION CENTER
RESIDENTIAL
WATER
MIXED-USE COMMERCIAL / RESIDENTIAL
CIVIC / CULTURAL
RELIGIOUS

Master plan

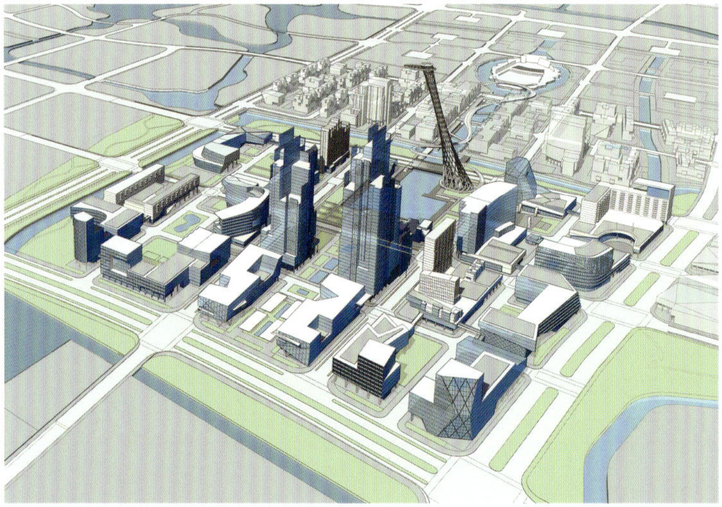

Photovoltaic facades

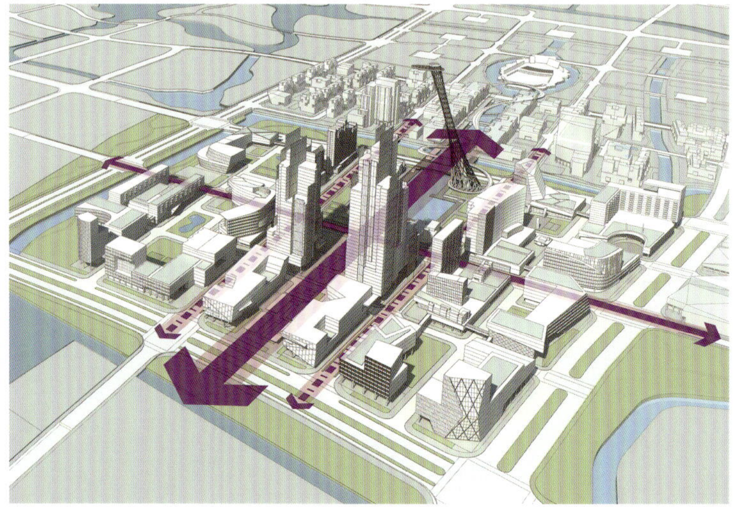

Organizational axis

Skyline

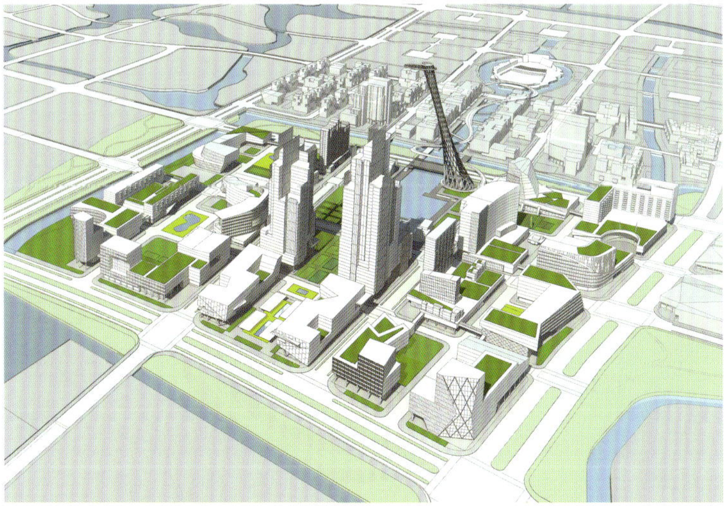

Open space network

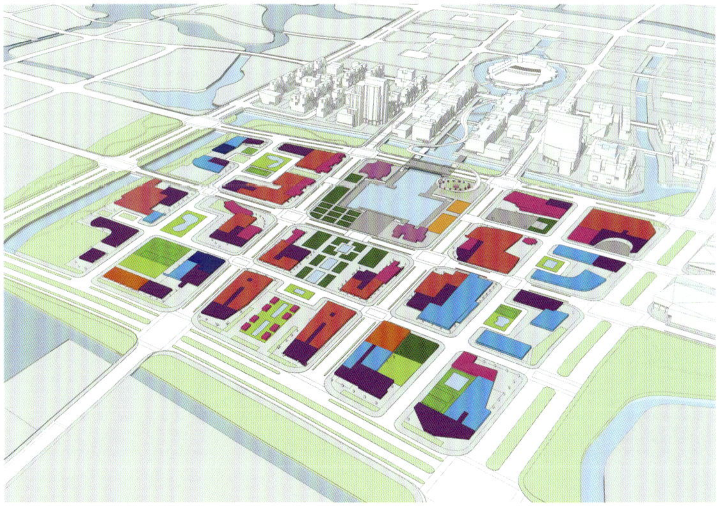

Ground floor uses

As cities grow, their traditional centers and districts often shift and change in their balance of uses and intensities. In Mumbai, the primary financial center of India, the two established business districts of Nariman Point and Bandra Kurla are reaching full capacity. The city elected to address this fluid context by developing a third financial district at Wadala, an area halfway between the historic Fort district on the south and the Mumbai International Airport on the north. The 247-acre site was acquired by the Mumbai Metropolitan Region Development Authority (MMRDA) because of its strategic location and connectivity to existing and planned metropolitan infrastructure, including a new commuter rail line being built to and from the site. City officials established a program that included over 40 million square feet of commercial office and retail, high-rise housing, and an array of cultural and public uses. Similar to the Beijing CBD, the new location in Wadala would help to preserve the historic core and essential urban character of Nariman Point.

Building on the city's historic spatial and landscape traditions and combining social and cultural vitality with the region's electronic

WADALA CENTRAL BUSINESS DISTRICT
MUMBAI, INDIA

AWARD
- First Place, International Design Competition

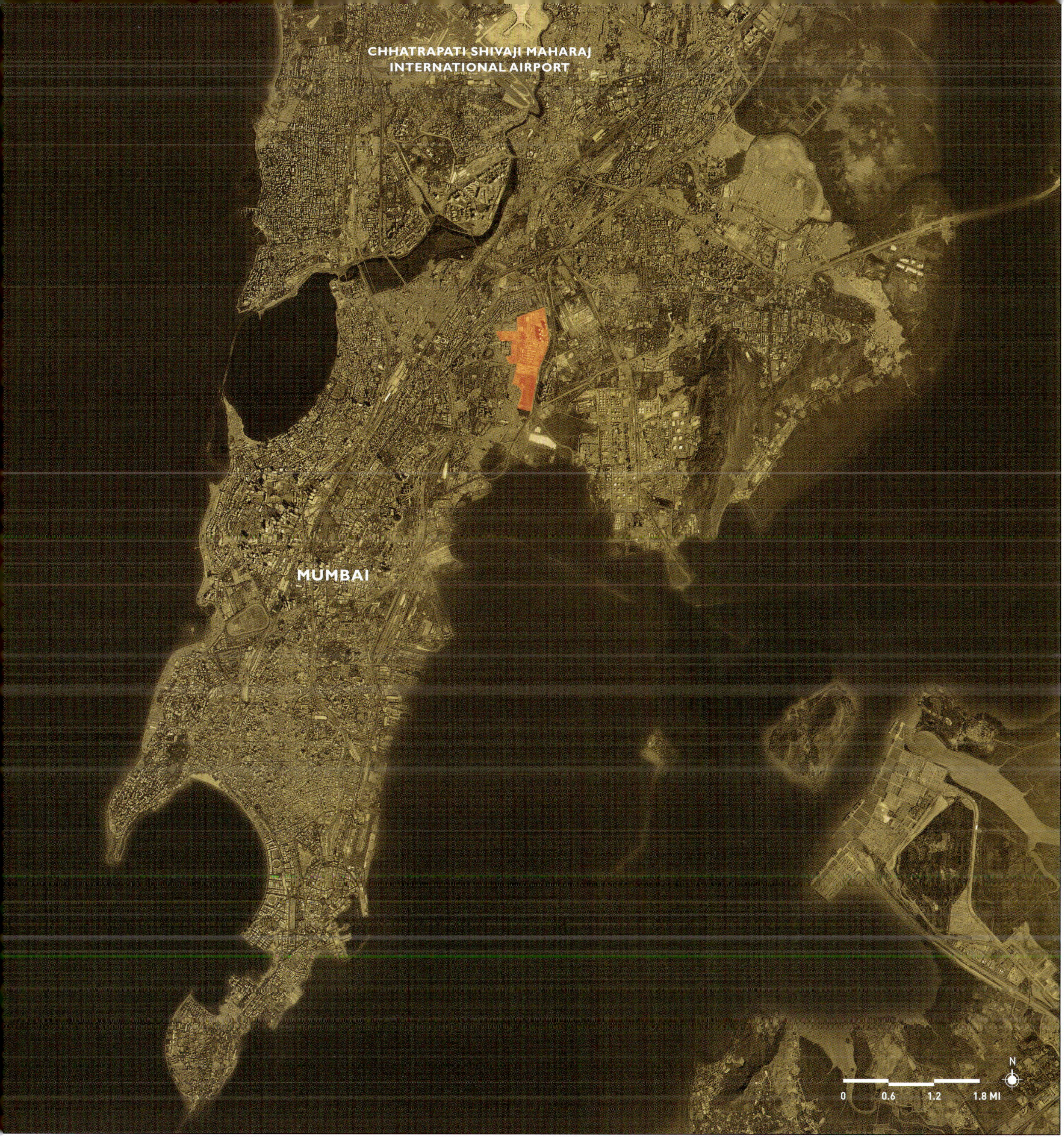
CHHATRAPATI SHIVAJI MAHARAJ
INTERNATIONAL AIRPORT
MUMBAI
N
0
0.6
1.2
1.8 MI

connectedness, the plan proposes predominately commercial office uses while also including diverse types of residential development within the same zone. Active, pedestrian-serving uses are encouraged at ground and lower levels. At two key locations, the plan encourages business-serving hotels, and a focused retail street anchors the largely residential western area of the plan. The block structure provides practical dimensions for the development of major commercial buildings while providing convenient access for enhanced walkability as well as limited vehicular access. The plan incorporates three commuter rail stations currently under construction. In addition to requiring sustainable principles and emerging trends of nature-based practices, the architecture will be modern and highly variegated, reflecting optimism about global markets and commerce.

RAIL
WADALA DEPOT STATION
A
B
C
D
E
F
F
G
CENTRAL PARK
NEW CUFFE PARADE DEVELOPMENT
PROPOSED STATION
70 m
SOUTH PARK
BHAKTI PARK STATION
WETLANDS/ MANGROVES
Residential
Hotel
Retail Street
Commercial/ Transportation
Office/ Resi - Ground Lvl Retail Permitted
Office/ Resi - Ground Lvl Retail Required
Park Space
Open Space
N
0
250
500 FT

Land use

1. CENTRAL PARK
2. AMPHITHEATER
3. NEW CUFFE PARADE SITE
4. LANDMARK BUILDING
5. RETAIL STREET
6. RETAIL MALL + OFFICE TOWERS
7. MULTIMODAL "HUB" + RETAIL ANCHOR
8. HOTEL SITE
9. WORKFORCE HOUSING
10. GATEWAY BUILDINGS
11. LINEAR OPEN SPACE WITH"BIO-SWALES"
12. SOUTH PARK
13. MANGROVE FOREST PRESERVE/ SALT PANS
14. RECREATIONAL OPEN SPACE
15. SCHOOL
16. POTENTIAL NEW MONORAIL TO BKC & AIRPORT
N
0
250
500 FT

Master plan

BLOCK COMPARISON: HISTORIC STUDY

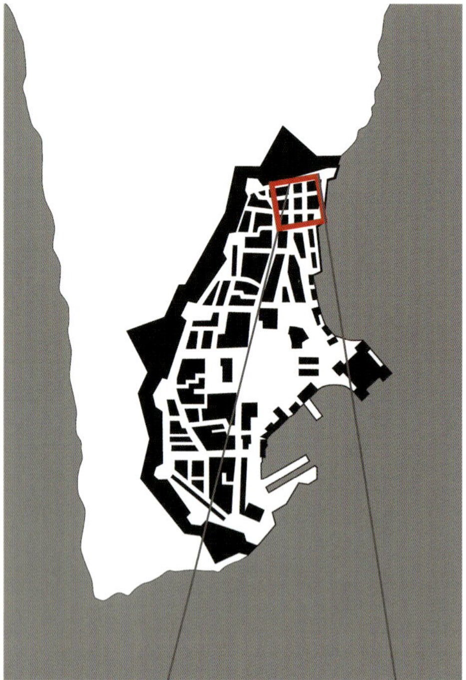

1838 - Fort area

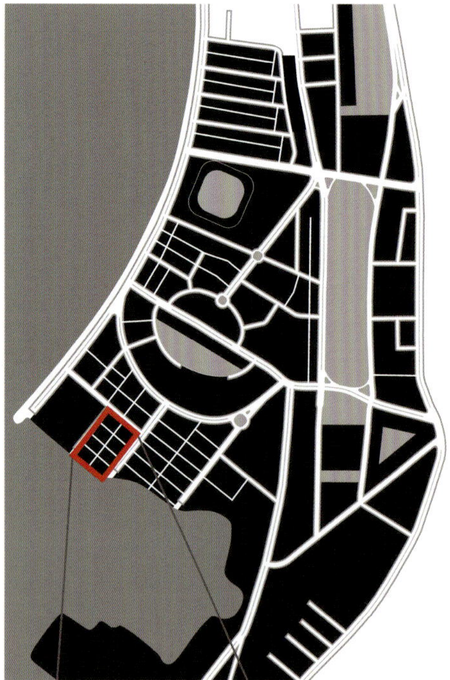

Nariman Point

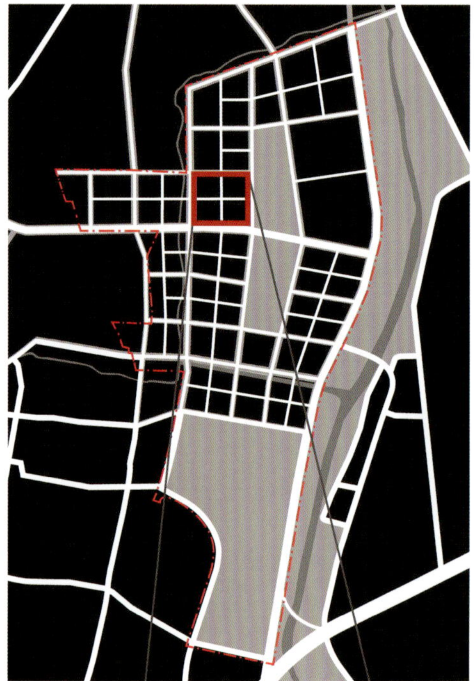

Proposed Wadala site plan

MUMBAI SMALL BLOCK EVOLUTION: GRAIN CHANGE

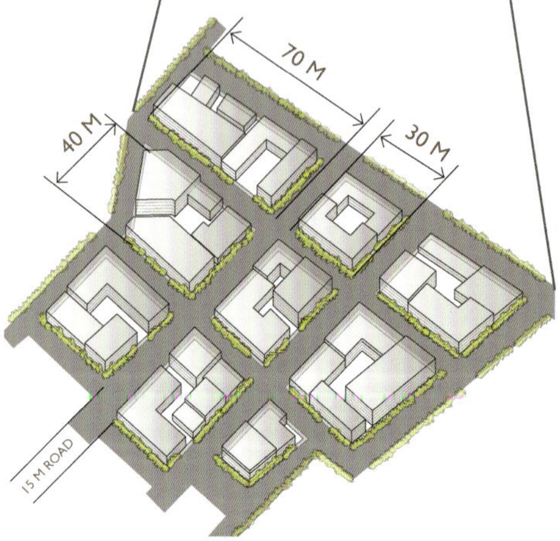

Historic fort area block

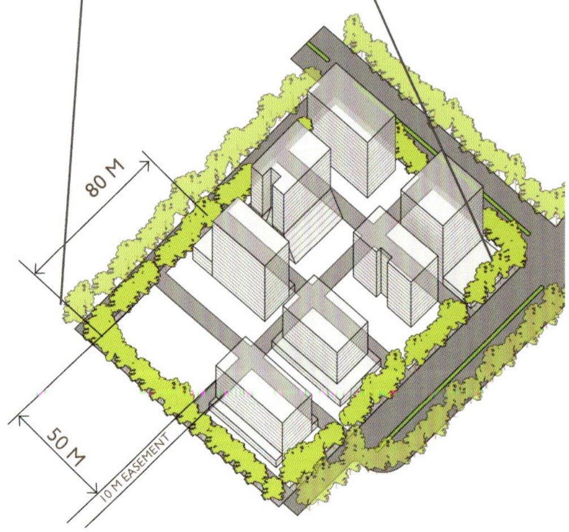

Nariman Point block

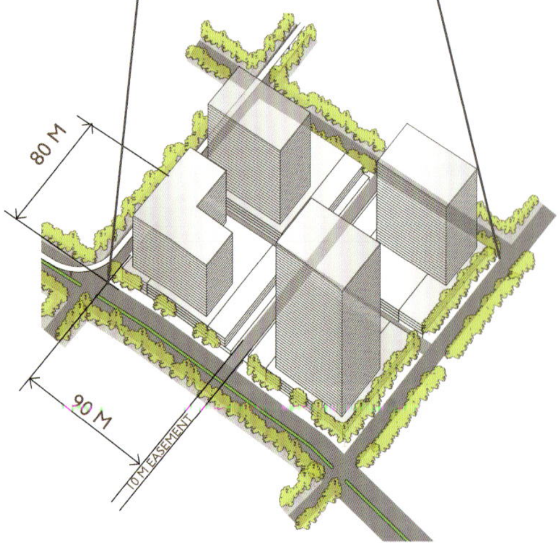

Proposed Wadala block size

WADALA MASTER PLAN DEVELOPABLE AREA

SITE AREA	square meters
Total Site Area (includes salt pans/preserves)	1,092,400
Committed New Cuffe Parade Parcel	92,600
Total Site Area Remaining	**999,800**

WADALA COMMERCIAL CENTER (WCC)	FSI	square meters
Total Potential Development	**4.0**	**3,999,200**

Program Distribution (for WCC)*	% *	square meters
Commercial Office	63%	2,519,496
Hotel	7%	279,944
Retail	6%	239,952
Residential	18%	719,856
Civic	6%	239,952
TOTAL DEVELOPMENT	**100%**	**3,999,200**

* Program Distribution based upon case study of La Defense in Paris, France

AIR RIGHTS TRANSFER BANK
2,665,900M2 = Total Air Rights Transfer Potential

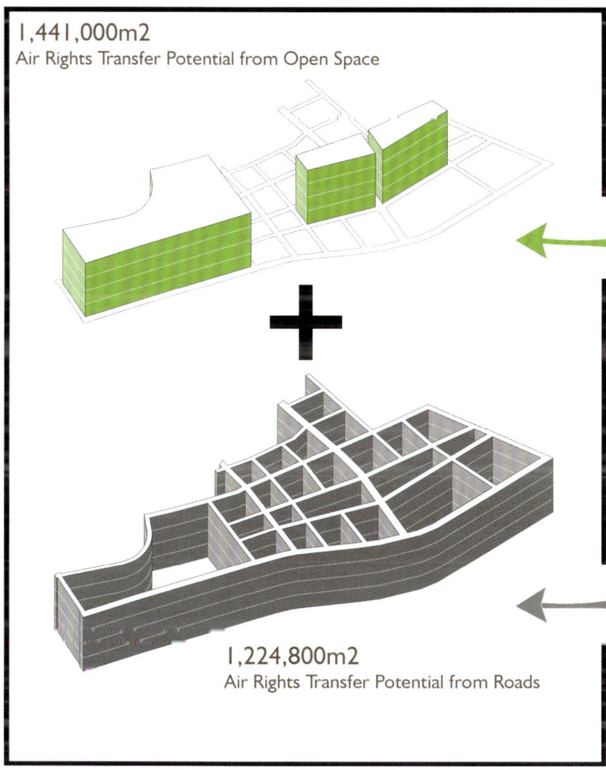

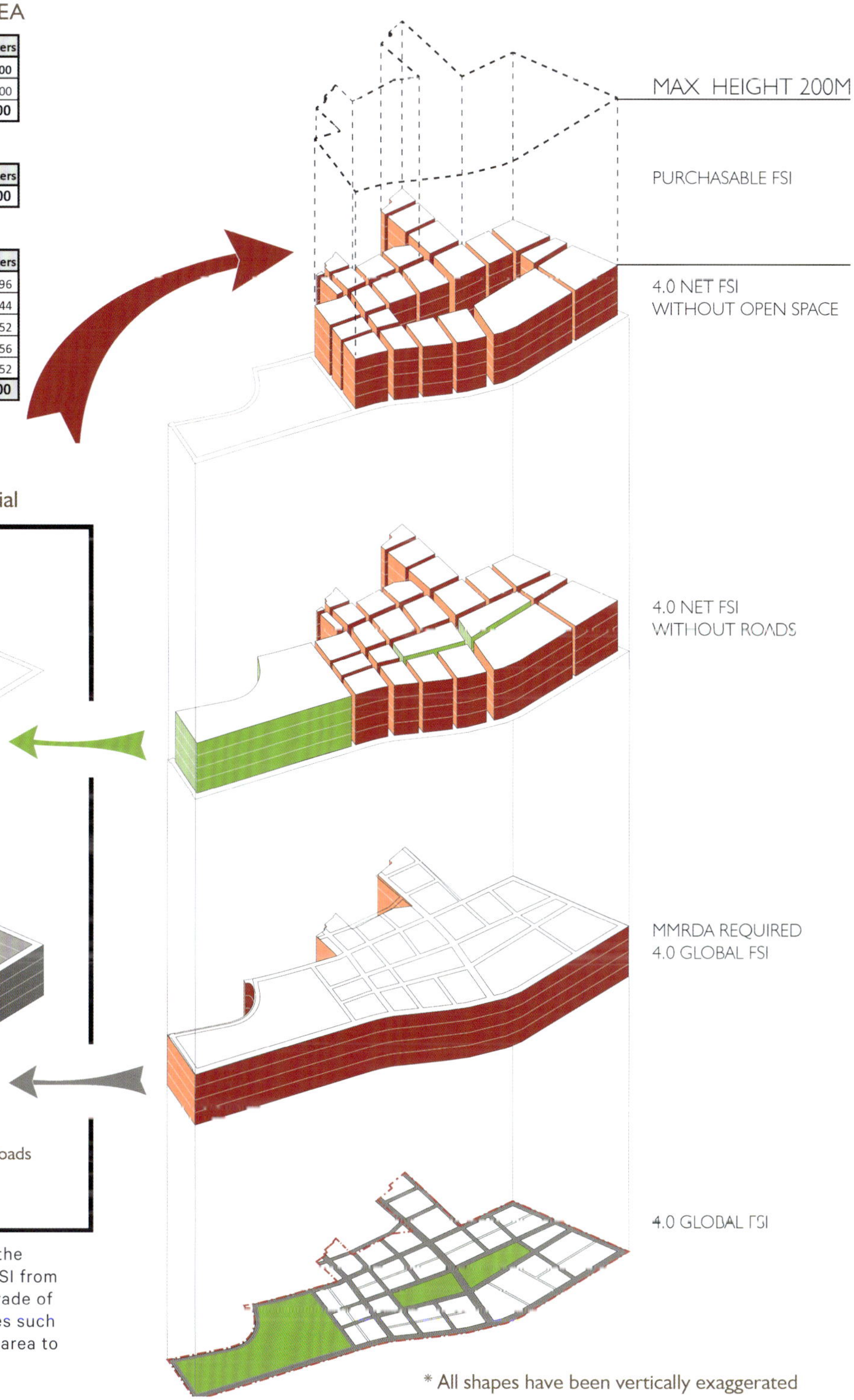

A Global FSI of 4.0 was applied over the entire site with the ability for individual developers to purchase additional FSI from an 'Air Rights Transfer Bank.' This 'bank' allows for the trade of development potential from public roads and open spaces such as the planned Central Park and the protected salt pans area to individual development parcels.

Analysis of developable area and transferable development rights of the commercial district

In 2005, most of the southern area of Chengdu County was farmland, rolling hills, and forests. With the relocation of Chengdu's city hall to the south, growth from the city center was headed there, though much of the land was currently undeveloped and unplanned. With the economic boom in the region and impending wave of urbanization, the need became apparent for a southern satellite center to meet the demands of Chengdu's international business community. A 4200-plus-acre site along the major north-south highway became the logical location for such a new district.

The planning concept for Luxe Lakes proposes that selected valleys are converted to lakes and adjoining rolling hills are made available for development. This allows development to have water access and attractive water views. The plan aims to balance urban development with environmental protection, with nearly 70 percent of the land area set aside for open space, including parks, forest preserves, existing orchards, and water ways including lakes and canals. The remaining land area would be used for a mixed-use town center, housing, offices for creative industry, an arts village, schools and a university, and a resort district. Research incubator start-ups and small production facilities are located adjacent to the university labs, classrooms, and researcher housing. The educational system becomes integrated with private industry and includes the opportunity for life-long learning experiences.

LUXE LAKES ECO-CITY
CHENGDU, SICHUAN, CHINA

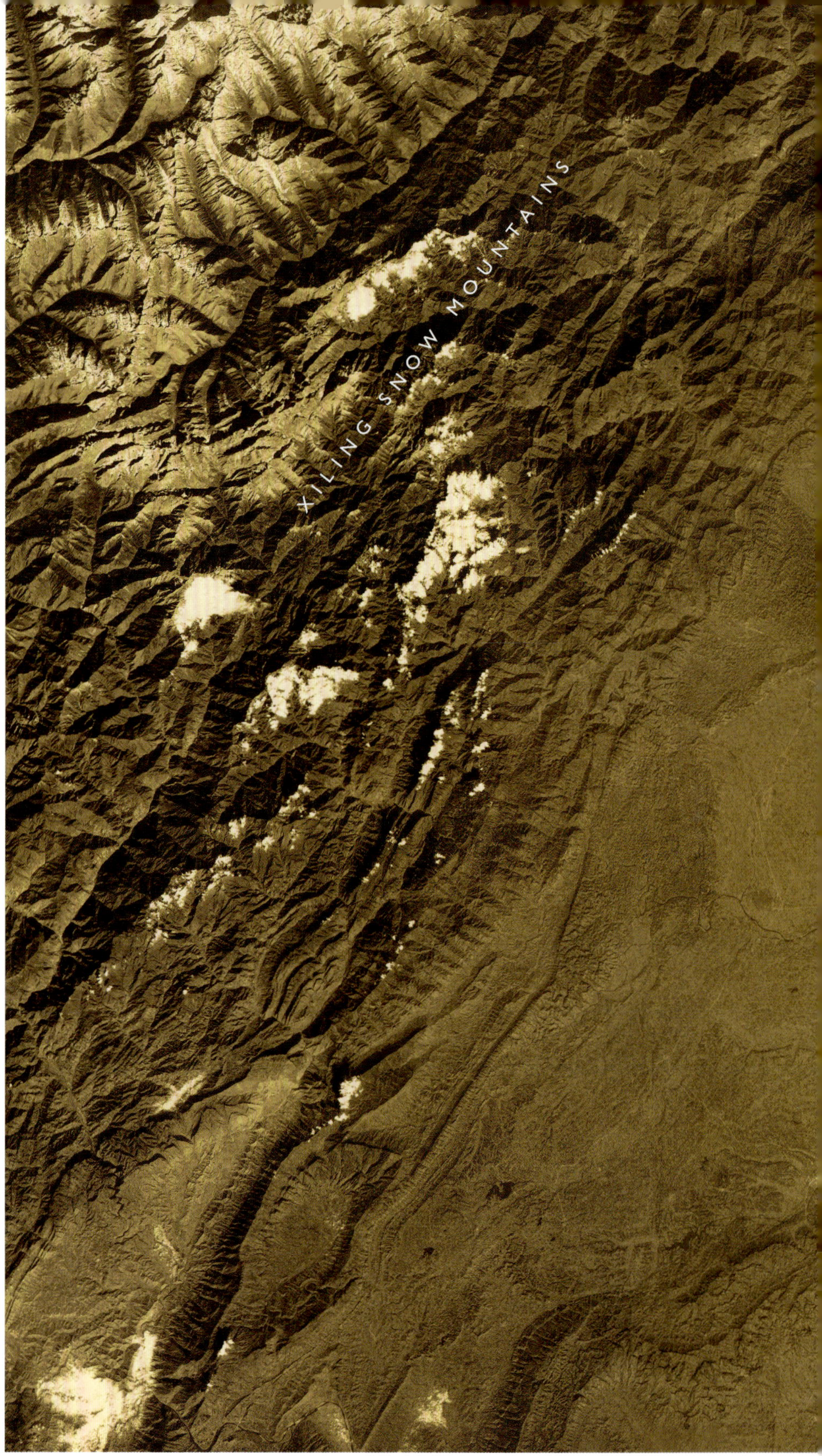

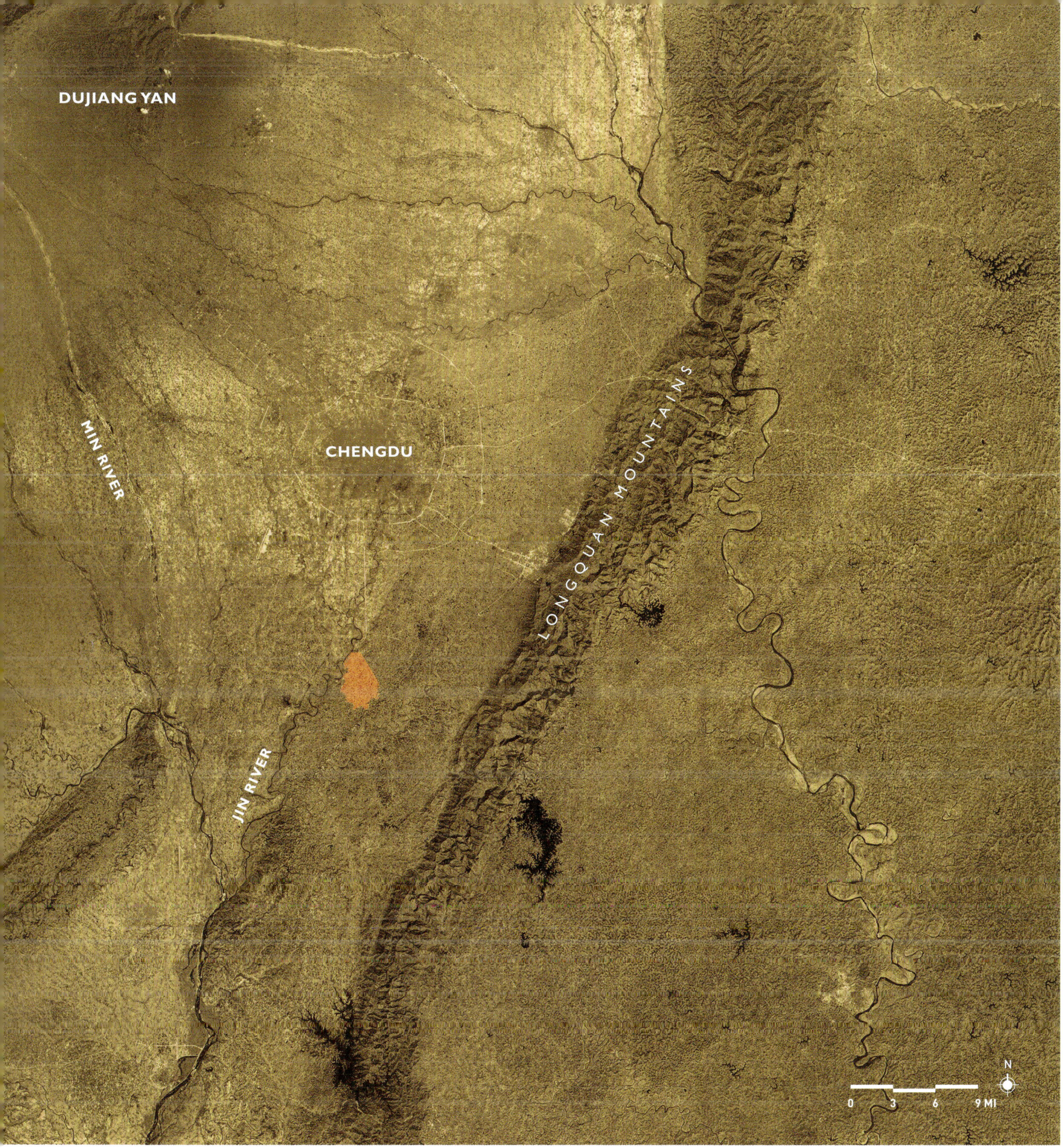
DUJIANG YAN
CHENGDU
MIN RIVER
LONGQUAN MOUNTAINS
JIN RIVER
N
0
3
6
9 MI

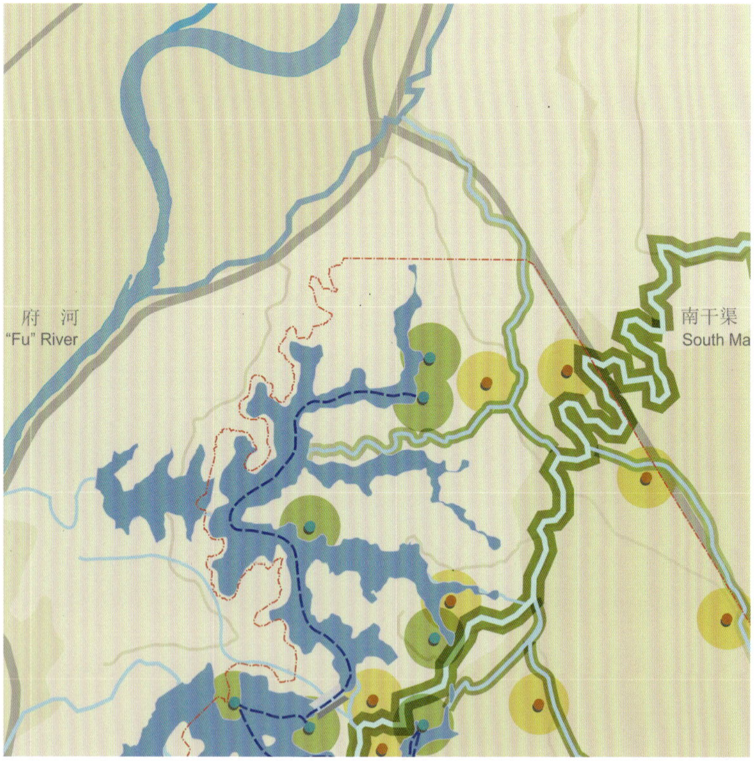

Two rivers, canals, and forest

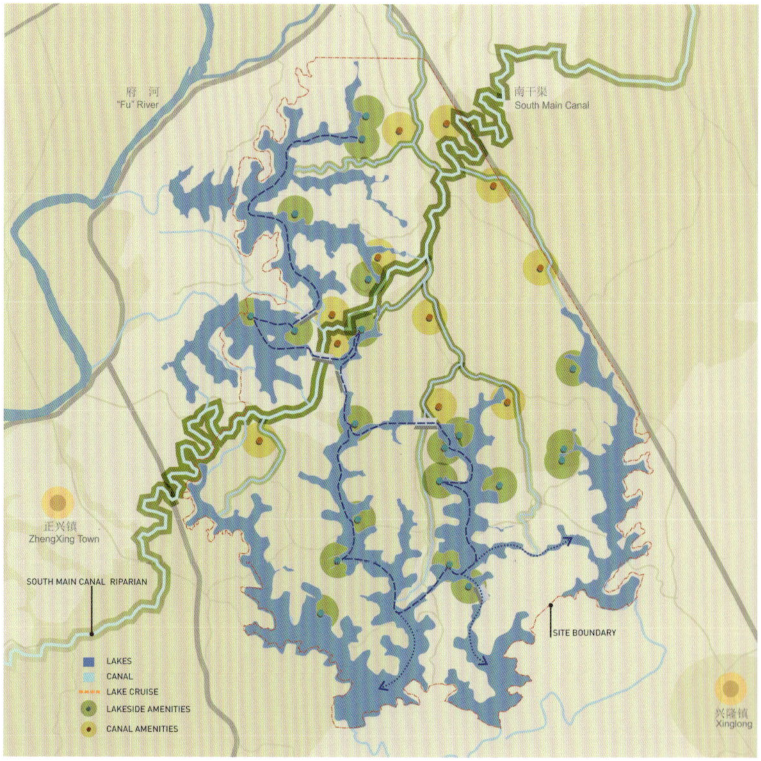

Proposed lake system

Lakefront development

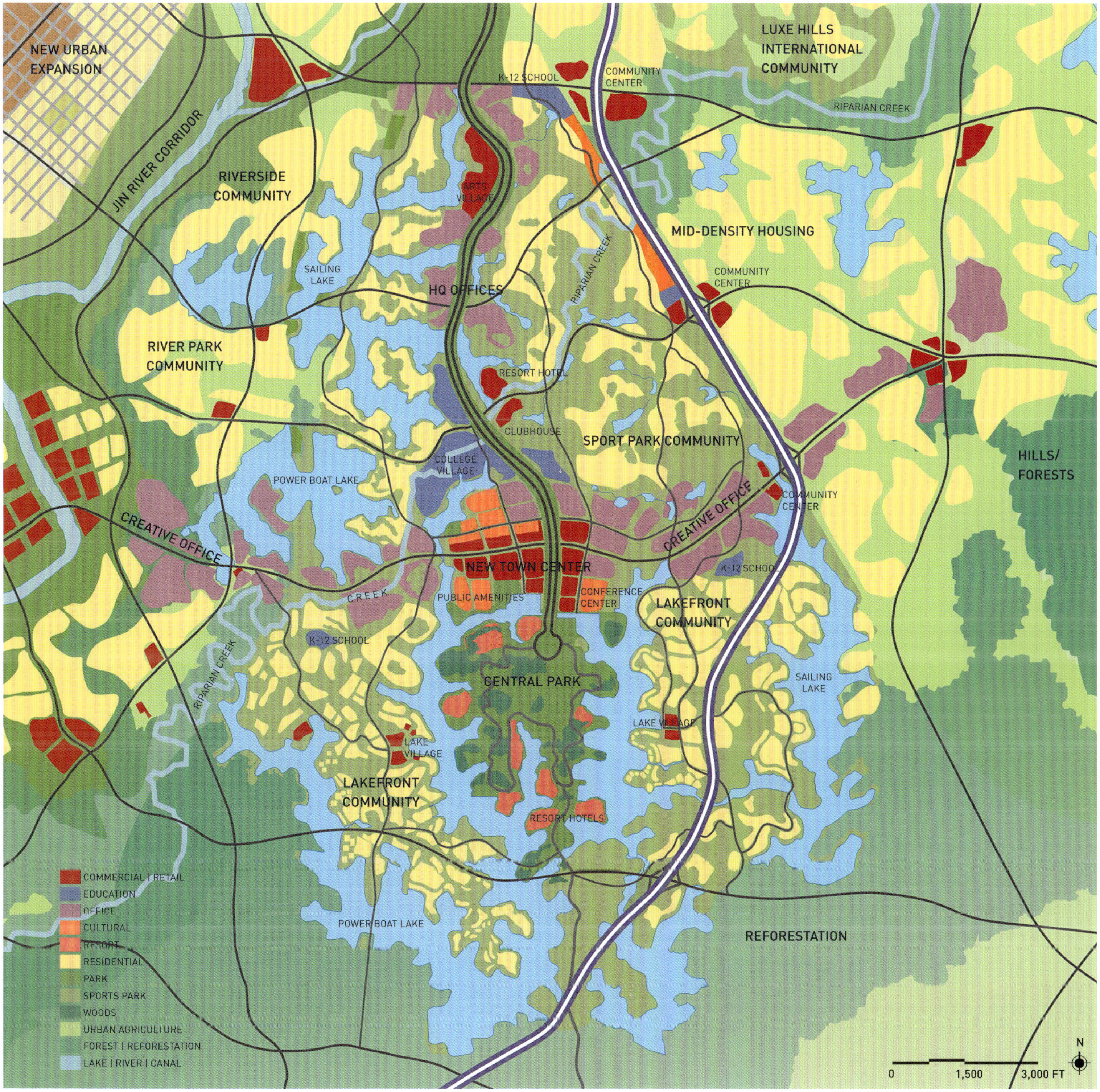
NEW URBAN EXPANSION
LUXE HILLS INTERNATIONAL COMMUNITY
K-12 SCHOOL
COMMUNITY CENTER
RIPARIAN CREEK
JIN RIVER CORRIDOR
RIVERSIDE COMMUNITY
ARTS VILLAGE
MID-DENSITY HOUSING
SAILING LAKE
HQ OFFICES
RIPARIAN CREEK
COMMUNITY CENTER
RIVER PARK COMMUNITY
RESORT HOTEL
CLUBHOUSE
SPORT PARK COMMUNITY
HILLS/ FORESTS
COLLEGE VILLAGE
POWER BOAT LAKE
CREATIVE OFFICE
COMMUNITY CENTER
CREATIVE OFFICE
NEW TOWN CENTER
K-12 SCHOOL
CREEK
PUBLIC AMENITIES
CONFERENCE CENTER
LAKEFRONT COMMUNITY
K-12 SCHOOL
RIPARIAN CREEK
CENTRAL PARK
SAILING LAKE
LAKE VILLAGE
LAKE VILLAGE
LAKEFRONT COMMUNITY
RESORT HOTELS
COMMERCIAL | RETAIL
EDUCATION
OFFICE
CULTURAL
RESORT
RESIDENTIAL
PARK
SPORTS PARK
WOODS
URBAN AGRICULTURE
FOREST | REFORESTATION
LAKE | RIVER | CANAL
POWER BOAT LAKE
REFORESTATION
N
0
1,500
3,000 FT

Master plan

Rampant expansion in rapidly growing urban regions typically has failed to achieve urban densities and character, instead spreading residential uses across the landscape at increasingly greater distances from urban services and employment. Already the second largest city in Nevada, Henderson is absorbing much of the growth in the Las Vegas Valley, with undistinguished suburban enclaves of single-family homes and strip retail development spread across the desert landscape. Recent growth along the I-15 freeway corridor, which links Southern California with Las Vegas, and the city's desire to evolve beyond its suburban past, have positioned Henderson's westside to become a major new mixed-use urban district for the greater Las Vegas region. The Henderson West project seeks to be the center for this new urban district that provides a mixed-use, high-density hub for the western area, serving as well as a prototype for future development elsewhere in the Valley.

The Henderson West master plan is built upon environmental principles to minimize the effect of extreme heat and winds during summer months. Buildings and courtyards are oriented to provide protection from winds and shade for outdoor walking areas. Pedestrian pathways are integrated throughout the project passing through and around a variety of active and passive open spaces. The emphasis is on pedestrian movement with less dependence on the automobile. A mixture of housing, offices, retail, and entertainment

HENDERSON WEST
HENDERSON, NEVADA, USA

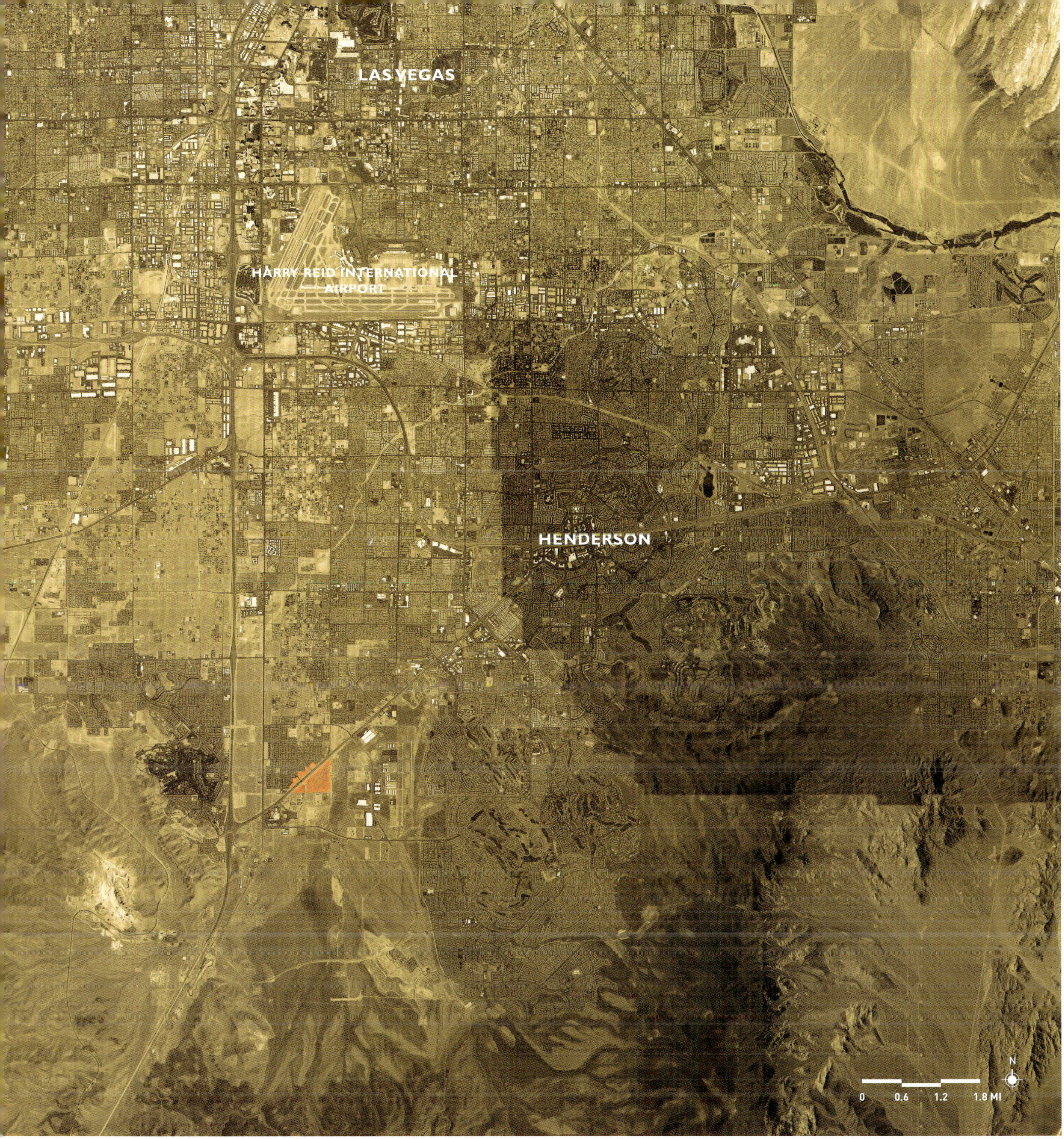
LAS VEGAS
HARRY REID INTERNATIONAL AIRPORT
HENDERSON
N
0
0.6
1.2
1.8 MI

uses provide amenities and a job-housing balance for those living in Henderson West, as well as attracting users from other nearby areas. Housing densities range from twenty-five dwelling units per acre on the low end to a maximum of 200 dwelling units per acre on the upper end. These densities are higher than other more traditional areas of Henderson where densities customarily are in the range of four to eight dwelling units per acre. The goal of the plan is to build upon a growing desire within the community for urban living including a variety of housing densities and amenities that accommodates a range of lifestyles, as well as to set a high standard for future development in the region.

Town square

Courtyard street corner

1. Neighborhood serving retail
2. Townhomes
3. Bike and community park
4. Supermarket with housing above
5. Convenience retail
6. Retail and garden terrace
7. Apartment housing
8. High-rise housing
9. Large retail
10. Mid-rise office
11. Courtyard housing
12. Anchor retail
13. Cinema
14. Retail with housing above
15. Civic building
16. Retail with office above
17. Central green
18. Hotel and meeting facilities
19. Amenity facilities
0
250
500 FT
N

Master plan

Central Green and café

Residential courtyard

Gateway bridge and Bike Park

Neighborhood park and brewery

The evolution of consumer preferences from brick and mortar to online shopping has led to the decline of shopping malls across the country, and the repurposing of these large, often centrally located sites offers opportunities to remove their essentially anti-urban features and restore them as additions to the fabric of their urban context. Westfield's thirty-five-acre Promenade Mall site, in the San Fernando Valley of Los Angeles, has been largely vacated and is poised for redevelopment. Years of planning by the City of Los Angeles and community have identified the neighborhood, including the mall site, as the "Downtown of the Valley." The City Council adopted in 2015 a Specific Plan (a focused land use plan under California law) called the Warner Center 2035 Plan, identifying the mall site for development as a dense mixed-use center with a floor area ratio (FAR) up to 5.0. A complex formula is specified in the plan for calculating density that favors affordable housing, small subdivision of large land holdings into small walkable city blocks, public open space and pedestrian ways, and active retail frontages on all streets within the district.

In accordance with the Specific Plan, the master plan for the mall site is organized around the concept of a traditional street grid — the age-old system that is simple and direct, flexible and open-ended — breaking the superblock of the now defunct mall into smaller development sites.

WESTFIELD PROMENADE
WARNER CENTER, CALIFORNIA, USA

WARNER CENTER
PIERCE COLLEGE
N
0 600 1,200 1,800 FT

This makes the site more urban and hospitable for walking in well-landscaped street spaces with active storefront retail. Street parking is allowed in places, supplemented with additional subterranean parking. Spatially, the sense of place is urban, quite different from the suburban mall. The plan has more than seven acres of publicly accessible open space including a central park programmed for active use, a wide range of residential unit types including affordable housing, significant Class A and creative office space, lifestyle retail, two hotels, and an entertainment venue for athletic events and performances. The project is programmed as an environmentally resilient neighborhood drawing upon energy and water conservation principles. At 3.4 million square feet, the project will provide a vertically mixed-use environment for live/work/play in an urban setting that is the antithesis of the suburban mall it is replacing.

UNIBAIL-RODAMCO-WESTFIELD
UNIBAIL-RODAMCO-WESTFIELD
Westfield
W

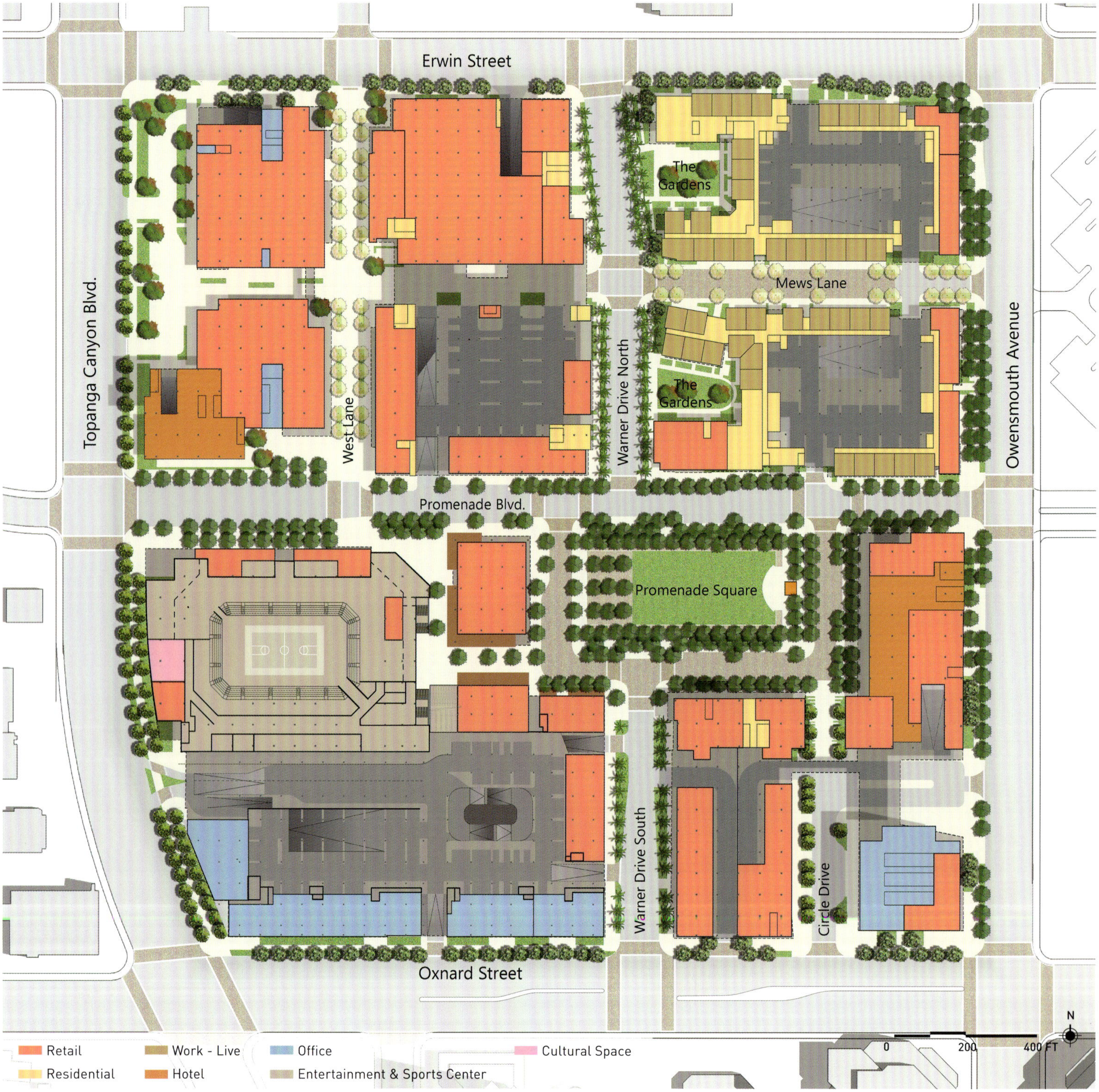

Ground level plan

Erwin Street
Topanga Canyon Blvd.
West Lane
Warner Drive North
The Gardens
The Gardens
Mews Lane
Owensmouth Avenue
Promenade Blvd.
Promenade Square
Warner Drive South
Circle Drive
Oxnard Street
N
0
200
400 FT
Retail
Residential
Work - Live
Hotel
Office
Entertainment & Sports Center
Cultural Space

Roof plan

Children's park at Promenade Square

Looking south on Warner Drive North

Owensmouth Avenue and Irwin Street

Topanga Canyon Boulevard and Irwin Street

The site for the 1968 World's Fair in San Antonio, Texas, called HemisFair, was planned for a 100-acre historically Hispanic neighborhood that was substantially erased by the fair's development. Once the fair completed its six-month run, the site was left as an essentially empty quarter, bordered by the downtown and the city's renowned Riverwalk, left for the ensuing decades to be carved opportunistically into a disparate array of low-intensity uses. The master planning effort, sponsored by the City of San Antonio and the HemisFair Park Area Redevelopment Corporation, a non-profit agency created by the City, came to be about history, memory, reparation and deference to the visions still alive in the many Latino families whose ancestors had been displaced.

Planning for the site's future fifty years later was very much an open workshop process involving many of the descendants of those who had lived there in a rigorous public workshop process that included sessions with over 700 participants. Questions were deliberately open-ended: What makes San Antonio unique? Who should receive the benefit from the property, residents or tourists? What should be the program for the 100-acre site? What type of housing? What about public open space? Instead of the conventional planning process where the professional planner develops alternatives, the community break-out groups designed twenty-eight concepts for the site which then were reduced to seven generic types of plans

HEMISFAIR PARK REDEVELOPMENT
SAN ANTONIO, TEXAS, USA

SAN ANTONIO
RIVER WALK
N
0 600 1,200 1,800 FT

and ultimately to one plan, selected and refined by additional workshops.

The resulting plan included more than 2,000 housing units, both market rate and affordable units recalling the mix that had existed before the fair. Citizens sought to restore the historic road system to reconnect to surrounding streets while dividing the large aggregated fair site into smaller scale neighborhood blocks. The plan recommended that the Convention Center, developed shortly after the fair in 1968, be removed to allow for the development of a large city-owned Central Park; a site for new Convention facilities for Riverwalk visitors is provided a short distance away. Since elected officials participated in the public workshops from the beginning, when the plan was presented to the City Council, there was less than fifteen minutes of discussion before a unanimous Council vote approved the plan.

Master Plan Features

1 Reinstatement of the historic street grid removed in the 1960s

2 Expand Convention Center to the east, remove outdated facility from the northwestern site area

3 Preservation and reuse of the remaining historic structures on the site through restoration of their historic street context

4 Location and character definition of three major parks and a greenway system to connect them

5 Height, setback, and use standards for new mixed-use development to reestablish street life and street character

6 Strategies for access and connectivity: parking, pedestrian and bike circulation, and connections with transit

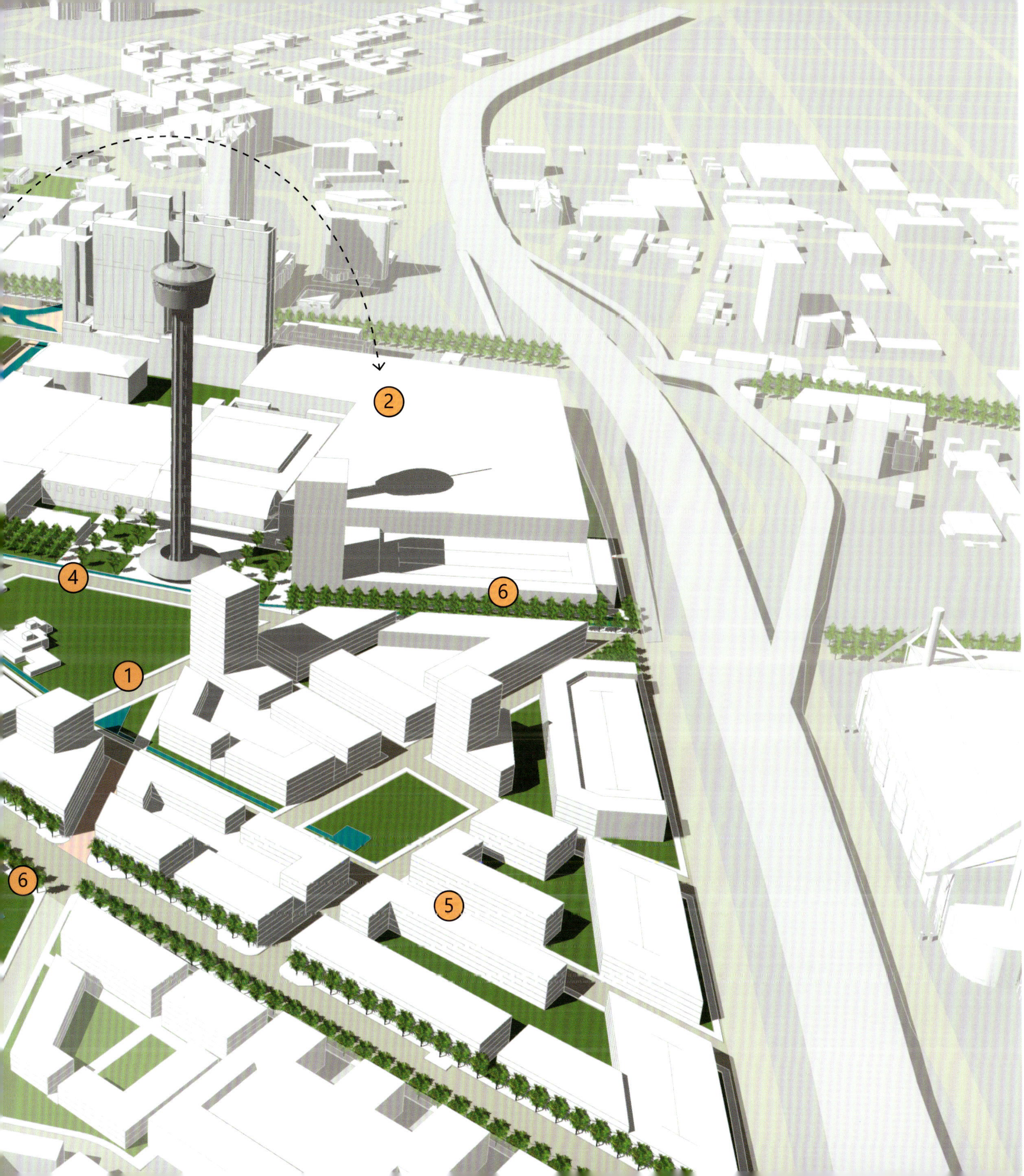
2
4
6
1
6
5

Public workshops

Public workshop

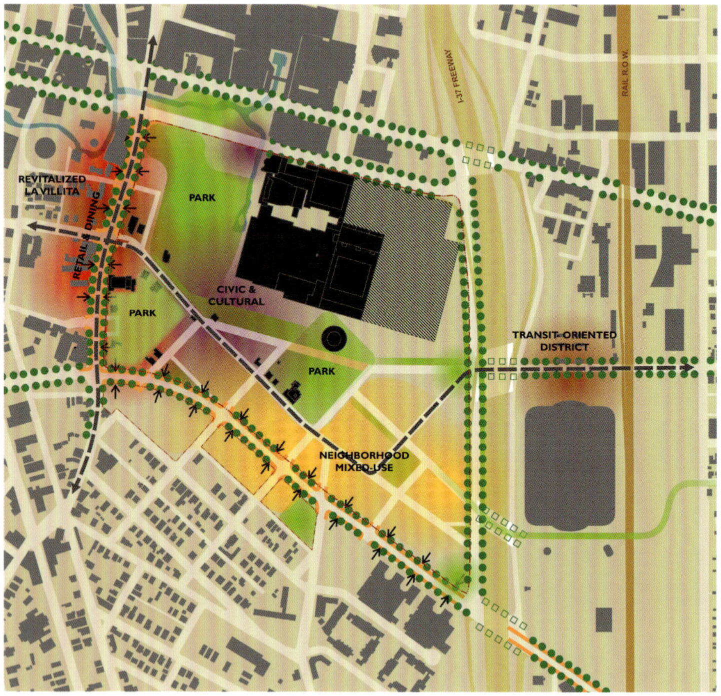

Concept plan

Open space

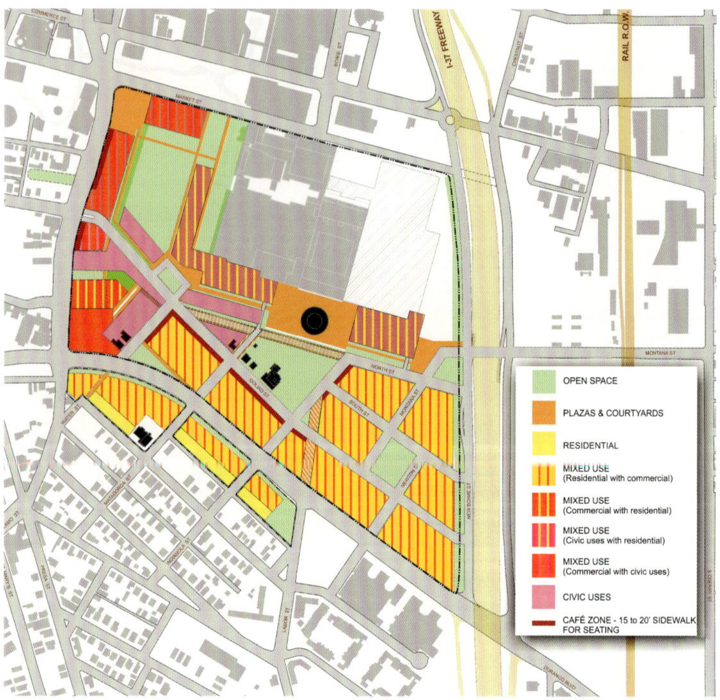

Land use

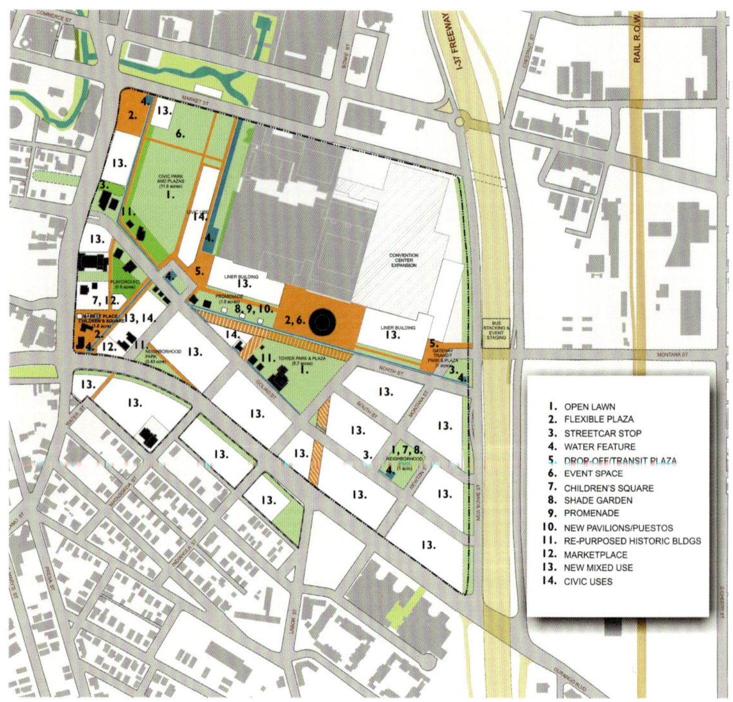

Program

COMMERCE ST
RIVERCENTER MALL
BOWIE ST
I-37 FREEWAY
CHESTNUT ST
RAIL R.O.W.
MARKET ST
LILA COCKRELL THEATER
GRAND HYATT HOTEL & CONDOS
LA VILLITA
HENRY B. GONZALES CONVENTION CENTER
CONVENTION CENTER EXPANSION AREA
SUNSET STATION
TOWER OF THE AMERICAS
MONTANA ST
ALAMODOME
LAVACA
MATAGORDA ST
INDIANOLA ST
PRESA ST
HEMISVIEW VILLAGE APARTMENTS
LABOR ST
BURNETT SCHOOL SITE
S CHERRY ST
DURANGO BLVD
N
0
250
500 FT

Master plan

Central Games Plaza

Promenade

Movie night at the park

Celebration at the park

Yanaguana Garden

As one of the largest additions to the urban fabric of Los Angeles, the 1,000-acre Playa Vista development that replaced the Howard Hughes Corporation's aeronautics engineering campus and airstrip was widely heralded as a new urbanist model of infill redevelopment. Upon completion and occupancy of its first phase, however, the project's developer, Playa Capital Company, undertook an evaluation of its earlier developments and determined that design standards needed revision so that Phase II projects would yield better streetscape and architecture of a higher quality. Prepared as a supplemental document to the Playa Vista Specific Plan, the resulting framework and standards are a form-based approach to establishing urban design character for the largest new development on the west side of Los Angeles.

A series of framework principles were defined to provide direction for future design and development, including: (1) establishing the street and park spaces as the most important element of public space with buildings that support their spatial definition; (2) establishing a distribution of compatible land uses and housing mix that supports a vibrant public realm; (3) defining an architecture that is straightforward and clear and that honors timeless architectural conventions; (4) controlling private parking access through planning and design that emphasizes a pedestrian-oriented streetscape; and (5) establishing a network of landscaped pedestrian paths as part of a walkable block structure that is more like the pedestrian scaled blocks of historical cities. Considerations also included detailed design guidelines for the project's mixed-use Town Center (which the firm eventually designed), to include 360,000 square feet of commercial development with more than 200 mixed-use housing units, some above the commercial development.

PLAYA VISTA PHASE II
LOS ANGELES, CALIFORNIA, USA

AWARDS
- APA California, Planning Award
- APA Los Angeles, Planning Award

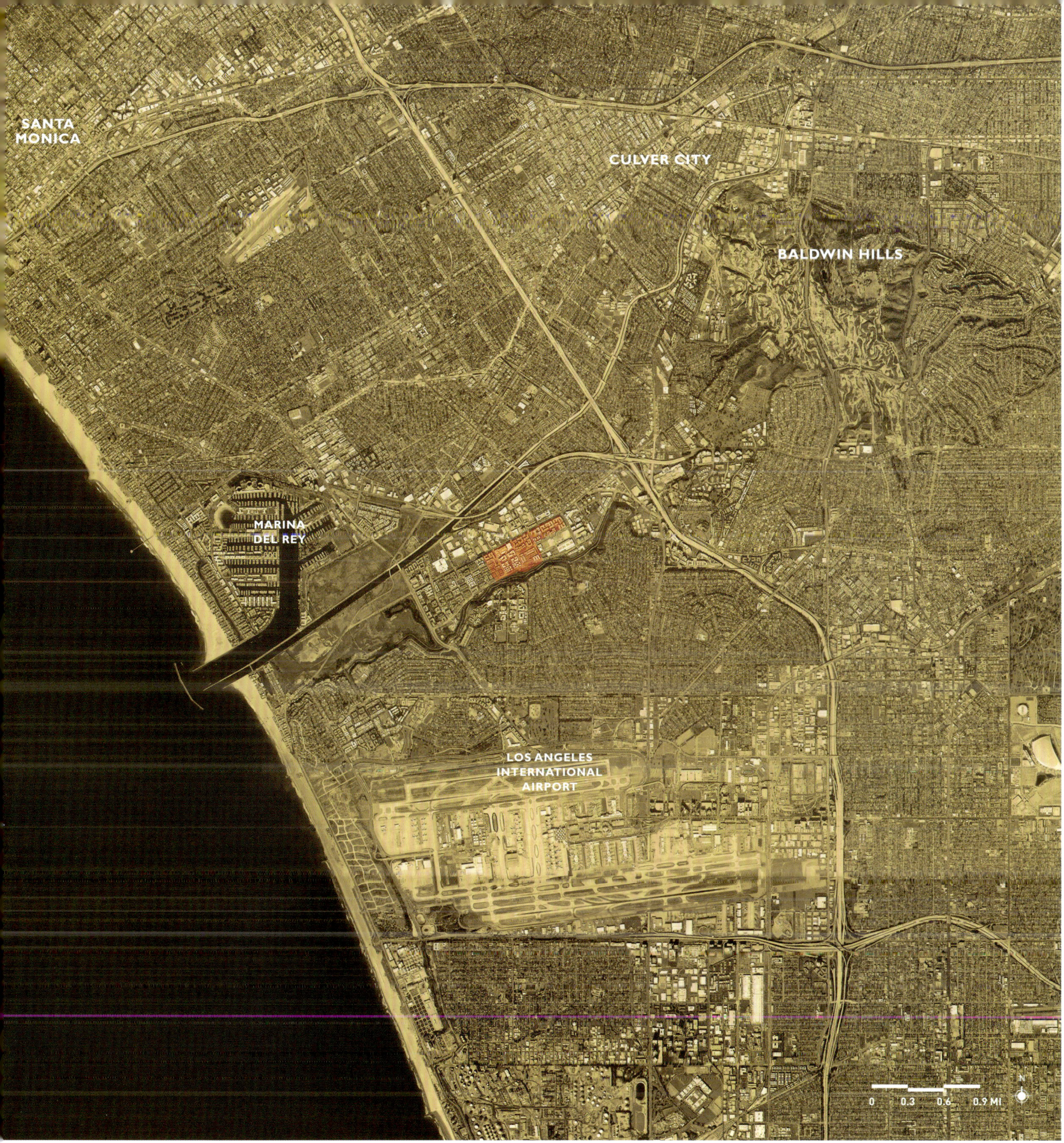
SANTA
MONICA
CULVER CITY
BALDWIN HILLS
MARINA
DEL REY
LOS ANGELES
INTERNATIONAL
AIRPORT
0 0.3 0.6 0.9 MI
N

LMU

The Village at Playa Vista

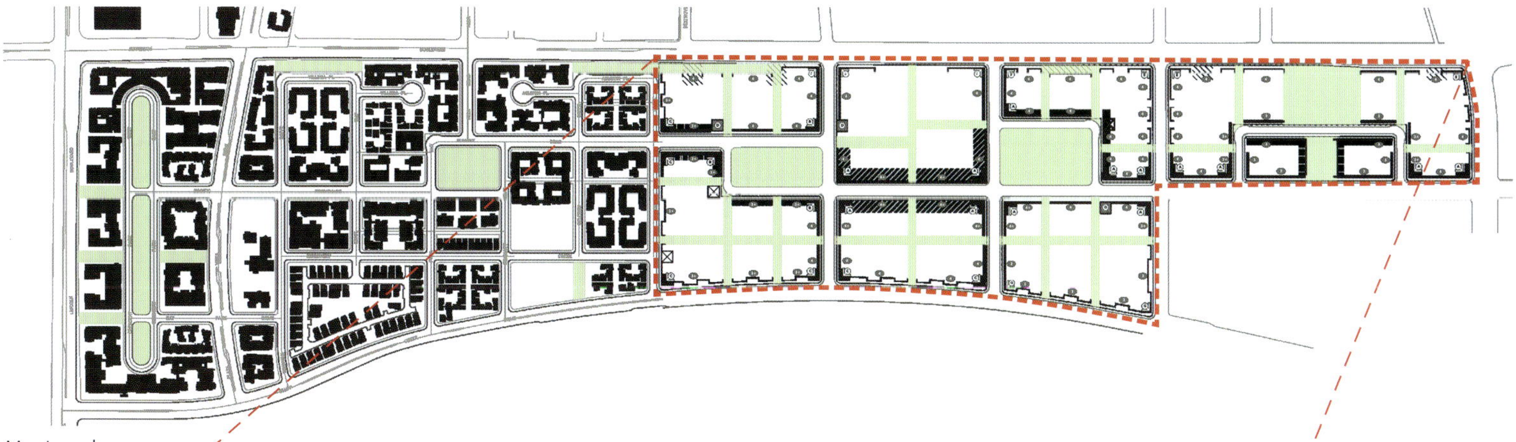

Master plan

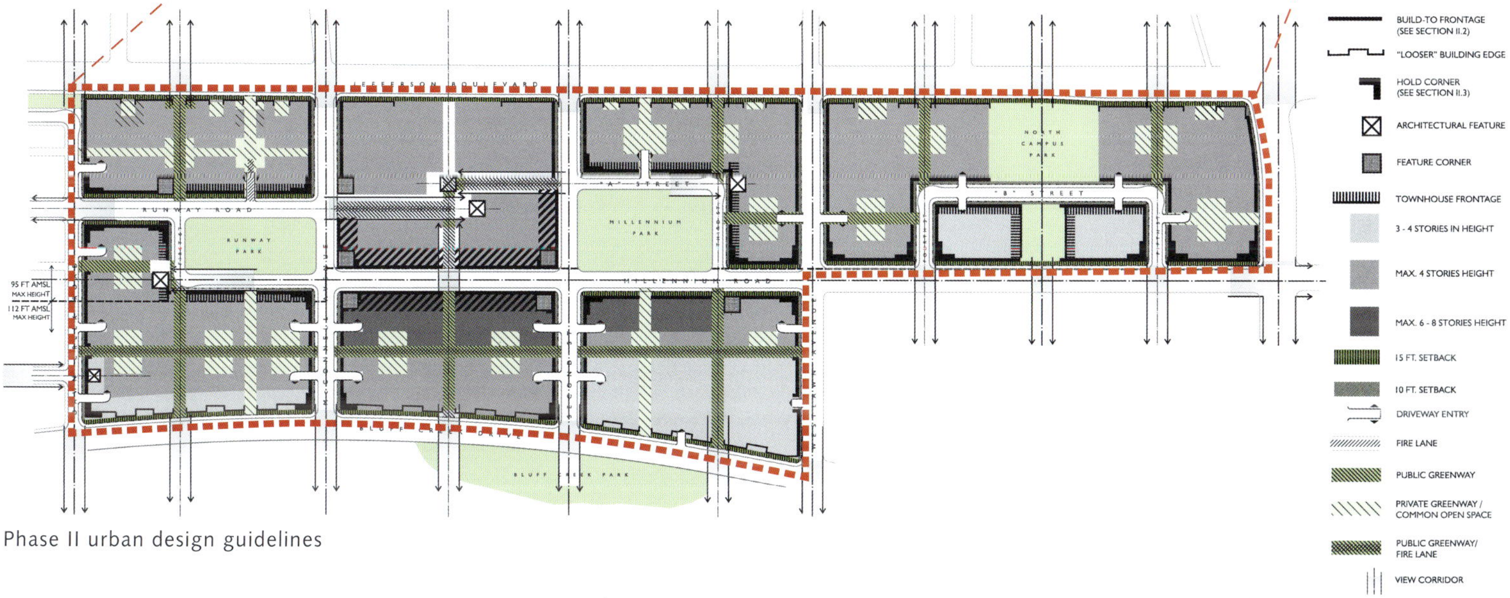

Phase II urban design guidelines

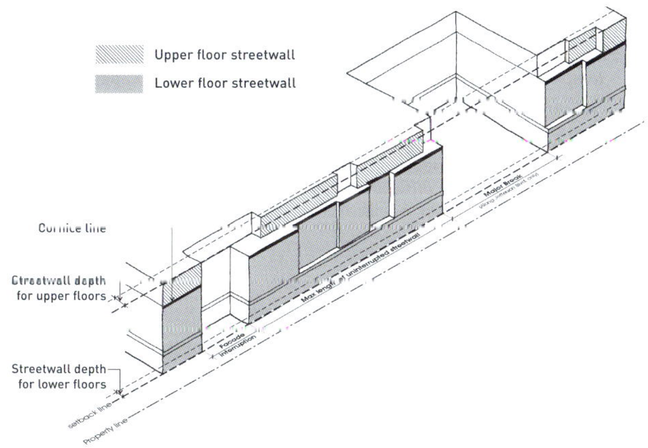

Streetwall standards

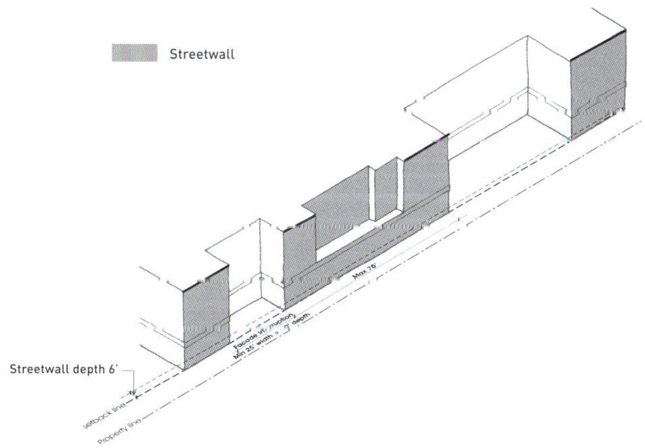

Streetwall standards

Playa Vista Phase II

The Village at Playa Vista

LEASING
LEASING

Like many cities in the United States, Los Angeles has experienced a reemergence of housing markets in its inner-city areas. Many of these areas are older manufacturing and industrial districts with "loft" type buildings that artists and others have sought to convert to housing. Although this trend is applauded by many, there has been growing concern among civic leaders that the increased value attributed to this growth is "pushing out" important employment necessary for an appropriate jobs-housing balance. Two adjacent property owners in the Lincoln Heights neighborhood of Los Angeles joined together in anticipation of working with the City of Los Angeles on a new specific plan for their neighborhood, ultimately adopted as the Cornfield Arroyo Seco Specific Plan. The city's goal for the specific plan was to encourage the retention of jobs in the area while allowing for housing conversions and infill. The property owners saw an opportunity to work with the city in mapping out improvements and legitimizing density trade-offs as incentives to property owners to retain employment while permitting housing within their holdings.

Building upon the Los Angeles Greenways Plan, the twenty-seven-acre Rivertown plan creates a new regional center for residents and workers within a strong framework of public open space connections, amenities, and urban institutions. It also provides a "land use bridge" linking the traditional culturally and geographically separate east and west sides of the city. The plan for the owners' properties anticipated zoning provisions and design guidelines that eventually became public policies, as planning for the properties was integrally tied to the public planning processes. Rivertown orients towards the Los Angeles River and proposes a new mixed-use neighborhood with a balance of jobs and housing, accessible open space, neighborhood parks, festive plazas, retail and community services, and a sensitive relationship with the existing environment and communities. The plan outlines methods for achieving neighborhood quality through appropriate distribution of uses and densities and defines strategies for implementation including density bonuses for an array of public benefits. The result is achievement of collective benefit through compromise of public and private interests. A balance was reached between the strong developer market for housing and the changing market for traditional industry, with the city supporting next generation industrial jobs with a strong tax base.

LA RIVERTOWN
LOS ANGELES, CALIFORNIA, USA

AWARDS

- AIA California Council, Urban Design Award
- AIA Los Angeles, NEXT LA Award
- ASLA California Council, Urban Design Award

HOLLYWOOD
DODGER STADIUM
LOS ANGELES
L.A. RIVER
USC
N
0
0.3
0.6
0.9 MI

San Fernando Blvd
Pasadena Ave
N. Broadway

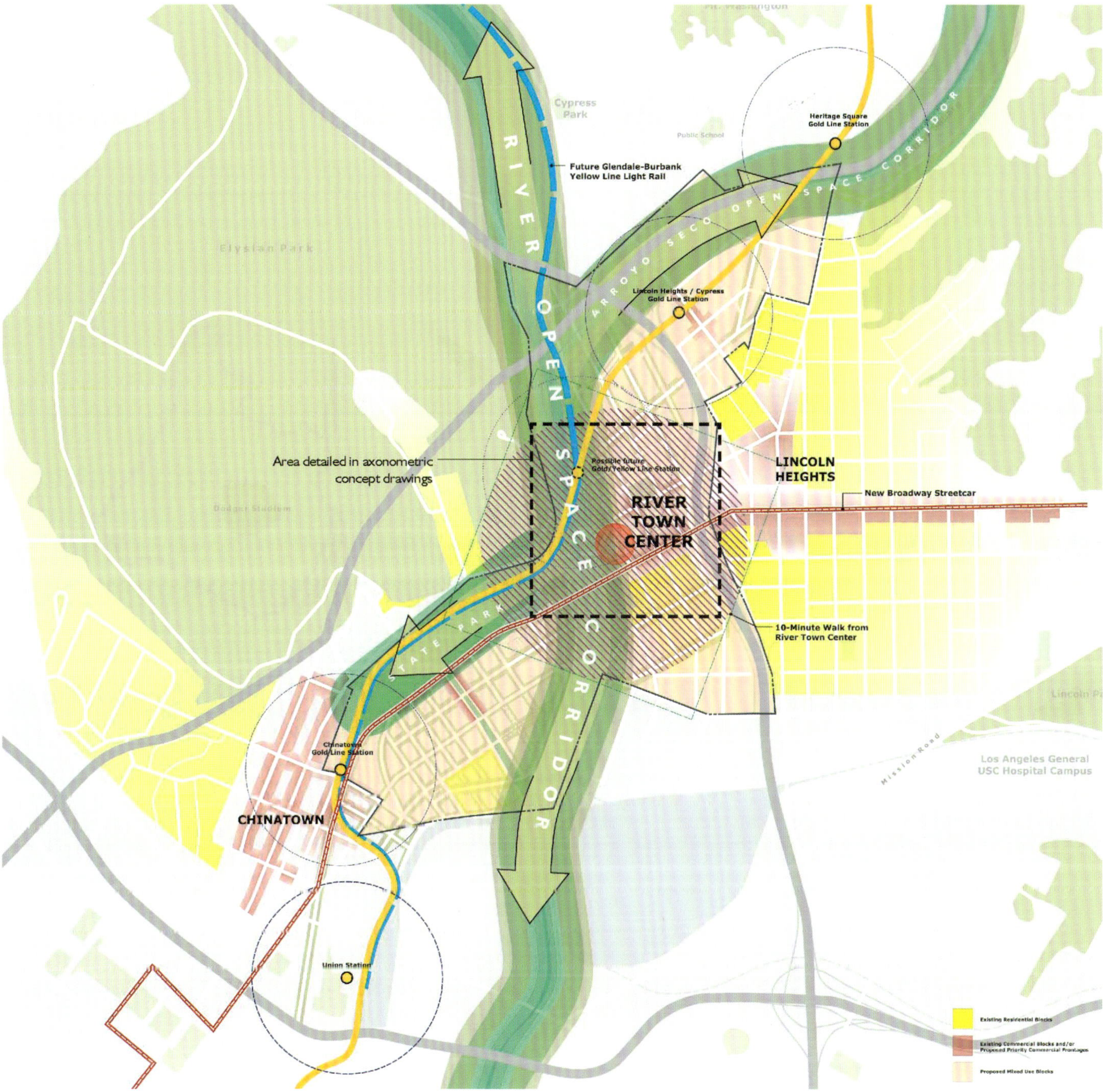

Framework plan

Transit Oriented Development concept

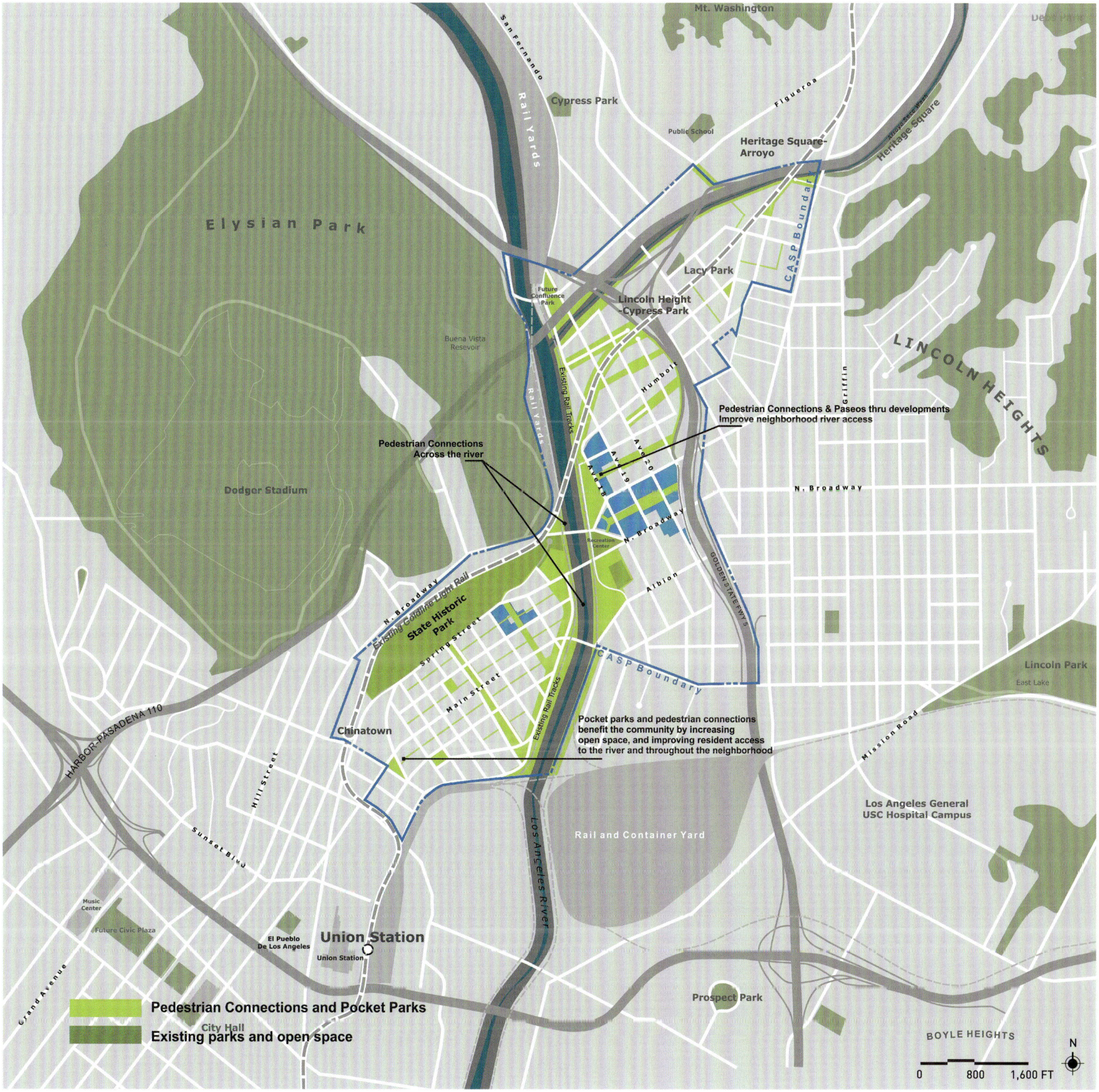

Open space and pedestrian connections

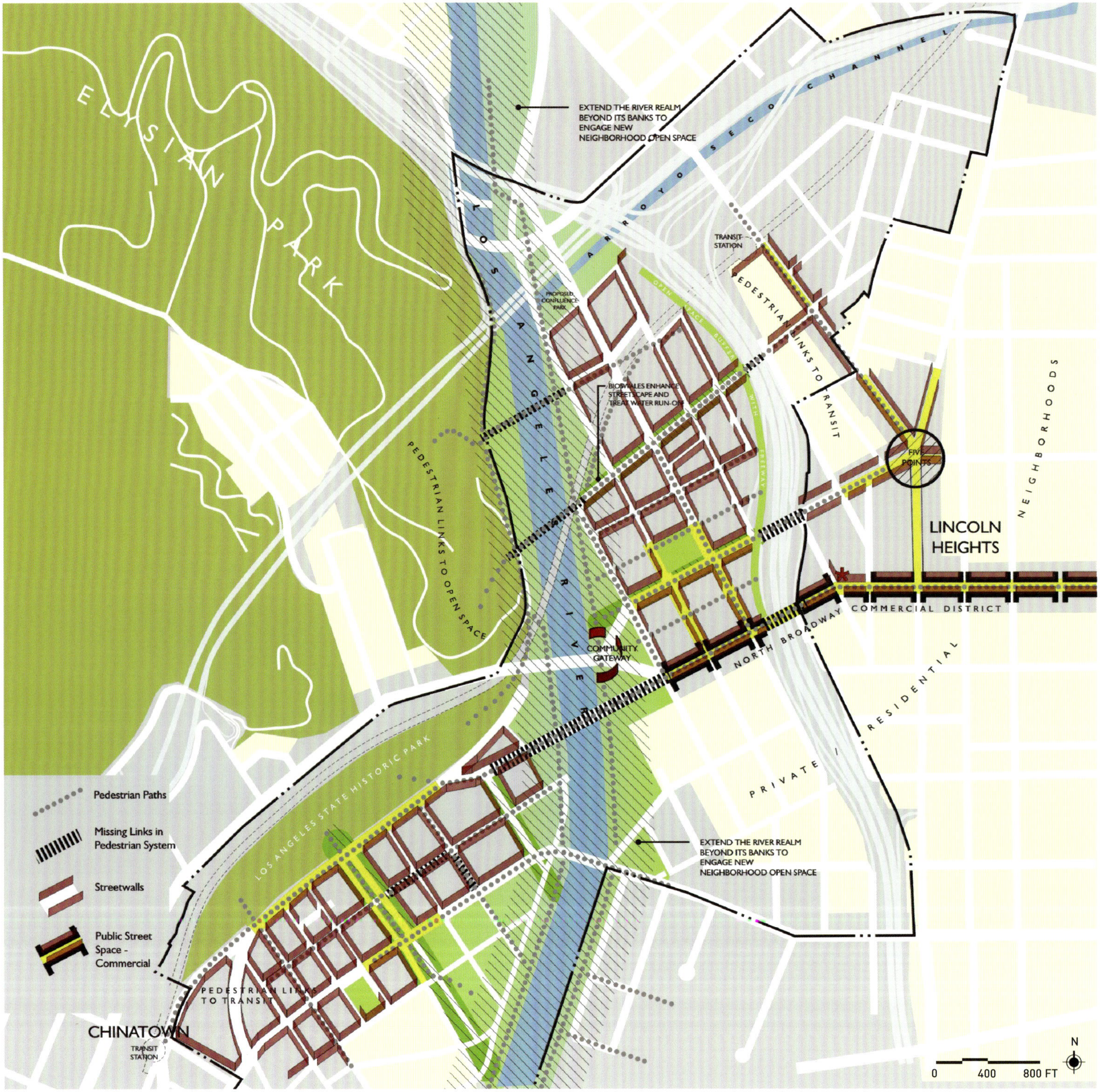

Block structure and streetwalls

Open space and view corridors

The streets and sidewalks and other modes of movement through a city are the critical glue that holds the city's various land uses together. When that glue fails, the city suffers and risks economic decline. Culver City, a separately incorporated city midway between downtown Los Angeles and the beach, sought to find solutions to existing city-wide issues like crippling daily through-traffic, particularly at rush hour, and the disconnected local street network that limits mobility between neighborhoods and across the city for those who live there. The Expo Light Rail Line, connecting Culver City to downtown, introduced a new catalyst for local mobility when it opened in 2012. This new connectivity to the region presented an opportunity to reenvision land use surrounding the station and exploring local mobility options within the city, including the transit hub and its surrounding neighborhoods.

The resulting plan, or visioning strategy, emerged from eight public workshops with community groups, City staff, and general public input to the project's interactive website, with the goal to increase the viability of alternative mobility modes for residents and other users by developing more and better choices. Recommendations for both near-term improvements

CULVER CITY TRANSIT ORIENTED DEVELOPMENT
CULVER CITY, CALIFORNIA, USA

AWARD
- APA California, Planning Award

UCLA
SANTA MONICA
CULVER CITY
BALDWIN HILLS
MARINA
DEL REY
N
0 1,500 3,000 4,500 FT

and longer-term strategies include a perimeter parking and circulation plan to discourage cut-through traffic; improved access points to major employment centers; a system of flexible, on-demand micro-transit with dedicated street lanes and strategic connections; a Complete Streets redesign for Washington Boulevard as the area's main spine; a comprehensive network of bike routes and bike facilities; more frequent and improved crosswalks for pedestrian priority and other neighborhood protection measures; an expanded transit oriented development district with a new specific plan; and a robust transit demand management program ultimately for city-wide application. The strategies embody the community's priorities: pedestrians first, transit next, then bikes, and cars last.

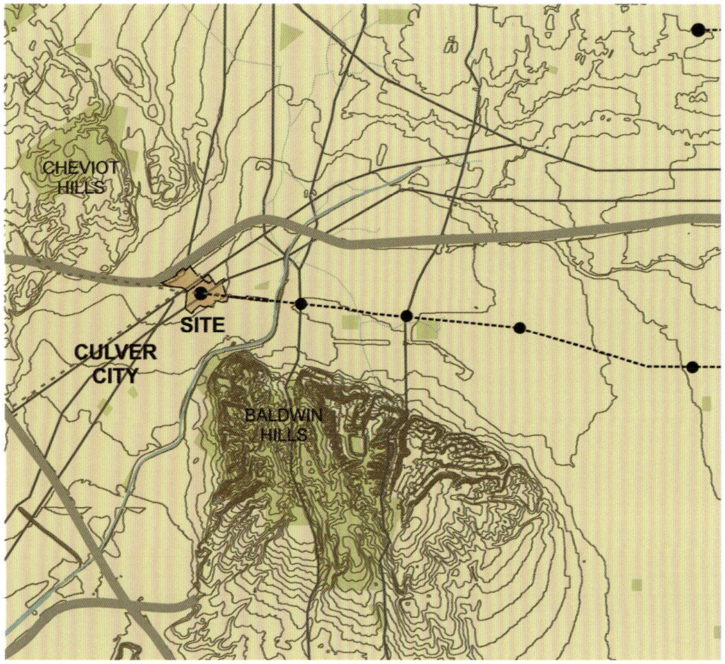

Regional setting

Existing road systems, freeway, and rail

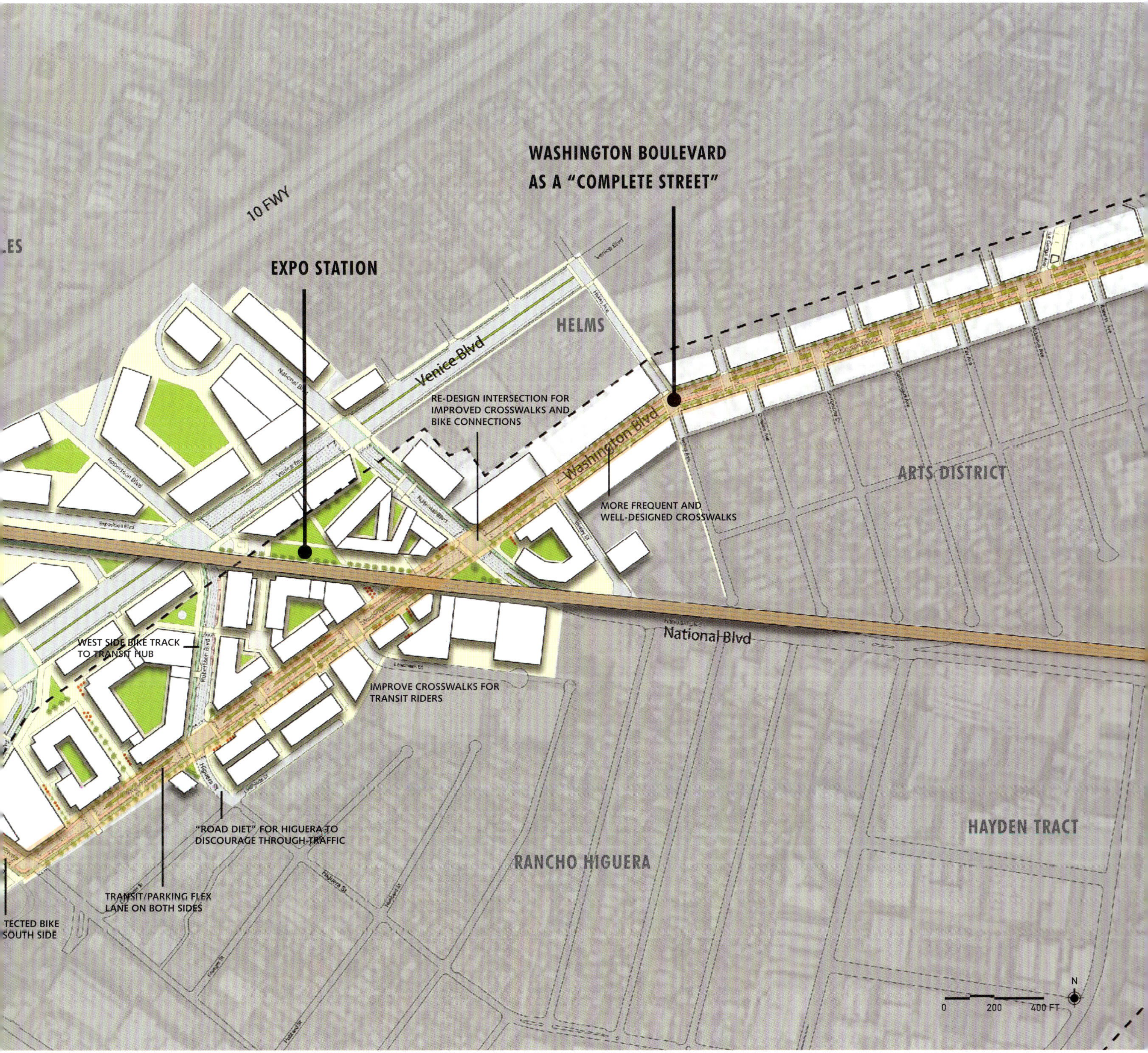
WASHINGTON BOULEVARD
AS A "COMPLETE STREET"
10 FWY
EXPO STATION
HELMS
Venice Blvd
Washington Blvd
RE-DESIGN INTERSECTION FOR IMPROVED CROSSWALKS AND BIKE CONNECTIONS
MORE FREQUENT AND WELL-DESIGNED CROSSWALKS
ARTS DISTRICT
National Blvd
WEST SIDE BIKE TRACK TO TRANSIT HUB
IMPROVE CROSSWALKS FOR TRANSIT RIDERS
"ROAD DIET" FOR HIGUERA TO DISCOURAGE THROUGH-TRAFFIC
TRANSIT/PARKING FLEX LANE ON BOTH SIDES
TECTED BIKE SOUTH SIDE
RANCHO HIGUERA
HAYDEN TRACT
0
200
400 FT
N

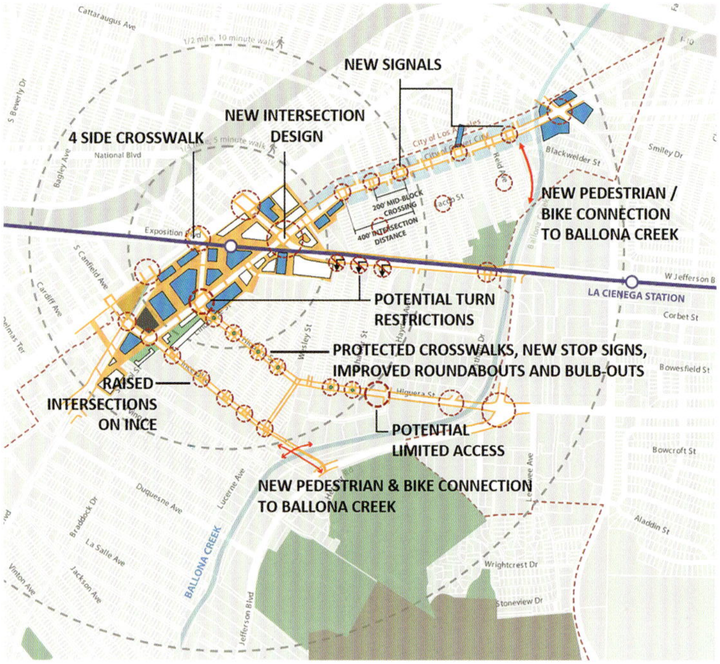

Pedestrian network recommendations

Variable network of traffic to minimize conflicts with other modes

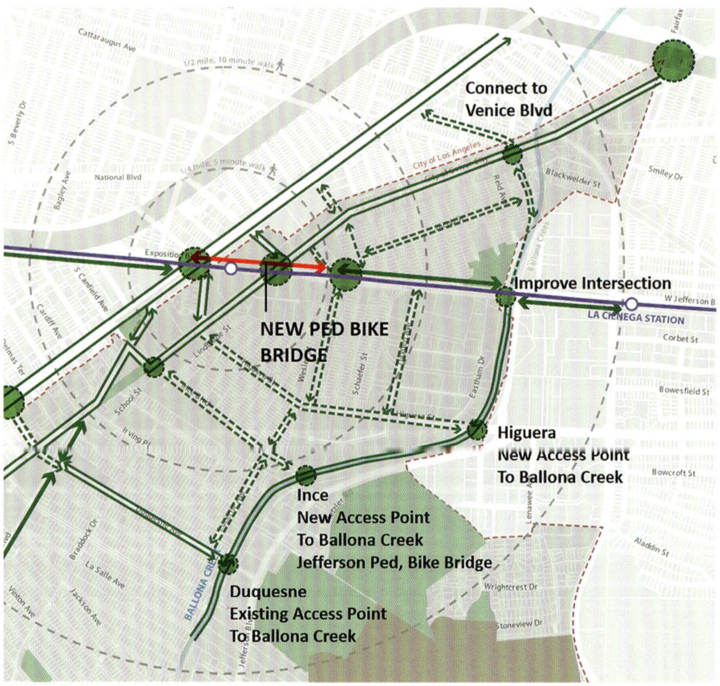

Bicycle network

Vehicular traffic management

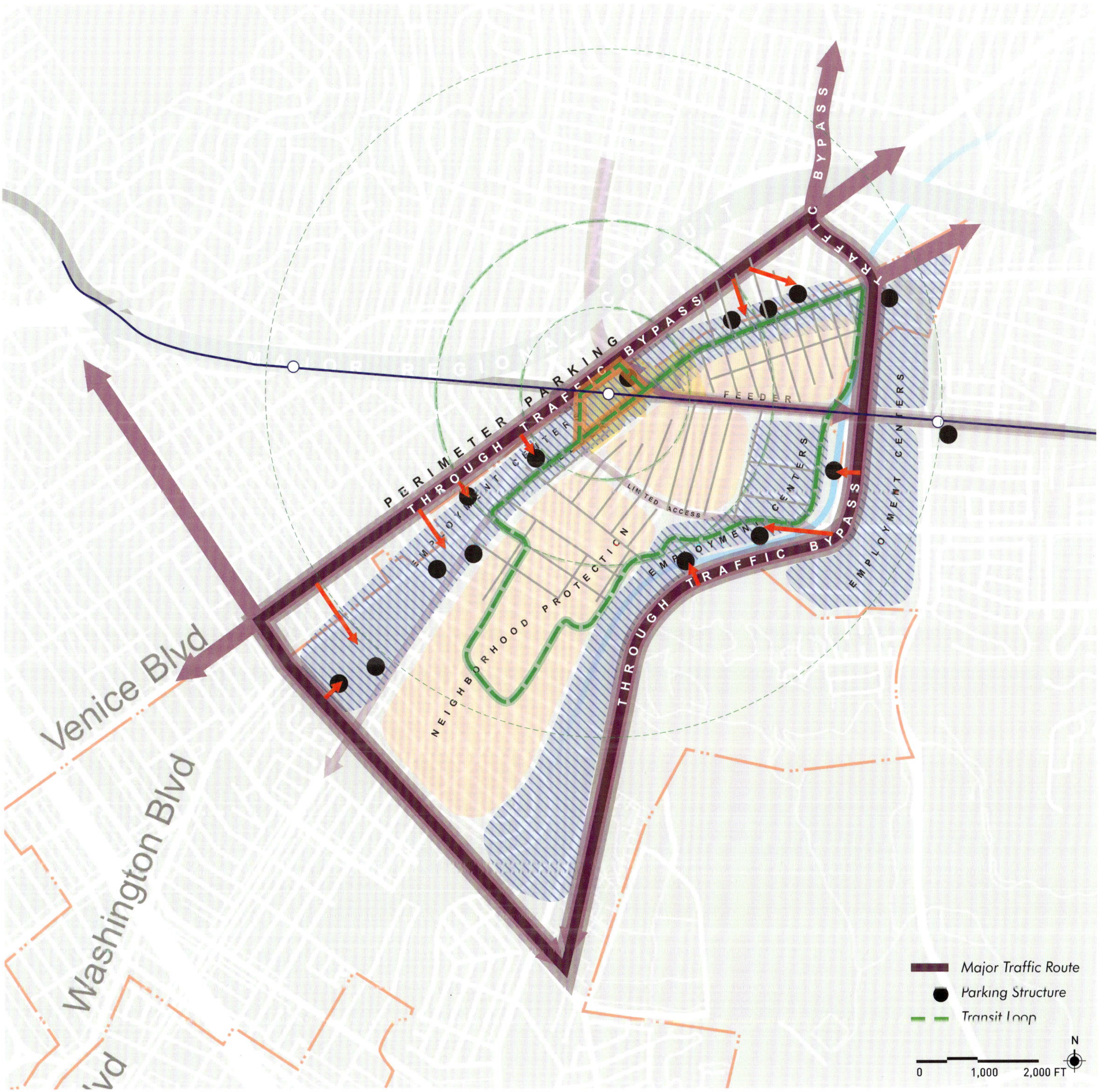

Recommendations for traffic diversion: conserve and protect the character of existing residential neighborhood quality

City bike tour

Workshop breakout sessions

Workshop citizen presentation

Culver City architects' panel

Public workshop

What remains in memory more: the overall impression of a city's grand boulevard, or the individual pieces that make it up? The streets and paths that stitch together the fabric of the city are the conduits of time and motion that allow the whole to come together and make sense, for better or worse. With "highway commercial" zoning that would encourage strip retail malls along the city's main vehicular route, Highway 111, the City of Indian Wells was poised to continue the auto-oriented strip retail development like other cities along the corridor. Seeing an opportunity to distinguish and differentiate itself, the City rezoned the 3.5-mile highway corridor limiting uses to landscape buffer and residential development. Despite strong support from the community, eleven highway property owners who were subject to the zone change filed lawsuits against the city for "downzoning" their properties. The council decided to adopt a Specific Plan for the highway frontage supporting its vision for the city.

The Specific Plan includes a combination of residential, resort, community, and open space uses. Research of the city's history discovered, for instance, that the highway right-of-way was once an airplane landing strip. The city also had been the location of many date groves, a few remnants of which still existed. During the nineteenth century, Indigenous tribes in the area dug holes with circular ramps deep into the earth in search of water. The team's research discovered the location of one of these wells within the highway corridor and included it in the plan for restoration. The Highway 111 plan proposed a landscape zone on both sides of the highway, prescribing a "formal" edge of date palms in multiple rows on the north side compatible with a major resort hotel and golf course there, and a more informal landscaped edge on the south side deferring to the smaller scale of its single-family homes. The project captured elements of the "real" desert, visually framing them, like California plein air desert paintings, as the desert plain, the mountains, and the sky—all now emblematic views from the road in Indian Wells.

HIGHWAY 111
INDIAN WELLS, CALIFORNIA, USA

AWARDS
- AIA National, Urban Design Award
- AIA Los Angeles, Urban Design Award
- Progressive Architecture Urban Design Award

COACHELLA VALLEY
INDIAN WELLS
0
0.5
1
1.5 MI
N

ELDORADO DR
INDIAN WELLS

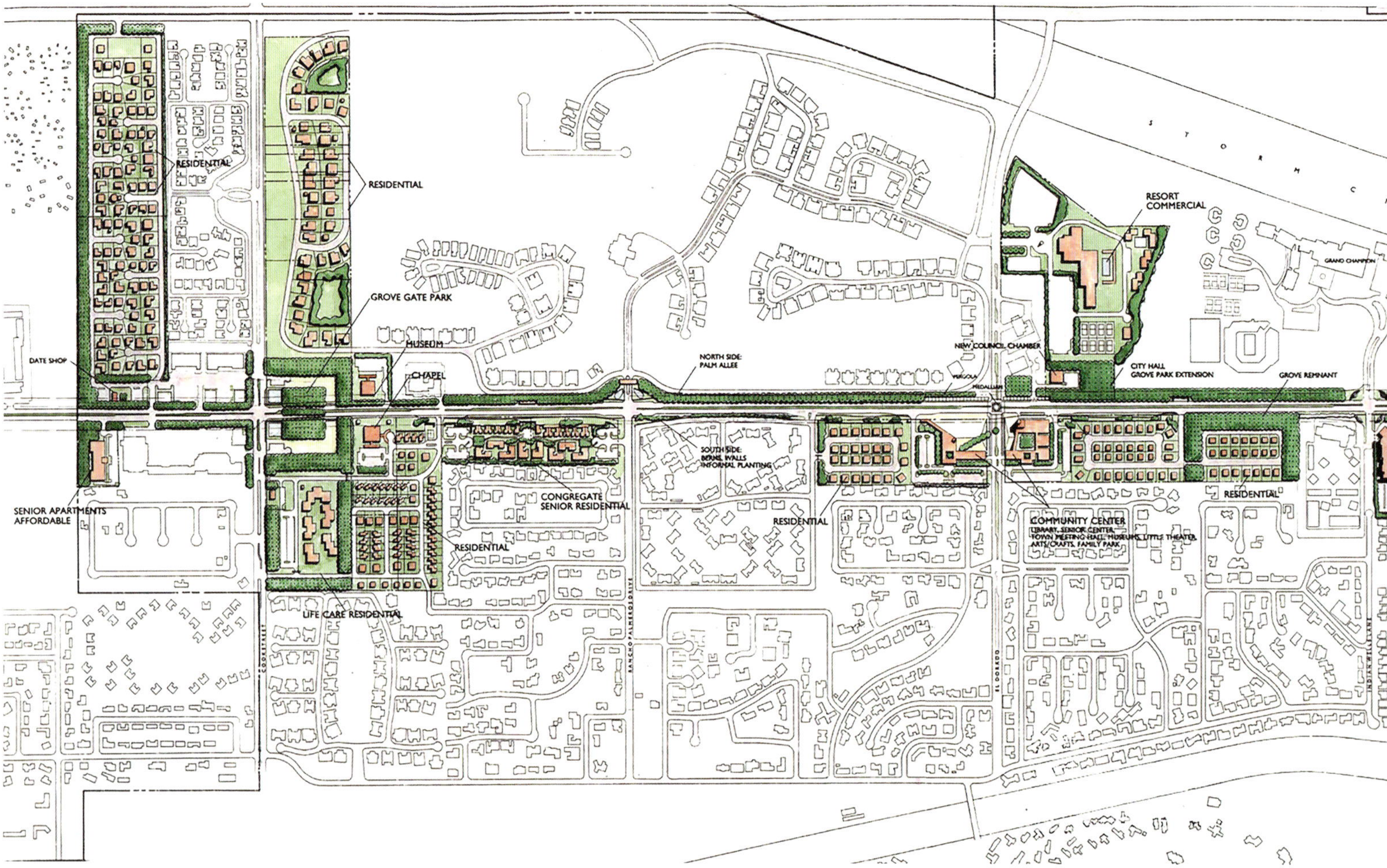

Master plan

View of Highway 111 looking west towards Grove Gate Park

Cahuilla Interpretive Center and Well

KEY

1. Grove Gate
2. Desert Garden Center
3. Desert Art Museum
4. Residential Node
5. Formal Palm Allee
6. Informal Edge
7. Civic Node
8. Existing City Hall
9. Community Center
10. Library Center
11. Resort Commerce Node
12. Arts / Music Center
13. Fountain
14. Natural History Museum
15. Cahuilla Interpretive Center
16. Wind Row Planting
17. Desert Golf Links
18. Point Happy
19. Strip Commercial
20. Mt. Eisenhower

Design principles

In the Grove Gate

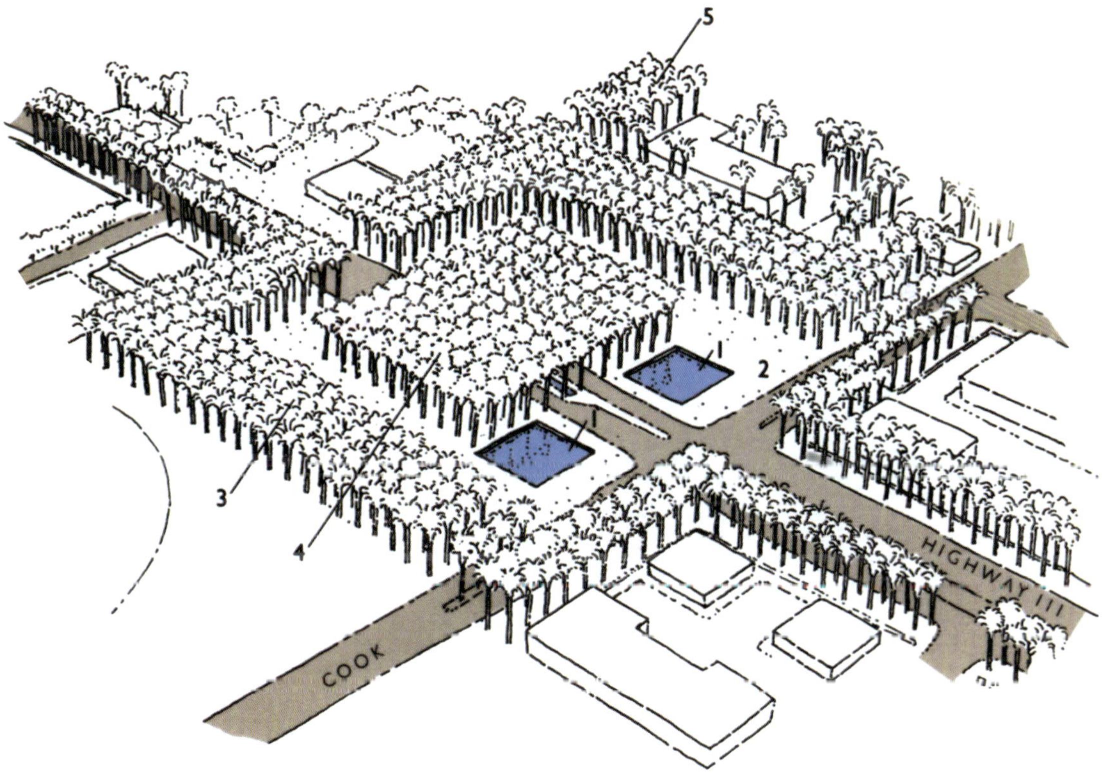

KEY

1. Reflecting Pools
2. Desert Landscape
3. Palm "Wall" Defines Outdoor "Room"
4. Grove Gate
5. Grove Remnant

Grove Gate

Desert view at civic node

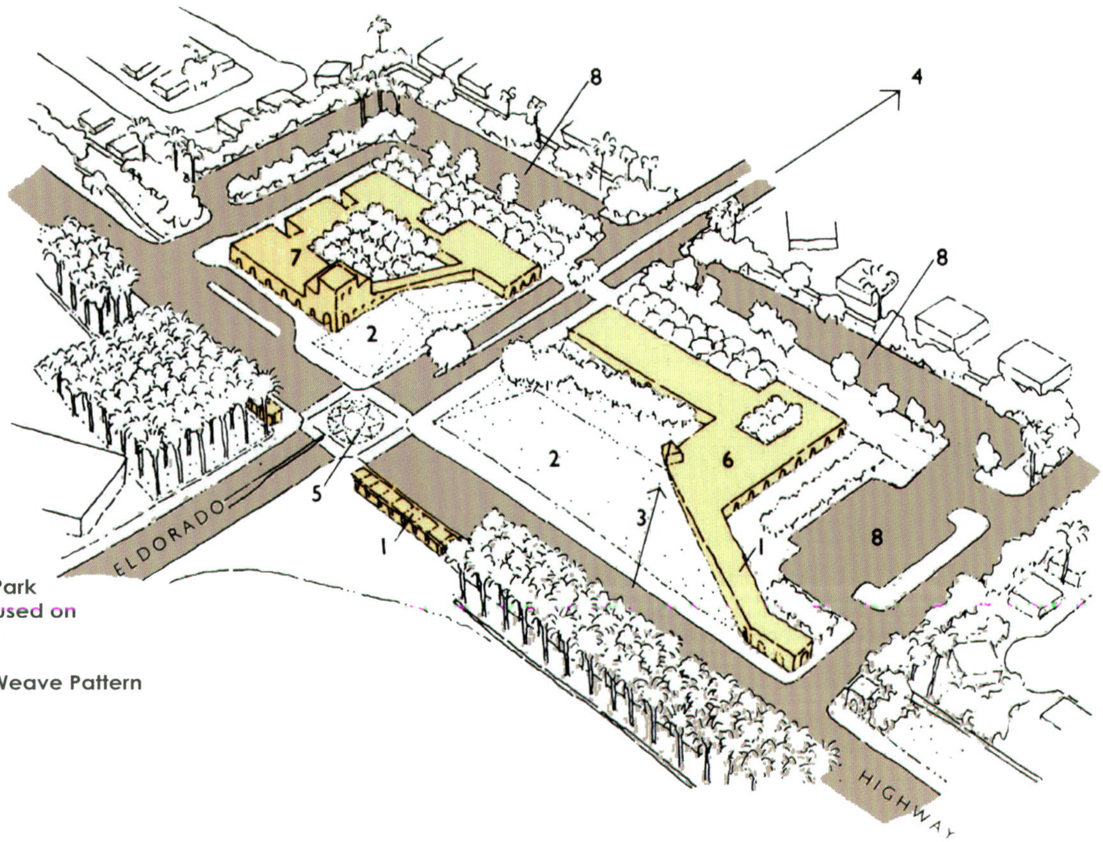

KEY

1. Arcade or Pergola
2. Bermed Natural Desert Park
3. Foreshortened Wall Focused on Reduced Scale Building
4. View to Mt. Eisenhower
5. Cahuilla Indian Basket Weave Pattern
6. Community Buildings
7. Library
8. Parking

Civic node

Axial view of fountain

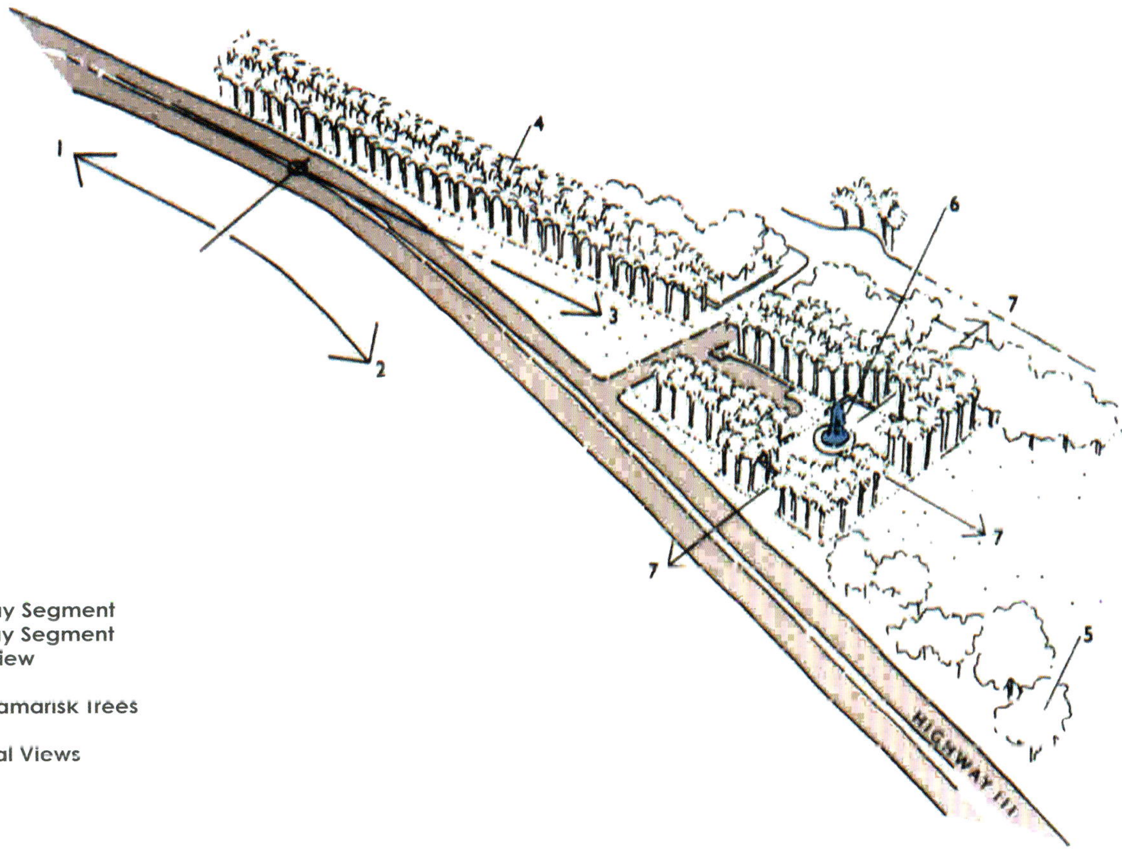

KEY

1. Straight Highway Segment
2. Curved Highway Segment
3. Primary Axial View
4. Palm Allee
5. Native Desert Tamarisk Trees
6. Fountain
7. Secondary Axial Views

Fountain

CITY CULTURE KNOWLEDGE REGION

The narrative of the Oklahoma Native American tribes' unique history is complex, unsettling, and little understood by most Americans. It is a story needing to be revealed, but because it is embraced by all Indigenous peoples, it must be told by the descendants of those who survived it and, as some asserted in this planning process, overcame its cruelties to become renewed and redefined as a people. Comprising the thirty-nine tribes of Oklahoma, each maintaining its deeply rooted historical identity, the Native American population today sought to tell the story of "Oklahoma Indians." It is a story forged in the hardships of the past, but one the tribes sought to tell through uplifting themes of diversity, adaptation, identity, and survival.

The idea to tell the story of the Oklahoma Indian originated with several tribal elders in the 1970s and finally gathered bipartisan support by a group of Oklahoma state senators by the mid 1990s. Thus began a twenty-five-year journey, beginning with the facility programming and site selection and later the architectural design for the museum you see today, which opened to the public in the autumn of 2021. With the schedule protracted by sporadic funding and lengthy deliberations among the various tribal interests, the design team used the time to better

FIRST AMERICANS MUSEUM
OKLAHOMA CITY, OKLAHOMA, USA

AWARDS

- AIA Next LA, Honor Award
- AIA Oklahoma City Chapter Merit Award
- AIA Los Angeles, Design Award
- National EPA Phoenix Award, Excellence in Brownfield Development
- ULI, Americas Awards for Excellence
- The Chicago Athenaeum, The American Architecture Award

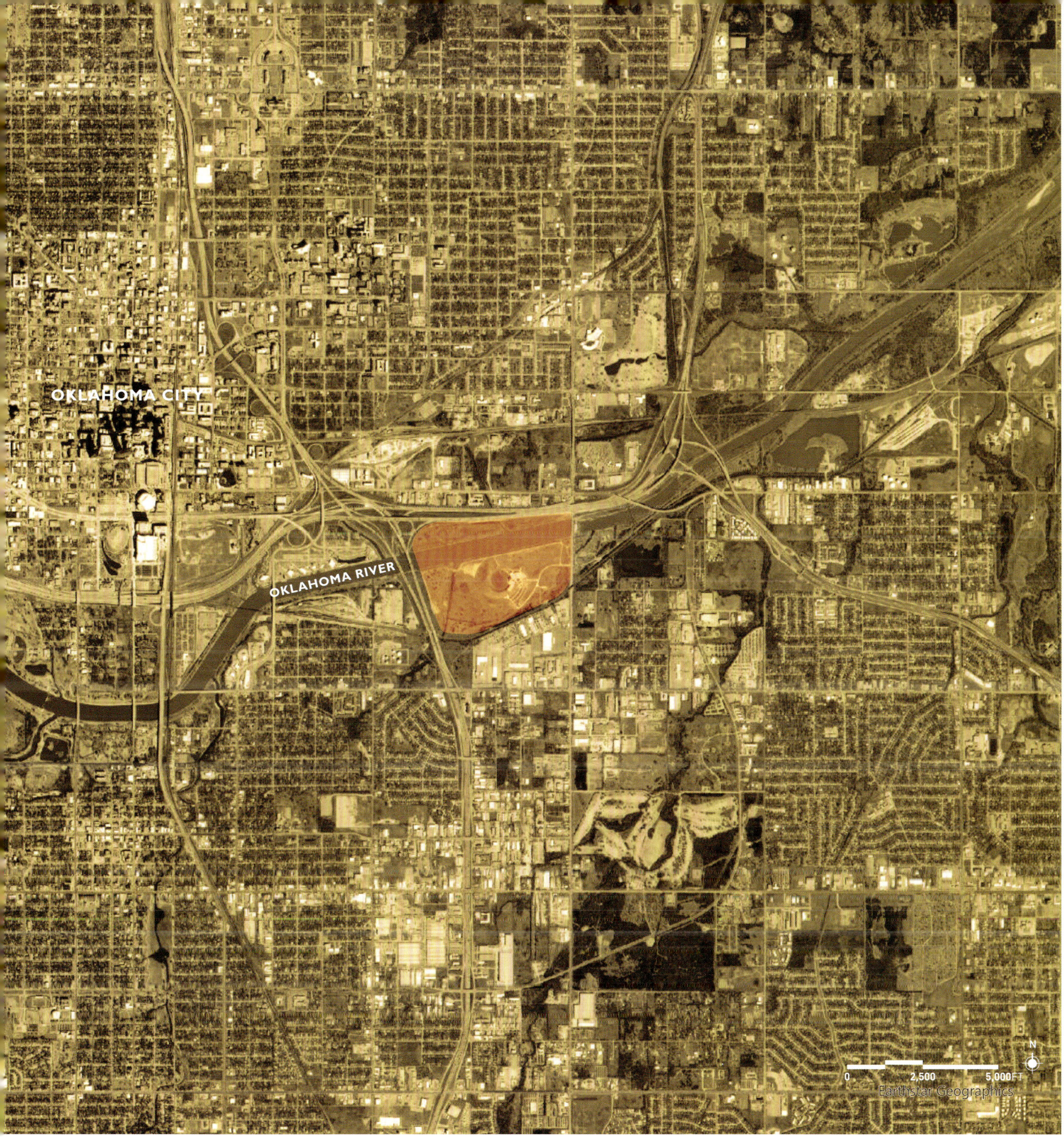
OKLAHOMA CITY
OKLAHOMA RIVER
N
0
2,500
5,000FT
Earthstar Geographics

understand Native people and to translate the understanding into a meaningful design. The First Americans Museum is their project, not ours, and as designers we believe it to be all the better for that.

The selection of Oklahoma City as the museum site was essential for telling the story. The site embodies the three origin ecologies of the various tribes (Plains, River, Woodlands). The tribes' restoration of the site from its history of resource exploitation as Oklahoma's "drilling site number one" offered an opportunity to tell of the circular history of the site and Indian way of nonlinear thinking, a holistic worldview that finds its reference points in nature. The museum's circular earth mound is an enormous solar "cosmological clock," highlighting the equinoxes; the intersecting circles signify Earth and the People, prehistory crossed by European introduction. Galleries tell the story of the Oklahoma Indian, with facilities for storytelling, tribal meetings, heritage research and tribal origins, and children's discoveries.

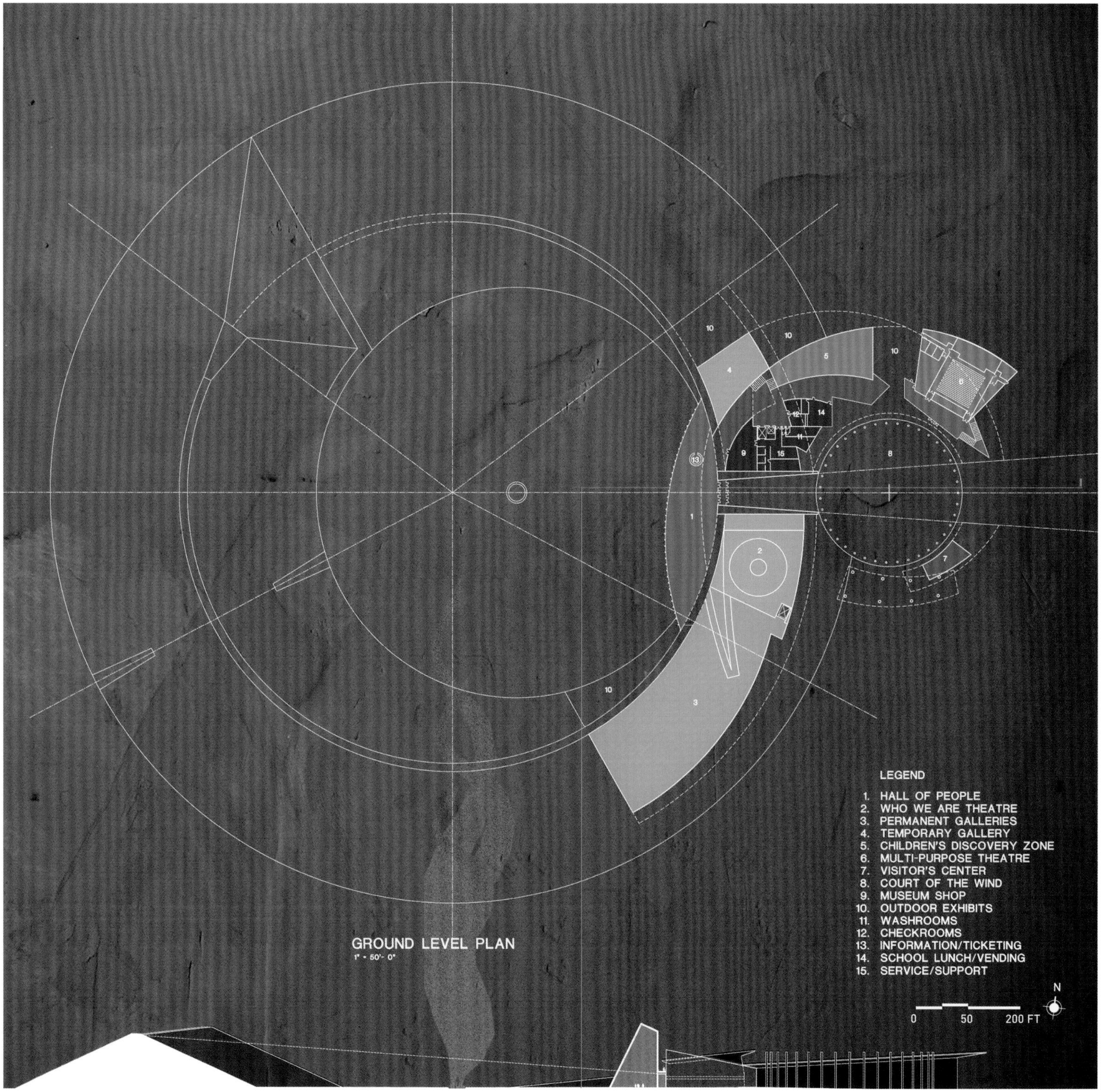

Ground level plan

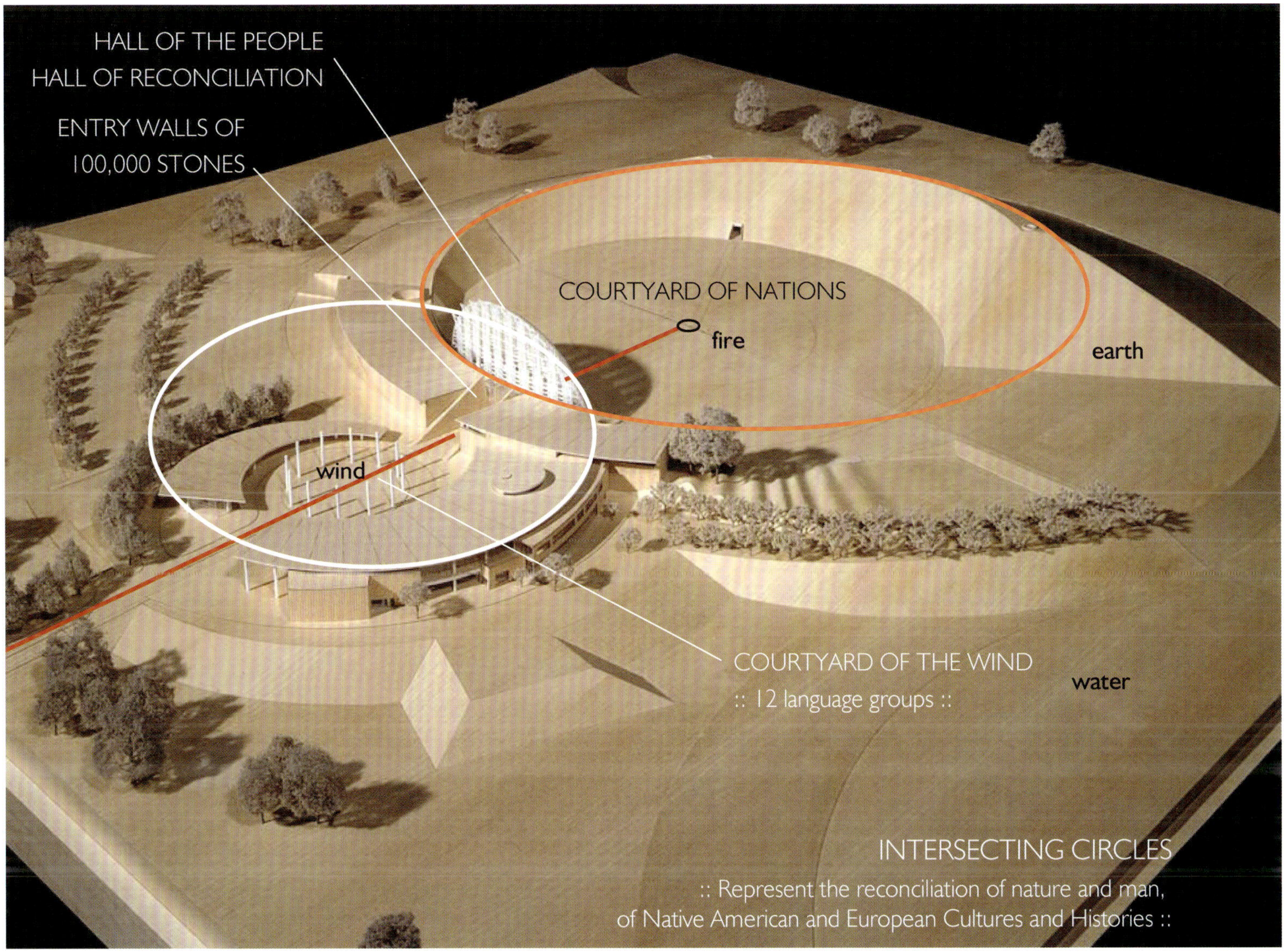

Intersecting circles

Physical model

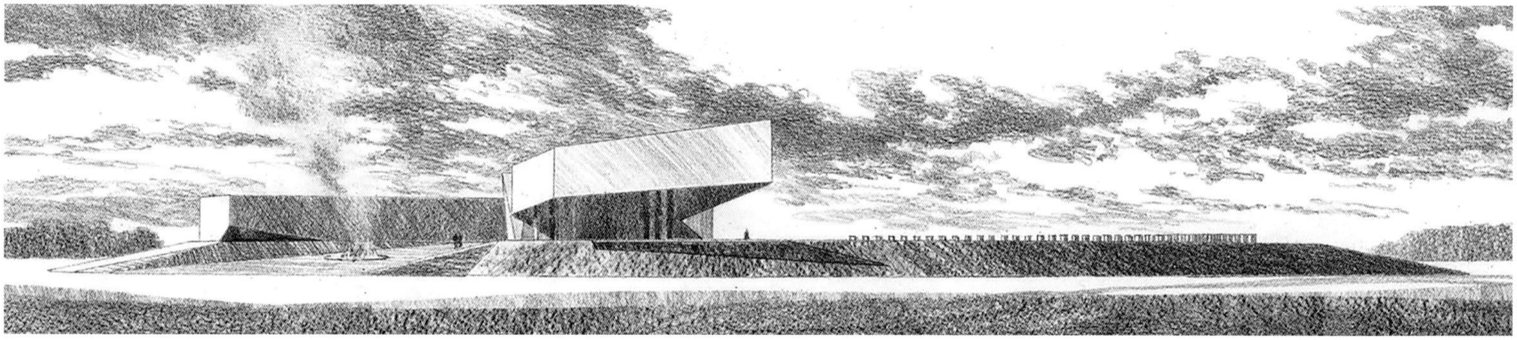

Alternative 1: On the Earth

Alternative 2: Of the Earth

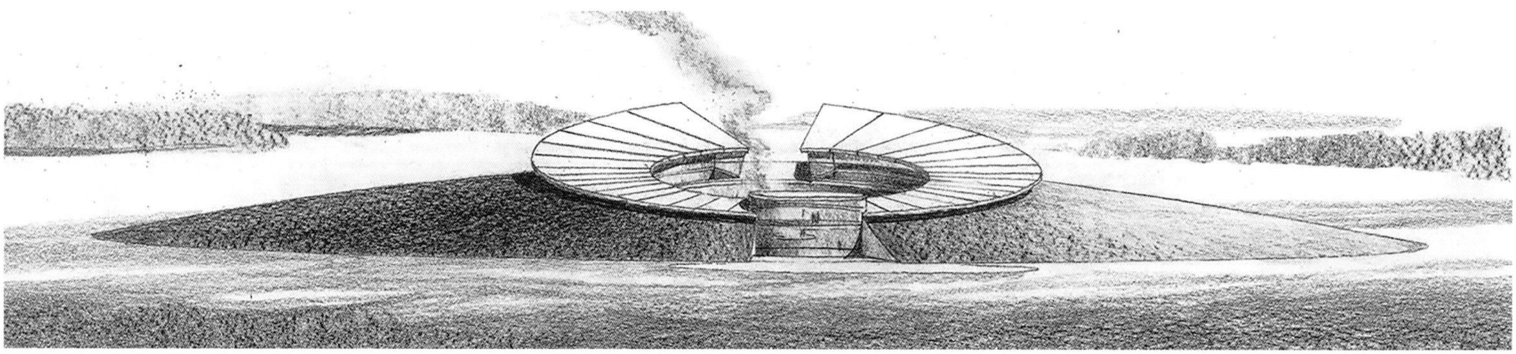

Alternative 3: In the Earth

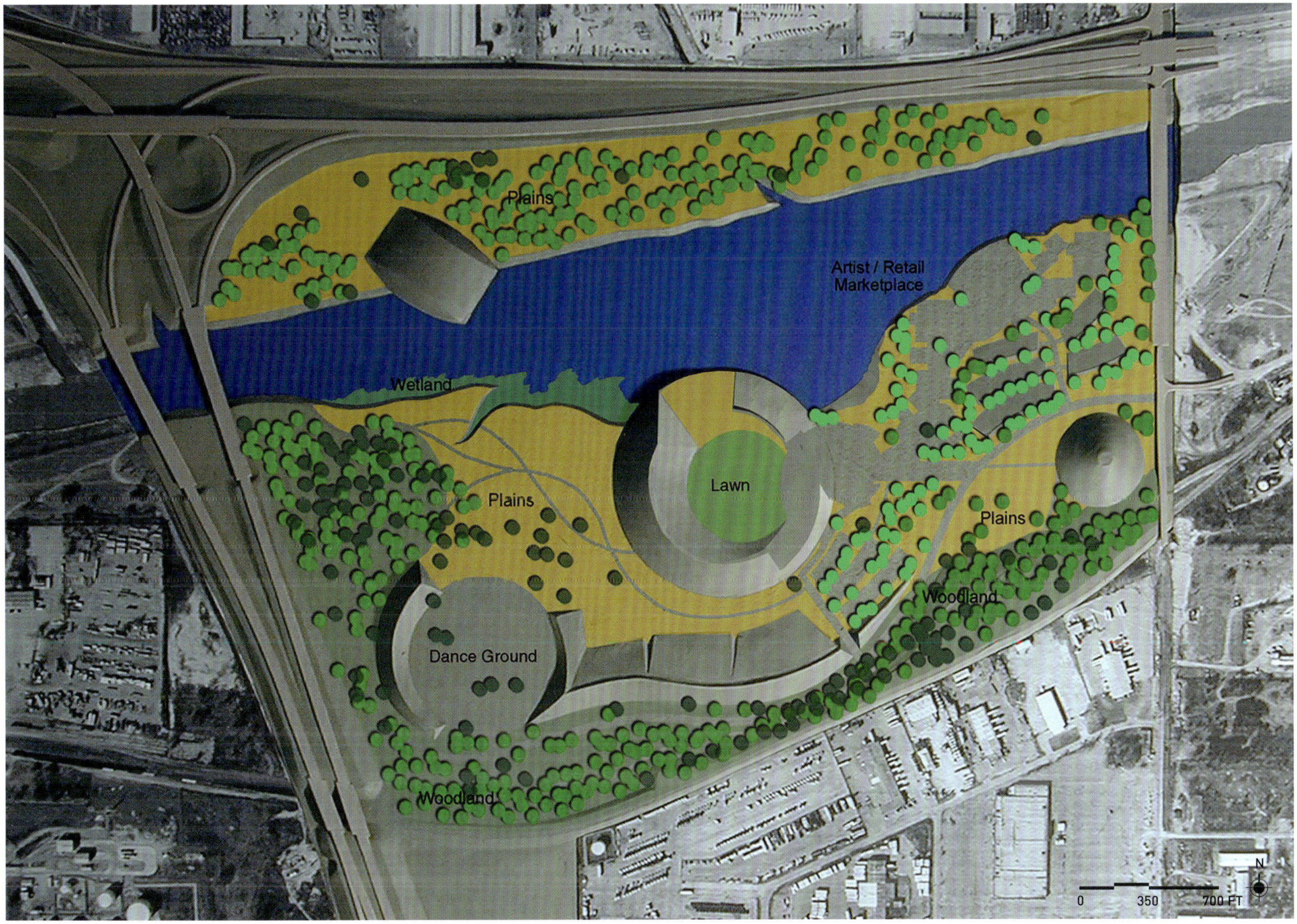

Three ecologies

Plains

Woodlands

River

HISTORIC AND INSPIRATION IMAGES

Wichita grass house

1930 crude oil production on site

Indian burial ground

Drum circle

Native American Eagle dance

Pow Wow — sacred social gathering

Workshops

Workshop

Aerial view of the museum

Summer solstice

Winter solstice

Equinox

Promontory walk

Gala at the museum

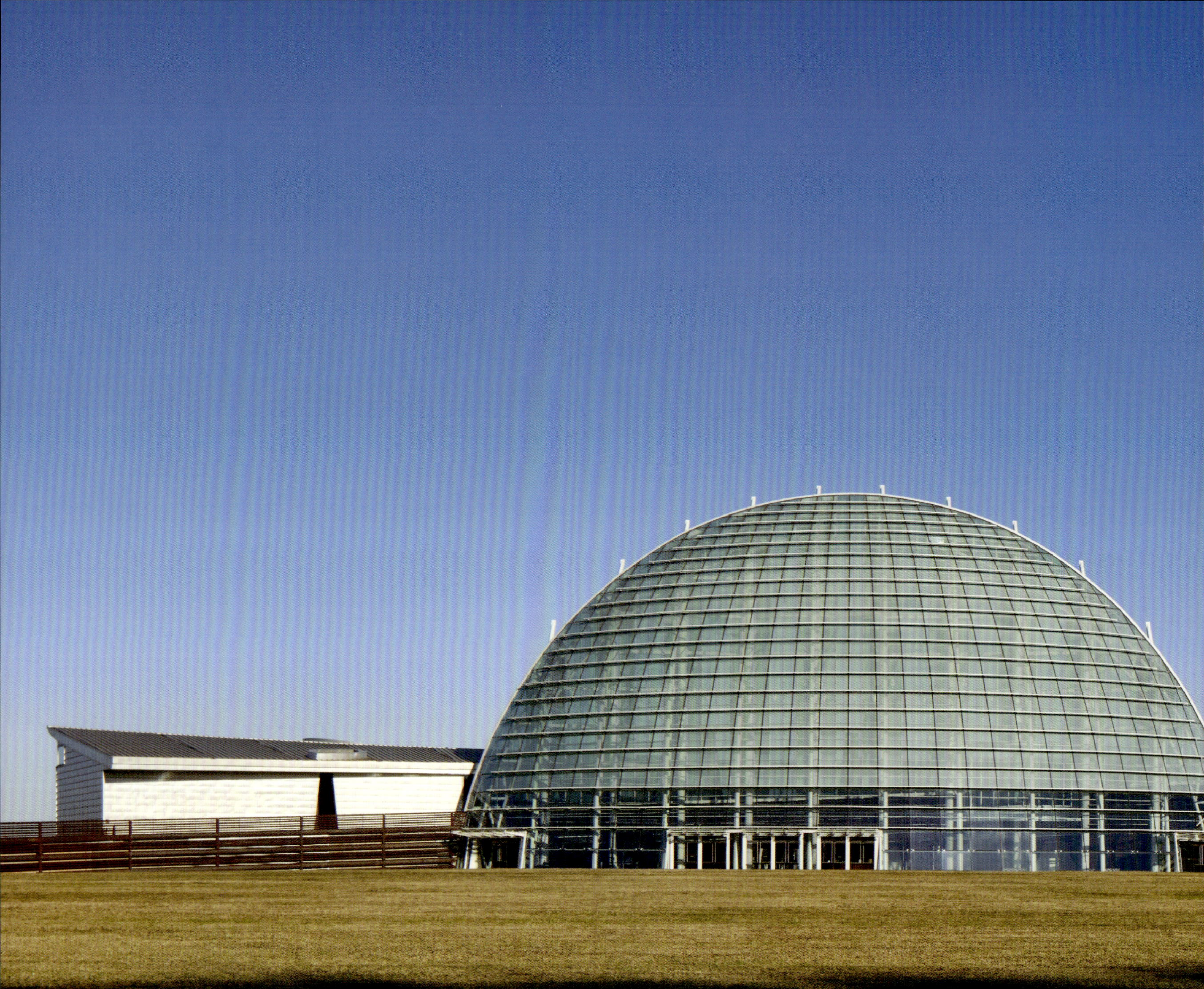

The culture of a city rests in its residential neighborhoods, each with its own identity and character, but all in their totality defining the meaning of their city. It is not surprising, then, that there should be lively debate when the time comes to bring change to some of that culture's character-defining landmarks. The historic piers of San Francisco are both iconic to the city and unique in their redevelopment potential. Piers 27, 29, and 31, located a half mile from the famous Fisherman's Wharf and Pier 39, are among the underutilized assets, with the potential for providing increased access and new uses for the waterfront. At the public hearing before the San Francisco Port Authority to choose between two master plan proposals for the piers' reuse, of which included a new YMCA, there was an outpouring of support for the YMCA. Support came from many neighborhoods of the city of all ages and races and swayed the Port Commissioners to award the project, despite an aggressively promoted submission from the competitor that had lobbied heavily in the neighboring community.

The plan paid deference to the passions of the communities for recreation and the waterfront. The dramatic transformation of that waterfront from predominantly light industry to mixed-use,

YMCA PIERS
SAN FRANCISCO, CALIFORNIA, USA

SAN FRANCISCO BAY
DOWNTOWN SAN FRANCISCO
N
0 300 600 900 FT

office, and commercial opens the doors to the Bay. The redevelopment plan proposed a new recreational mixed-use project in partnership with the YMCA, providing a unique opportunity to bring a diverse community to the water's edge with recreational activities in the true spirit of San Francisco. Active and passive recreation is programmed throughout the project in both indoors and outdoors. A range of unique open space environments are created by the plan, grouped into three major zones. A new cross-axial promenade is proposed as part of the overall circulation network. The promenade spans the entire project along the inner edge of the pier basins linking the Marine Center to the Northeast Wharf Plaza.

2002 aerial

Accessibility, circulation and opportunity

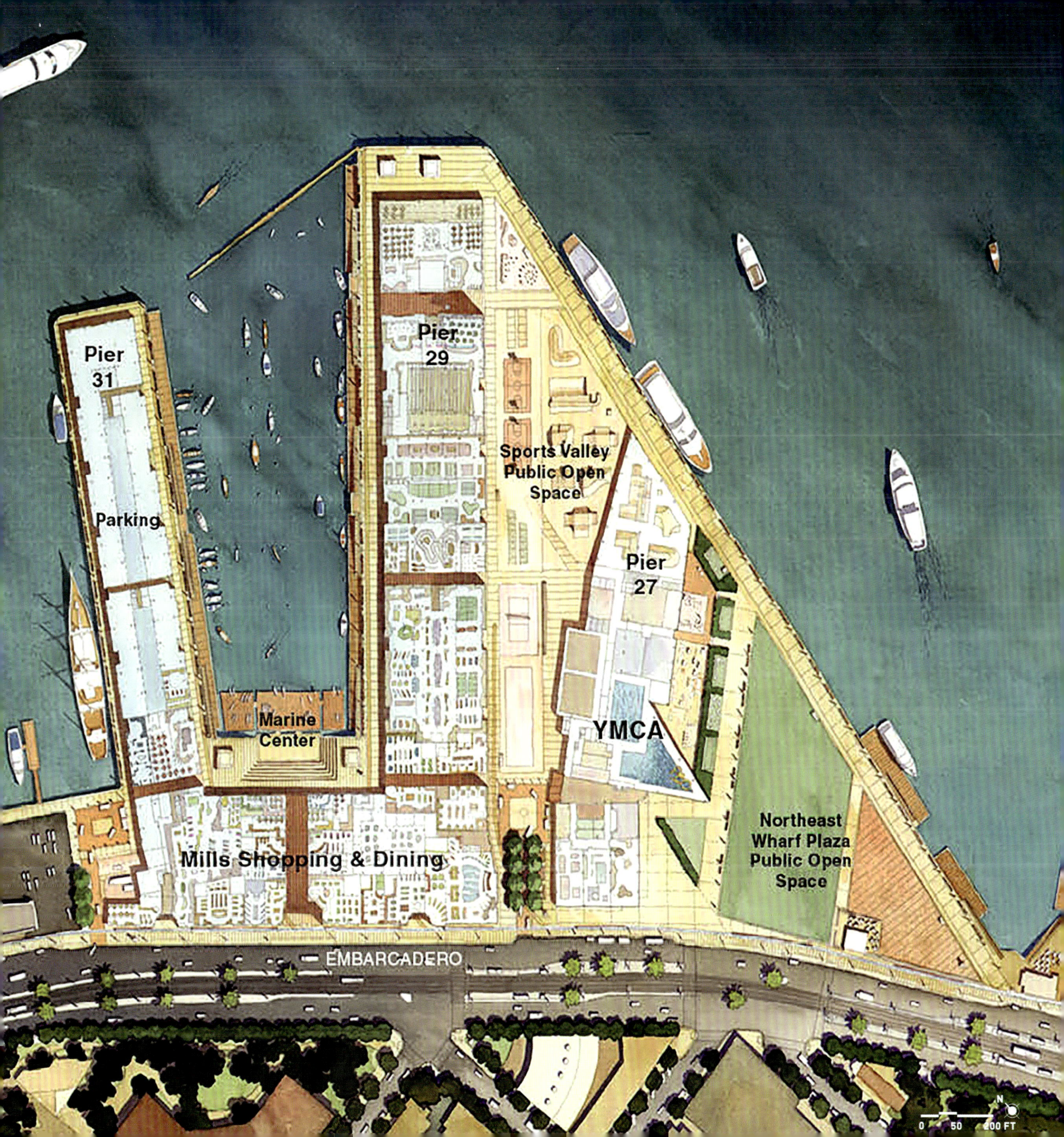
Pier 31
Parking
Pier 29
Marine Center
Sports Valley Public Open Space
Pier 27
YMCA
Mills Shopping & Dining
Northeast Wharf Plaza Public Open Space
EMBARCADERO
0 50 200 FT

Northeast Wharf Plaza

YMCA entrance

Sports Valley

Public gallery

Upper level

A record of war, service, survival, and restoration is written as a visual social history in the structures and landscapes of the West Los Angeles Veterans Affairs campus. This record has been rendered invisible in recent years — or at least as invisible as a 388-acre site in the midst of prosperous westside Los Angeles can be — by neglect and misuse. Originally deeded to the federal government in 1887 for use as a "Soldier's Home," the campus has degraded over time, with land, housing, and amenities unused and in disrepair. Under the terms of a court-ordered settlement honoring stipulations in the original 1887 deed, the U.S. Department of Veteran Affairs (VA) was directed to prepare a master plan to revitalize the campus to be "Veteran-centric" once again. The resultant Draft Master Plan Framework is one of a series of steps toward revitalization of the West Los Angeles Campus for veterans' use and represents a commitment to restore and reactivate the site to play the role for which it was historically intended, as a "Veterans Home" for veterans.

The Master Plan Framework will guide the VA in determining and implementing the most effective use of the campus for veterans, particularly homeless Veterans, including underserved

WEST LA VA CAMPUS
LOS ANGELES, CALIFORNIA, USA

AWARDS
- APA California, Urban Design Award
- APA Los Angeles, Planning Award

GETTY CENTER
UCLA
BEVERLY HILLS
WESTWOOD
SANTA MONICA
N
0 0.2 0.4 0.6 MI

populations such as female veterans, aging veterans, and those who are severely physically or mentally disabled. The Framework envisions a long-term build-out focused on housing and services for veterans, restores and enhances the site's historic legacy, conserves and repairs its natural setting, and facilitates and promotes reintegration of veterans into civilian life. The plan is based on principles of community design as a home for all veterans, composed of diverse but well-defined mixed-use neighborhoods forming, in the broadest sense, a therapeutic community setting for veterans to live and reintegrate into civilian society. The Master Plan Framework establishes a Central Square as a community focal point and mixed-use center for veterans' activities; reuse of the site's industrial area as a veteran reintegration zone with continuing education, job training, veteran business incubator space, and programs for the arts; access to the site from the Metro subway; enhanced health care facilities, including new research laboratories and graduated care facilities for aging veterans.

N
0
100
200 FT

Existing site

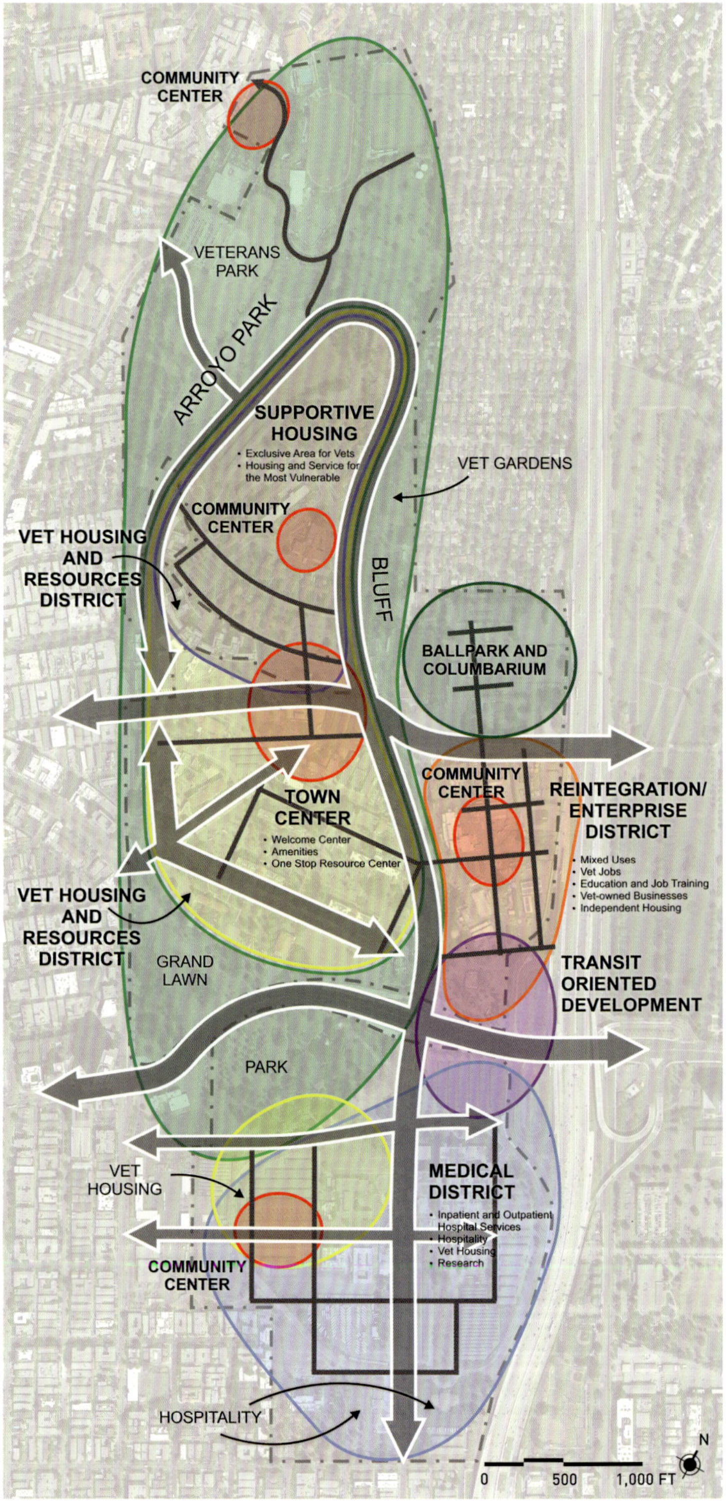

Plan concept

Master plan

Land use

Wadsworth Chapel

Reintegration enterprise district

Town Center plaza

If the hills and canyons of Southern California seem somehow familiar even to those who have never visited, it is at least in part because they have been in the background of movies and television seen by millions. One such location is Walt Disney's 890-acre Golden Oak Ranch, located in Santa Clarita, California, that has been used for film production since the 1950s. The rustic setting, sweeping vistas, and ability to build large-scale sets have made Golden Oak Ranch an important location for outdoor film, television, and commercial productions. Despite these advantages, the lack of indoor production space limits the usability of this location. Disney | ABC Studios at The Ranch have created a major new movie and TV studio by combining the benefits of a large outdoor filming venue with a highly controlled and efficient indoor soundstages complex.

The site for Disney | ABC Studios at The Ranch preserves the natural setting of Golden Oak Ranch and Placerita Canyon by locating the studio with its soundstages on a fifty-six-acre site in the westernmost portion of the property, directly adjacent to the State Route 14 freeway. This preserves 90 percent of the Ranch's natural area for outdoor shooting and locates the remaining state-of-the-art soundstages and associated production support facilities as a buffer between the Ranch and the highway. The plan calls for a minimum of eight and maximum of twelve, 20,000-square-foot television stages with production offices attached to the exterior walls to provide convenient access from staff offices to the studio while giving the sound stage a smaller scaled façade. Studio mill facilities have a central location to the sound stages. Studio administration and producer bungalows as well as amenities such as the commissary and gym are located overlooking the natural stream course of the canyon below. The vegetation and natural open space of Placerita Creek are an amenity to the adjoining studio complex, which the studio's extensive habitat restoration plan is designed to restore, revegetate, and enhance the natural environment with native and riparian plant species.

DISNEY ABC STUDIOS
SANTA CLARITA, CALIFORNIA, USA

SANTA CLARITA
SAN FERNANDO
0
0.2
0.4
0.6 MI
N

AL FORSTER '09

Studio entrance

Master plan

Building Number and Use

1–12 Soundstages

13 Warehouse

14 Central Utility Plant and Associated Exterior Equipment

15–16 Administration

17, 26 Writers/Producers Bungalows

18, 19, 22, 27, 30, 31 Production Offices

20, 21, 23, 24, 32, 33 Mills

25 Commissary

29 Electrical Substation

Circulation diagram

Access Point

Truck Circulation

Truck/ Equipment Parking

Car Circulation

Service Roads

P Surface Parking

P Permeable Surface/ Conditional Parking

Production zone

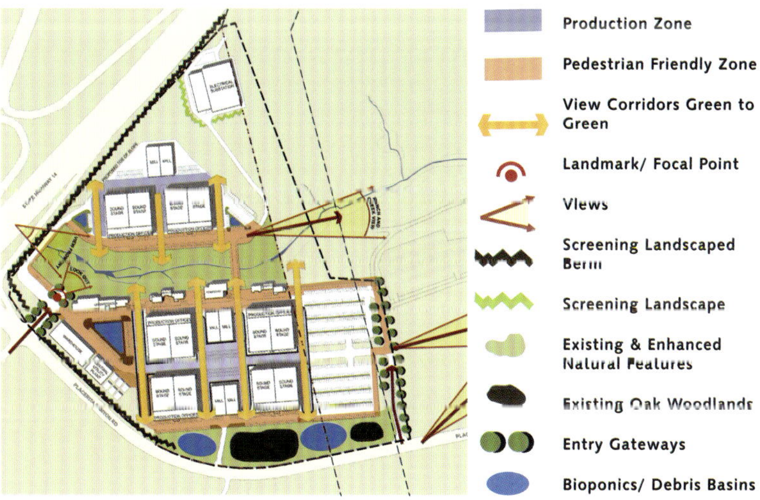

Urban design features

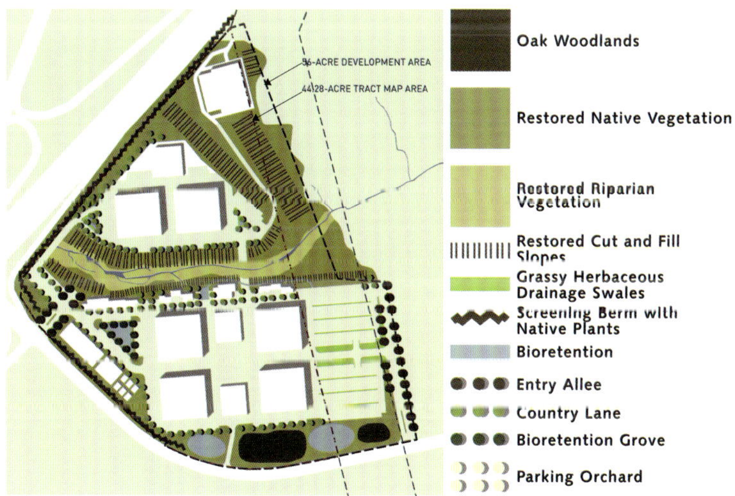

Landscape strategy

In contrast to earlier generations of studios where the backlot is the leftover space behind the sound stages, the plan for the DreamWorks SKG studio in Playa Vista, conceived as the first new motion picture studio in Los Angeles in over sixty years, makes the backlot the front lot at the center of the studio complex, creating an inviting, well-landscaped outdoor space upon entry. The studio plan celebrates its origins in two of Southern California's mythic industries of the past—aircraft and cinema—and heralds the coming of age of the region's hallmark industries of the future—multimedia entertainment and communications technology.

Collaborating with Steven Spielberg and his production designer, Rick Carter, the plan for the 100-acre Entertainment, Media and Technology District was specifically scenographic, beginning with experiential points of view and exploiting the principles of perspective and scale to enhance illusions of distance and open space within the site. Because the experience of viewpoints is different from various locations on the site, special attention was focused on the progression of imagery and the relative part each building and space plays as the point from which a person views the surrounding site, as well as the role it plays as an object or space to be viewed. It is a small step from scenographic site design to cinematographic production design techniques, and Spielberg's intention was to create an environment that could be used in future feature film shoots. The two approaches, from two distinct disciplines, were closely linked in both intent and technique, and the guidelines for the design of the campus drew equally from both.

DREAMWORKS SKG STUDIO
LOS ANGELES, CALIFORNIA, USA

SANTA MONICA
MARINA DEL REY
PLAYA VISTA
LOS ANGELES INTERNATIONAL AIRPORT
N
0 0.3 0.6 0.9 MI

Working on Spielberg's conceptual idea

On-site charrette at Howard Hughes's offices

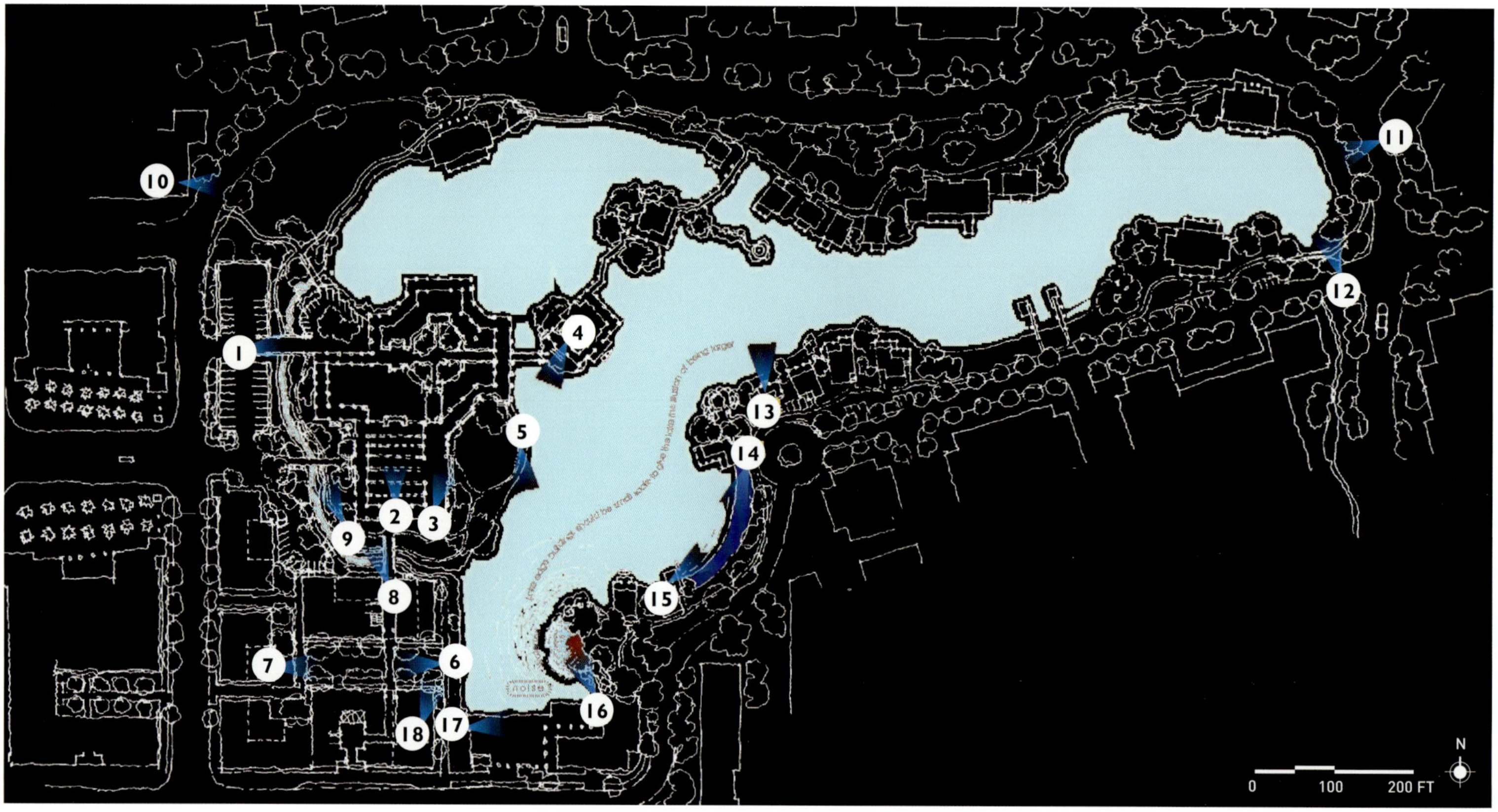

Location of key site views

14. Lake view

2. Headquarters living room

3. Porch

6. Internal campus street

CITY
CULTURE
KNOWLEDGE
REGION

Amgen, one of the world's largest biotechnology companies, found that its new opportunistically assembled campus in a former commercial-industrial park lacked coherence and functional efficiency and was distinctly out of step with Amgen's creative scientific culture. The company codified its values, and one in particular — "to collaborate, communicate and be accountable" — spoke to one of the core planning principles, which the CEO presented as a challenge: make this campus about the "spaces in between" where the exchange of information and the nurturing of knowledge happens, not about the buildings that form them. For Amgen, in other words, space is the object. Thus, the campus plan that emerged was less about the buildings and their specific functions (in fact, their flexibility has proven instrumental over the years in adapting to changing operations and work styles), and more about the opportunities for spontaneous interactions in a framework of interconnected open spaces, an especially effective part of the work environment given the benign climate of Thousand Oaks. Ultimately, the master plan introduced coherence, civility, and quality of place to a disjointed site.

Amgen's master plan was seen by management as a vehicle for creating gathering places for informal collegial meetings while providing for creative product development. Since the suburban business park was never

AMGEN
THOUSAND OAKS, CALIFORNIA, USA

MOORPARK
THOUSAND OAKS
N
0
0.4
0.8
1.2 MI

conceived of as a unified corporate campus, roads and buildings needed to be repurposed or eliminated. Two major pedestrian/open space axes were established, one north-south — "The Terrace" — to tie the administrative core to the clinical manufacturing facilities, and one east-west — "The Paseo" — to link the administrative functions with the research centers. A large Central Green was located at the cross-axis for all company meetings. The northerly end of The Terrace, compactly defined by the three administrative buildings that also contain cafés, a fitness center, and other services, has become a bustling hub of daily interaction. The quality of the campus environment has been a powerful tool for the company's successful recruitment and retention of a qualified workforce.

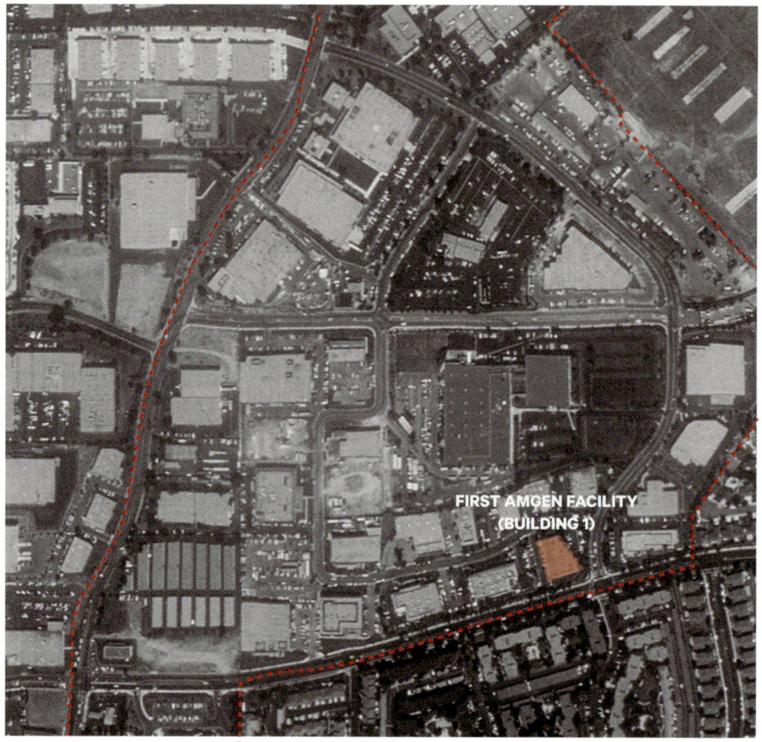

1989

2022

N
0
200
400 FT

Urban design provisions

Open space concept

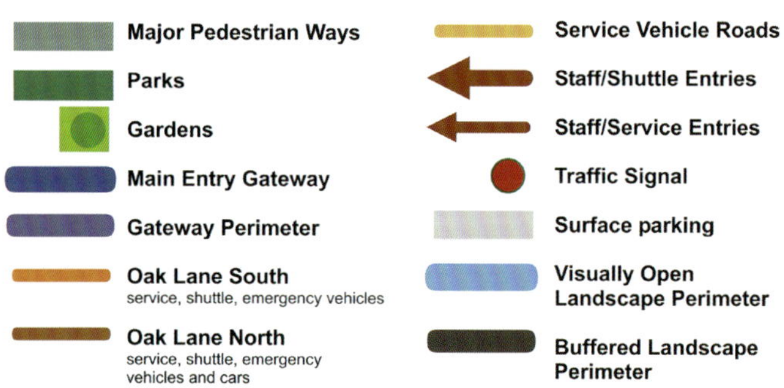

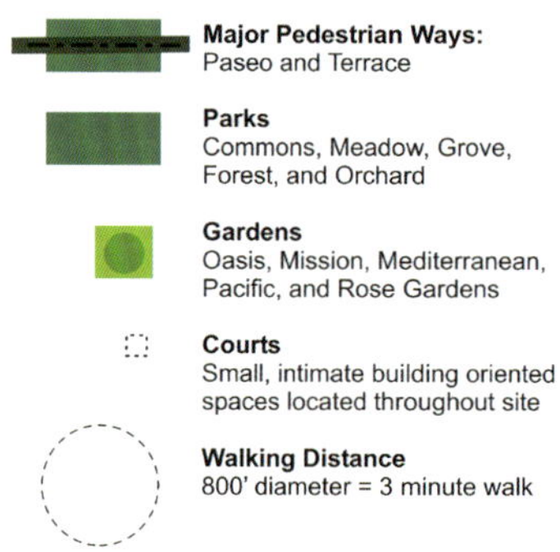

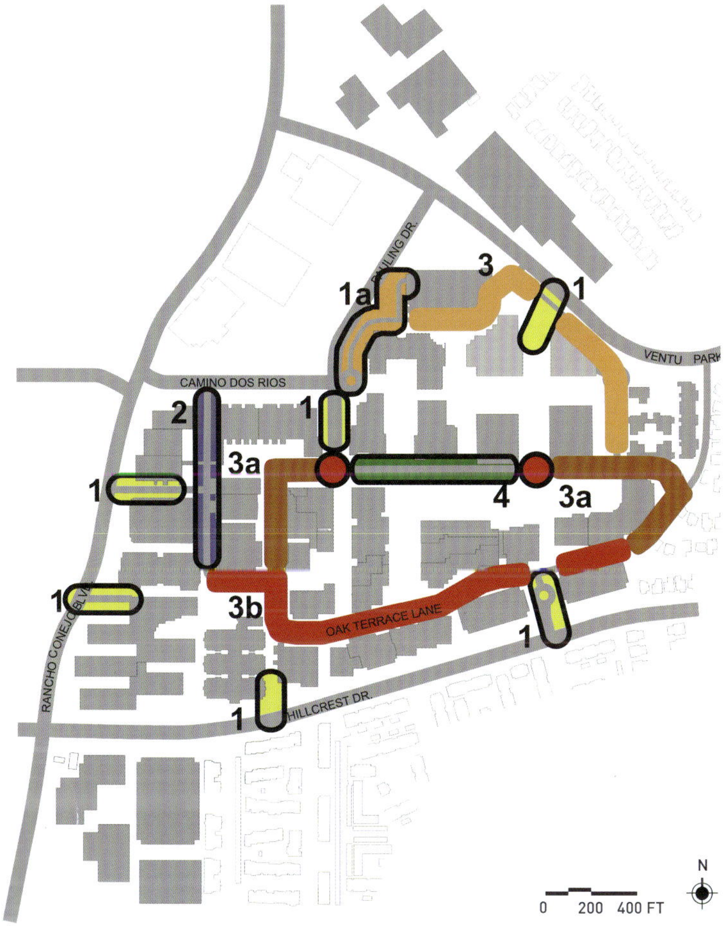

Emergency/ service vehicle route studies

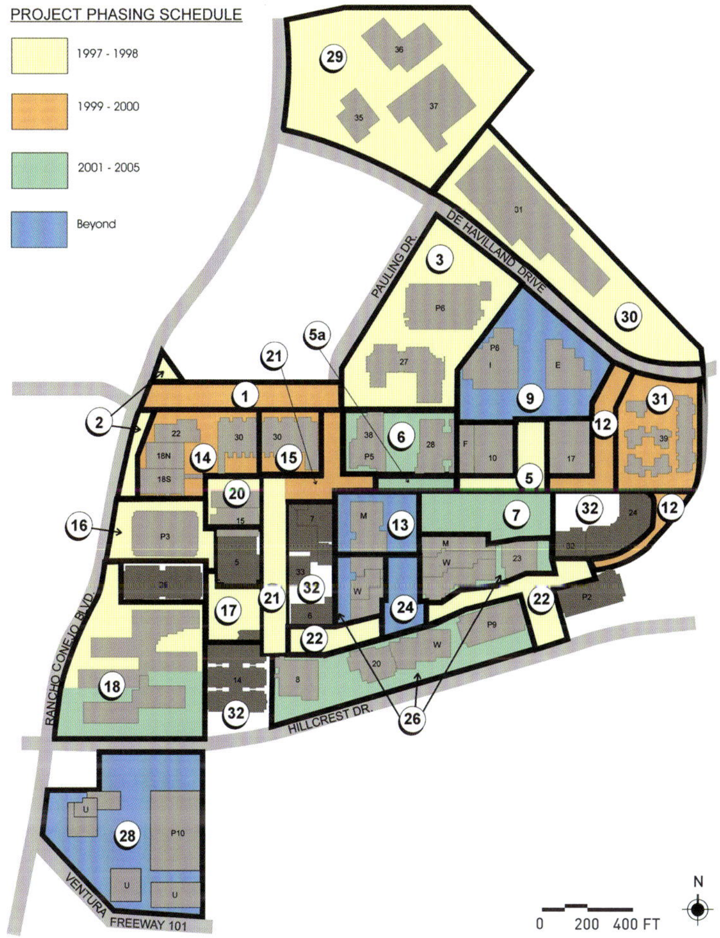

Phasing

1 **Entry**
Cars, Amgen service, vendors, emergency

1a **Main Entry**
Cars, VIPs, shuttle, Amgen service, vendors, emergency

2 **Utility Road**
Amgen service, vendors, emergency

3 **Periphery Road**
Cars, shuttle, Amgen service, vendors, emergency

3a **Interior Loop Road**
Pedestrians, shuttle, Amgen service, emergency

3b **Interior Loop Service Road**
Pedestrians, shuttle, Amgen service, vendors, emergency

4 **Paseo**
Pedestrians, Amgen service, emergency

PROJECTS LIST

1. Amgen Center Drive — Final
2. Rancho Conejo Gateway — Final
3. Building 27 — Final
4. Building 9 Site Improvements — Interim
5. Paseo East & Building 10/17 Open Space — Final
5a. Paseo Central — Final
6. Paseo Completion (Buildings 28, 38 & PS5) — Final
7. Central Park — Final
8. Camino Dos Rios East (Buildings 10, 17 & GTE) & Private DeHavilland West — Interim
9. Meadow (Buildings 10, 17, E, I & PS8) — Final
10. Private DeHavilland Temporary Entry — Interim
11. Building 39 Temporary Open Space — Interim
12. Private DeHavilland and Building 24 Loop — Final
13. Building M
14. Building 30 Phase 1 (Process Development)
15. Building 30 Phase 2 (Quality Control)
16. Research Walk and PS3
17. Research Court — Final
18. Building 29 Site Improvements — Final
19. Building 29 South — Final
20. Building 15 Site Improvements — Interim
21. Oak Terrace West (Private Pauling, — Final
Paseo West) — Final
22. Oak Terrace South & Amgen
Court — Final
23. Oak Terrace Court (Temporary
Roadway) — Interim
24. Oak Terrace Court
25. Mfg. District Site Improvements — Final
26. Mfg. District Site Improvements — Interim
27. Building 34 (Visitor Center) — Final
28. Parcel U and PS10 — Interim
29. Sales and Marketing Center — Final
(Building 35, 36, 37 & Nursery) — Final
30. Building 31 (Distribution Center)
31. Building 39 (Day Care Center) — Final
32. Remainder — Final
Final

Entrance to The Terrace

Research court outdoor seating

Outdoor shaded seating

Outdoor conference pavilion

Outdoor conference pavilion

Main open space

Research court water feature

At Genentech's headquarters, the world's first publicly traded biotechnology company, the core planning objectives of creative interaction were much the same as for Amgen. The site, however, presented a different set of challenges. For one thing, the ninety-eight-acre South San Francisco campus sits on a cold and windy peninsula on San Francisco Bay, constraining the use of outdoor space. It is made up of a patchwork of intermittently acquired parcels that are in proximity but often not contiguous; businesses owned by others are interspersed among the Genentech owned parcels such that an internally organized and well-integrated campus structure is not possible. A more nodal plan was called for, one where building clusters can protect smaller, human-scaled courtyards from climatic elements.

Considering land assemblage, topography, views, adjacent uses, and operational structure, the master plan locates a central administrative hub composed of three buildings at the geographic center of the campus. The ground level of these buildings is rich in amenities, including food service, meeting rooms for conferencing, and exercise facilities. The central landscaped courtyard is well protected from winds off the Bay, while taking advantage of Bay views.

GENENTECH
SOUTH SAN FRANCISCO, CALIFORNIA, USA

SOUTH SAN FRANCISCO
SAN FRANCISCO INTERNATIONAL AIRPORT
0 0.2 0.4 0.6 MI
N

The hub is connected to a series of satellite enclaves organized along an existing encircling public road. While the hub is the center of activity for all Genentech employees, each satellite enclave has modest amenities and services. Each enclave is organized around a primary open space, linked to the greater campus by pathways, enhanced sidewalks and landscape, and a rapid shuttle system. The distributed placement of employee services and amenities work together to promote company culture and connectivity.

2022

N
0
200
400 FT

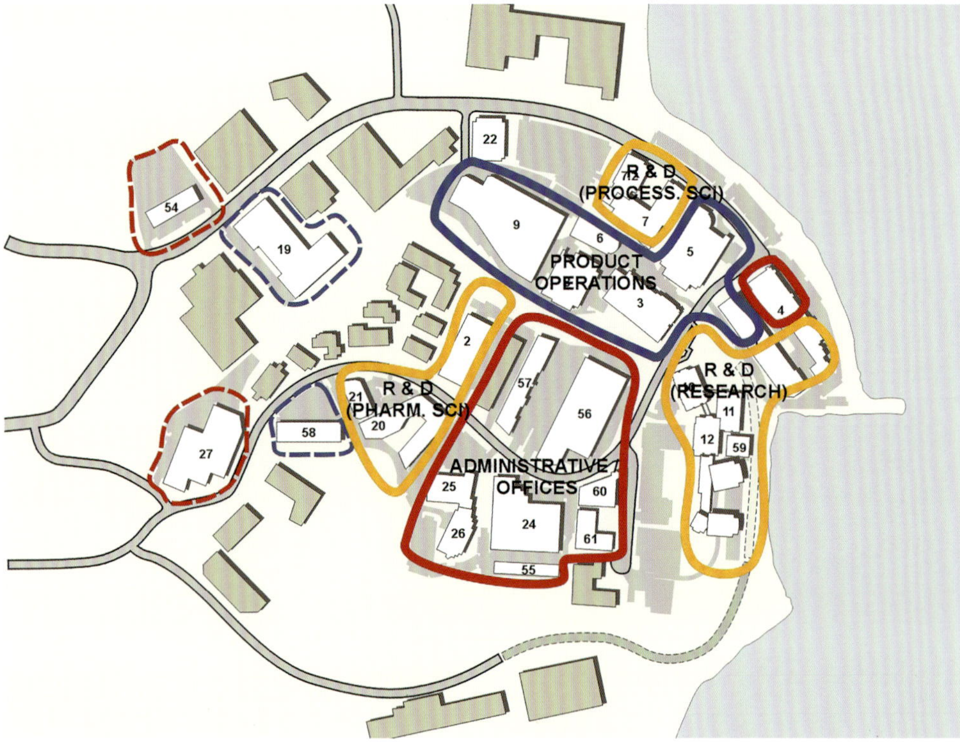

Land use zones

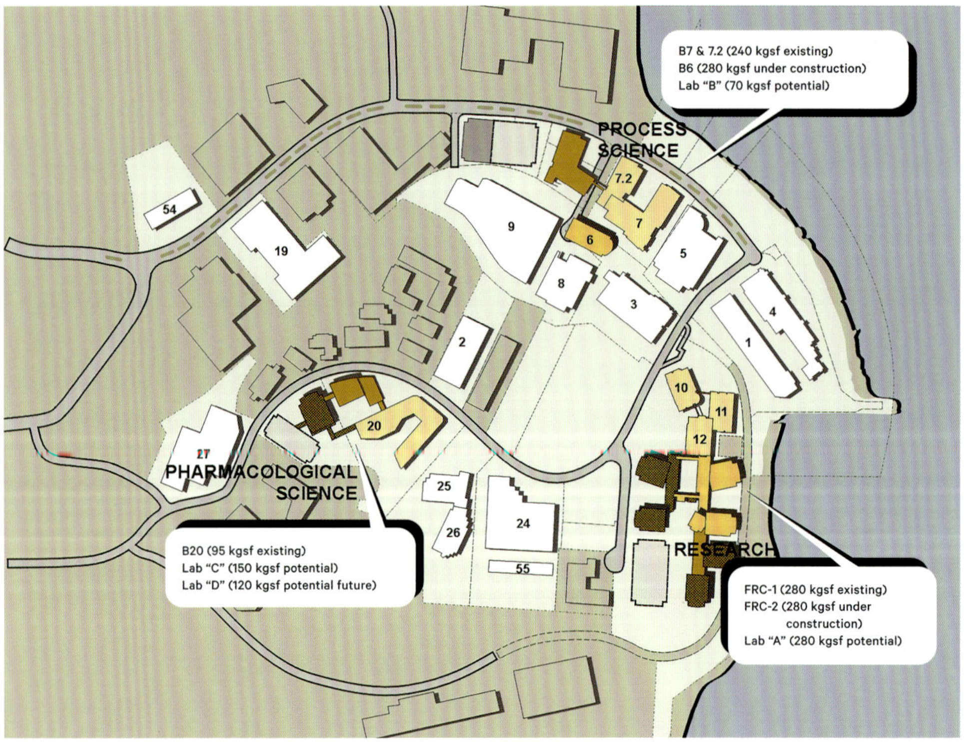

Campus clusters

Site aerial

The Master Plan for the Jet Propulsion Laboratory (JPL) in La Canada-Flintridge, California, puts forward a vision for the future of the Laboratory that maintains its preeminent position in the science and technology of space exploration, and firmly establishes it at the top of the list of the most desirable places in the world — if not the known universe — to work. For a ten-year horizon master plan of its 130-acre site, JPL sought to align its physical development program with its operations strategic plan while also addressing opportunities for better interdisciplinary employee interaction, and improvements to the quality of life at the Laboratory for purposes of recruitment and retention.

The master plan aligns with organizational strategies at many scales, realized through strategic building upgrades and improvements to landscaped areas. The plan clarifies the open space system to provide spatial identity and a campus armature connected to the nearby mountains and river course. A central pedestrian-oriented spine lined with amenities and services creates collaborative places to foster a professional community through exchange of information and collegial team building.

Buildings retain their highly flexible industrial character, as suitable for Mars Rover testbeds as for workspace or studio use. Flexibility and adaptation occur in older warehouses and large interior assembly buildings. The functional organization emerges and withdraws as new projects enter and old ones leave, activities changing with the assignment. Yet, the overall form of the campus remains the same. Other features include enhanced security; new visitor services to educate the public about space travel and related research; site selection for a new Flight Projects Center; and clear and adequate vehicular circulation and parking. The plan was generated from extensive dialogue with the Laboratory's staff, including scientists and leadership, about the future of the Laboratory, including ways that the site can best help support future research and development, making it a place that reflects the world's most advanced space exploration.

JET PROPULSION LABORATORY (JPL)
PASADENA, CALIFORNIA, USA

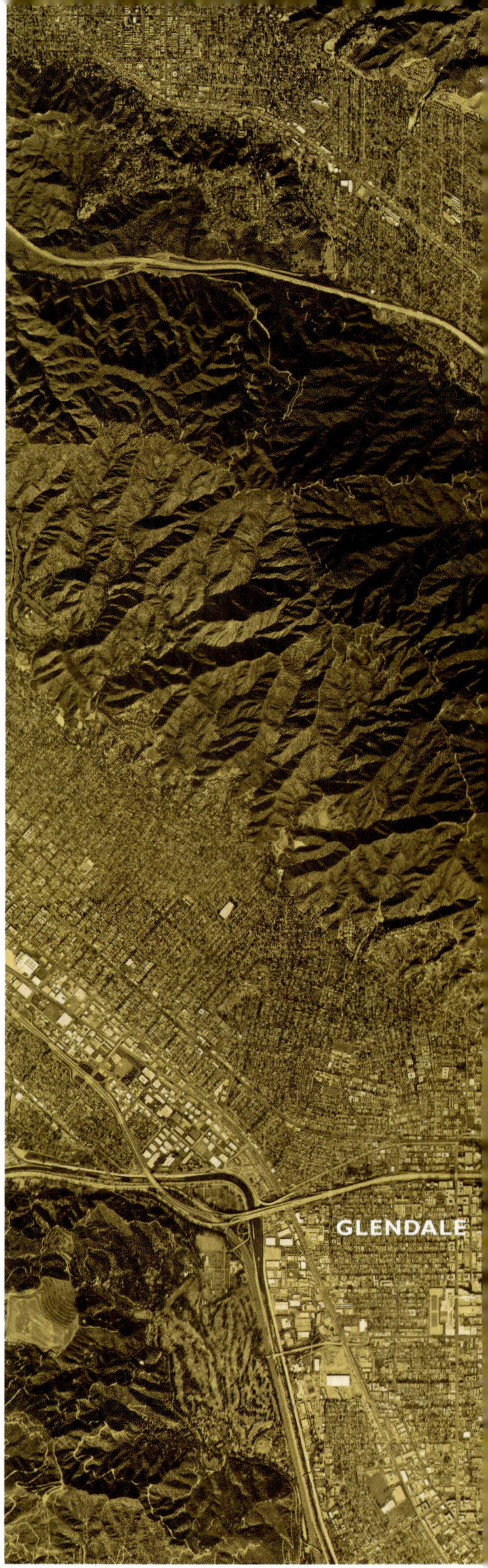

ROSE BOWL
OLD TOWN
PASADENA
CALIFORNIA
INSTITUTE OF
TECHNOLOGY
N
0 0.3 0.6 0.9 MI

1. View looking towards large open space

2. View of pedestrianized zone

0 100 200 FT
N

Open space framework

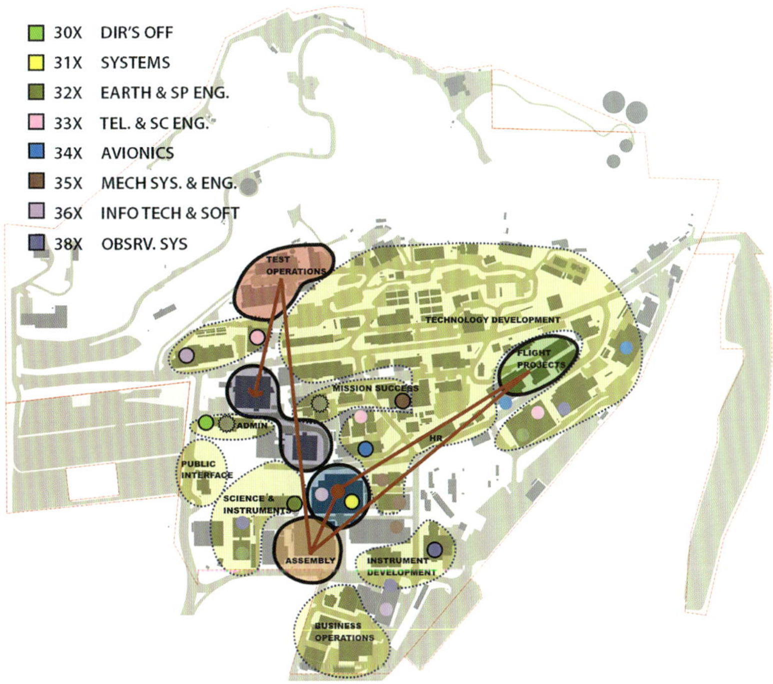

Current project flow and adjacencies

Hard and soft analysis

Assembly building for the 2020 Mars Rover first test drive

JPL campus

The Knowledge City's physical fabric is designed to be an environmental lesson in the virtues of well-planned urban living made legible. Houston's weak regional planning policies have allowed growth to sweep across the prairies and into floodplains, accommodated by levees that ironically have only added to the widespread problem of flooding. At the same time, local universities and colleges do not produce enough knowledge workers to feed Houston's expanding knowledge economy, resulting in an undersized science-engineering workforce. The Knowledge City plan addresses these problems through interconnected strategies of economic, educational, environmental, and urban development. The goal is to create an intense and resilient urban place in harmony with its natural features, in contrast to Houston's conventional low-density, car-dependent "rooftop" suburban enclaves.

The Knowledge City aims to become a leader in educating the region's workforce by providing STEM related education from kindergarten through jobs ("K thru J"). Joint degree programs are negotiated with several institutions of higher learning working together collaboratively. Collaboration spaces are in mixed-use buildings including housing, retail, recreational amenities, and other uses within the urban center of the project. The idea is that urban living itself involves an information exchange that facilitates learning for not just college level but for life-long enrichment.

Seventy percent of the site lies within the floodplain of the Brazos River. The plan locates its highest densities on higher ground, in the "Uplands" above the floodplain at a site adjoining Interstate Highway I-10. An open-ended grid and mixed-use blocks contain university education and vertically stacked multi-family housing in an ever-changing engagement of urban living and learning in the same vibrant place. The Uplands is also the site of the first phase of development, pursuing the owner's intent to start with education and employment, not suburban homes.

In the lower floodplain area, Island neighborhoods of densely compact housing with a retail village center elevate development above floodwater that then flows freely between the islands, not reliant upon a levee containment system. The islands are connected by bridges for vehicles, but also pedestrian walkways and bike lanes, and agricultural use continues in the residual open spaces. The whole of the city is a large-scale live-in demonstration of environmental principles and urban resilience — a didactic city.

KNOWLEDGE CITY
HOUSTON, TEXAS, USA

AWARD

- AIA Los Angeles, NEXT LA Award

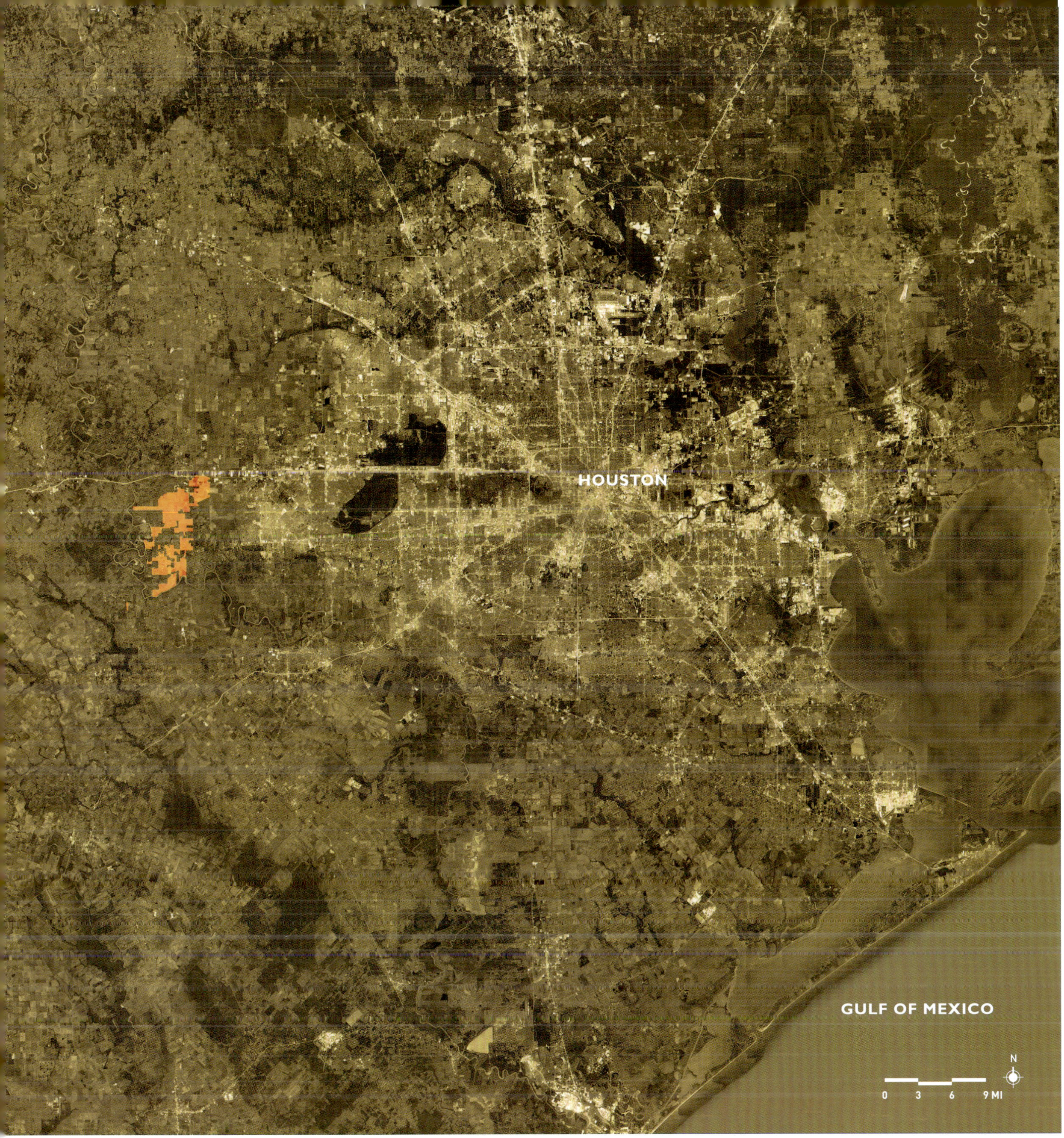
HOUSTON
GULF OF MEXICO
N
0 3 6 9 MI

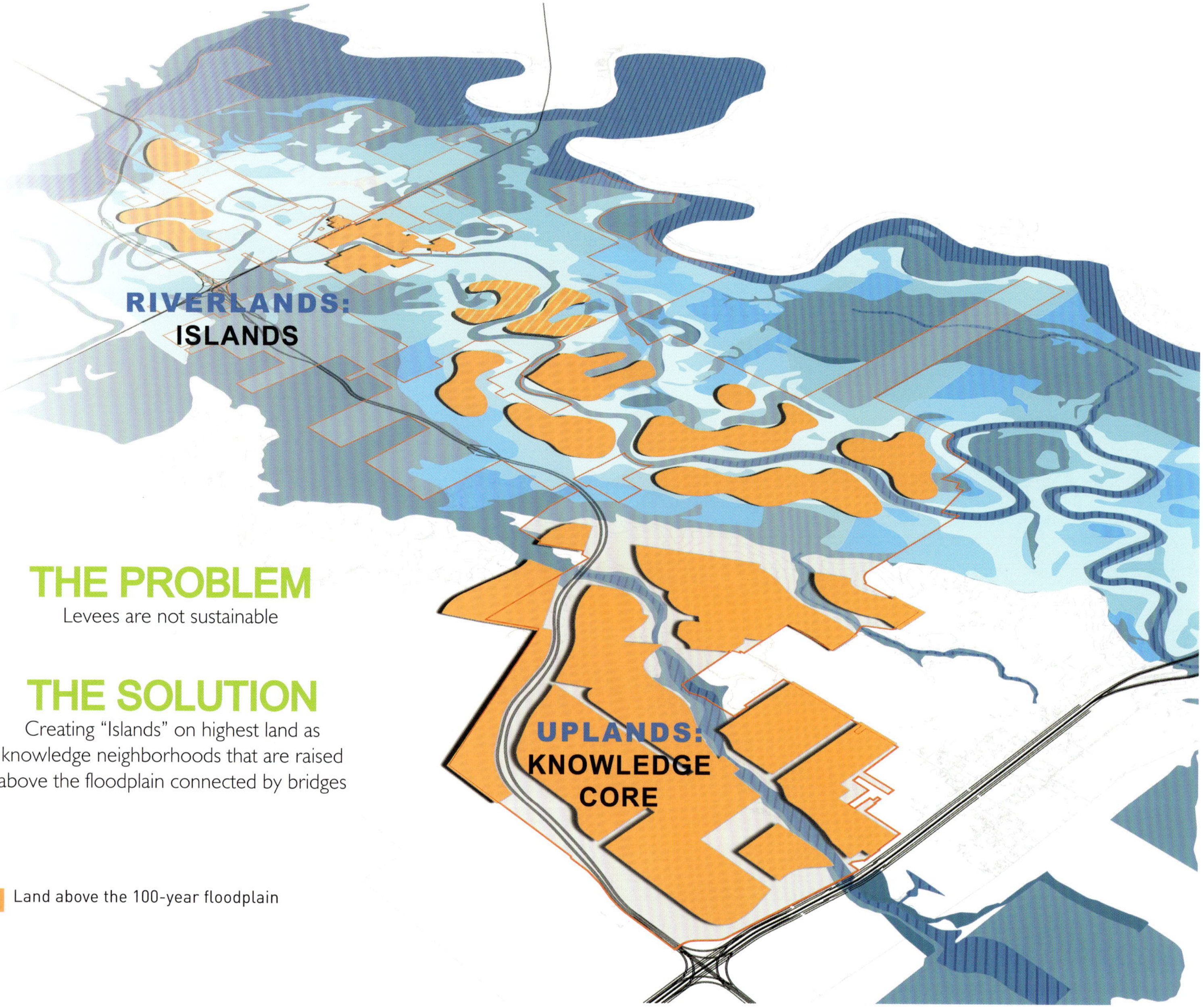

THE PROBLEM

Levees are not sustainable

THE SOLUTION

Creating "Islands" on highest land as knowledge neighborhoods that are raised above the floodplain connected by bridges

Land above the 100-year floodplain

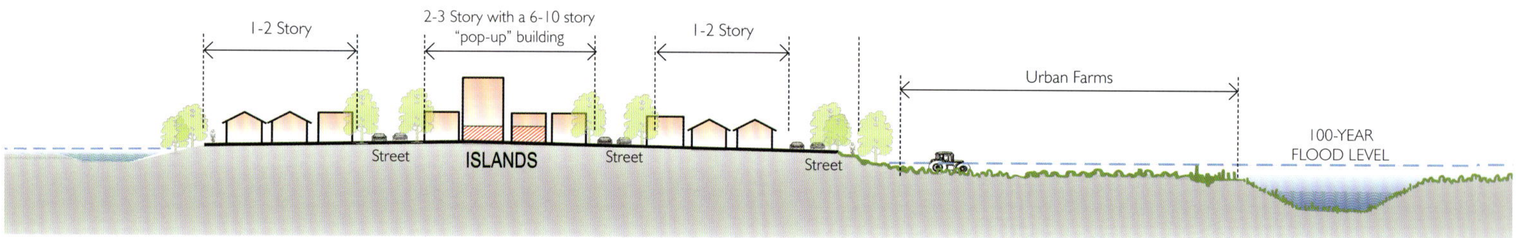

Typical section through one of the islands

JOBS FIRST

Project approach is job creation as priority instead of housing development

K-12
5,200 students

Community College
3,000 students

Work Force Training

Universities
15,000 students

Research & Industry
10,000 jobs

Corporate Services + Offices
40,000 jobs

Conservation, Recreation & Agriculture
Over 10,000 acres

Knowledge Neighborhoods
12,000 to 15,000 households

Synergistic relationship: education + employment

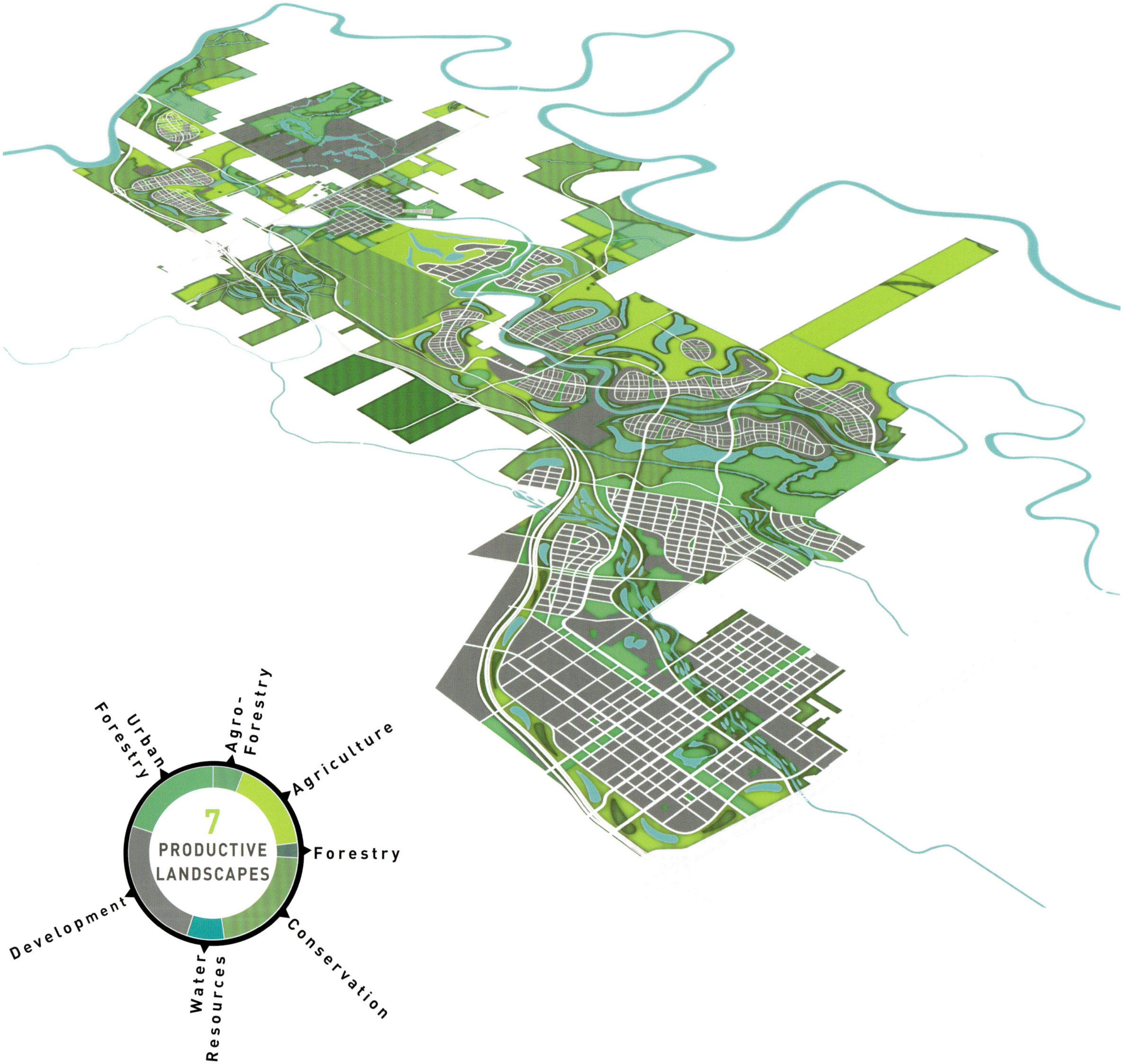

Types of productive landscapes

Open space

Central park

Blue greenway

(A) On-site wetland mitigation bank
(B) Local farming
(C) Wetland restoration
(D) Compact "islands" developed on raised ground instead of levees
(E) Transit connection throughout site
(F) Rooftop PV on all major buildings & street furniture
(G) Community-scale solar energy field
(H) Limited water supply from shallow aquifer - no water taken from deeper aquifer
(I) Agriculture & stormwater management buffer
(J) Regional BRT connection along I-10 Corridor
(K) Bike system throughout site
(L) 60% water supply from capture and reuse
(M) Mixed-use hubs served by transit in all neighborhoods
(N) Wetlands & creek habitat restored throughout the site
(O) Blue Greenway - stormwater management system & aquifer recharge
(P) Shuttle routes within the Knowledge Core
(Q) Mixed-use compact development
(R) Wastewater Treatment for reuse & recycling

Sustainability

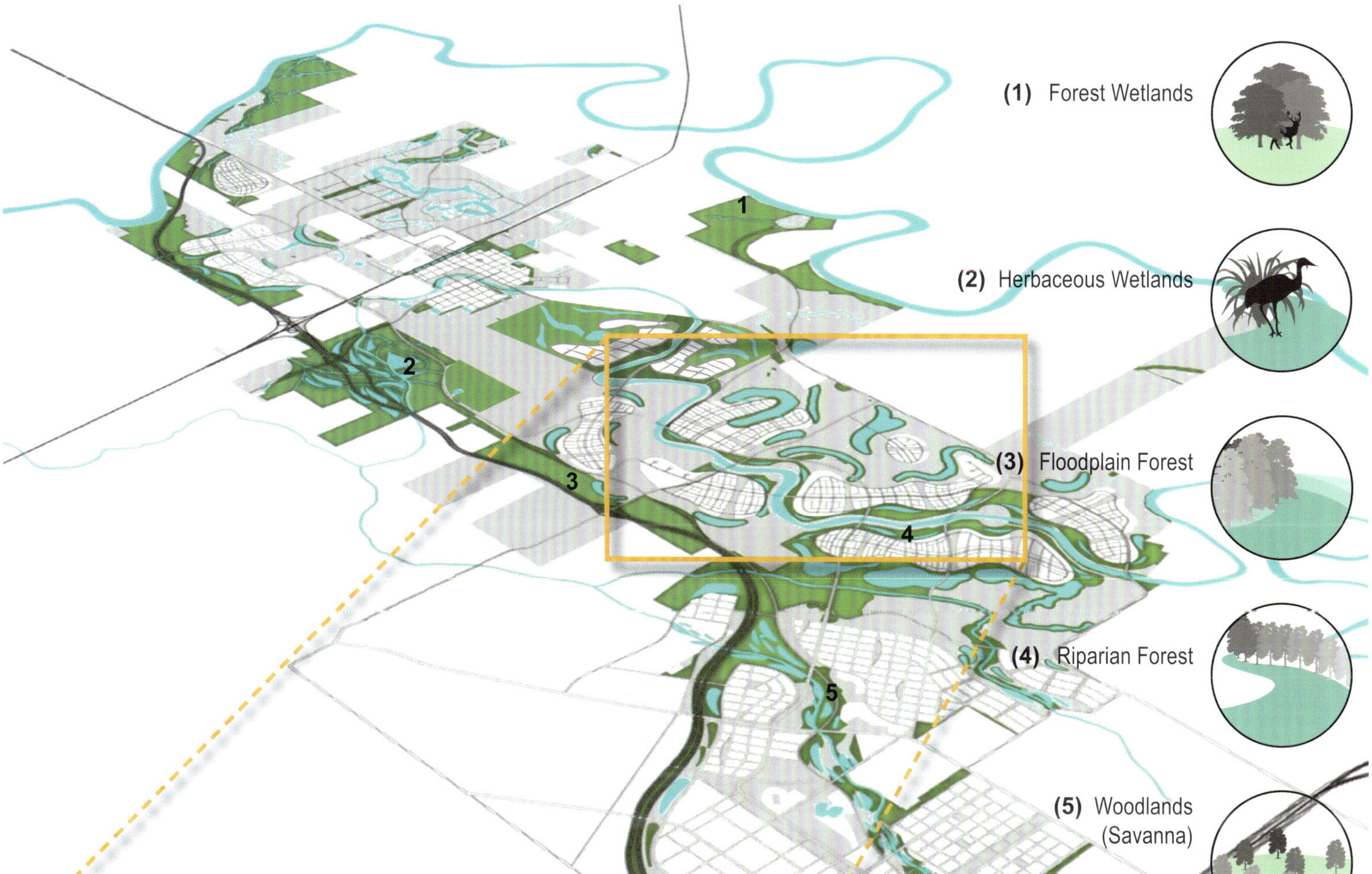

Compact development "islands" are created on higher land to protect existing wetlands

Conservation

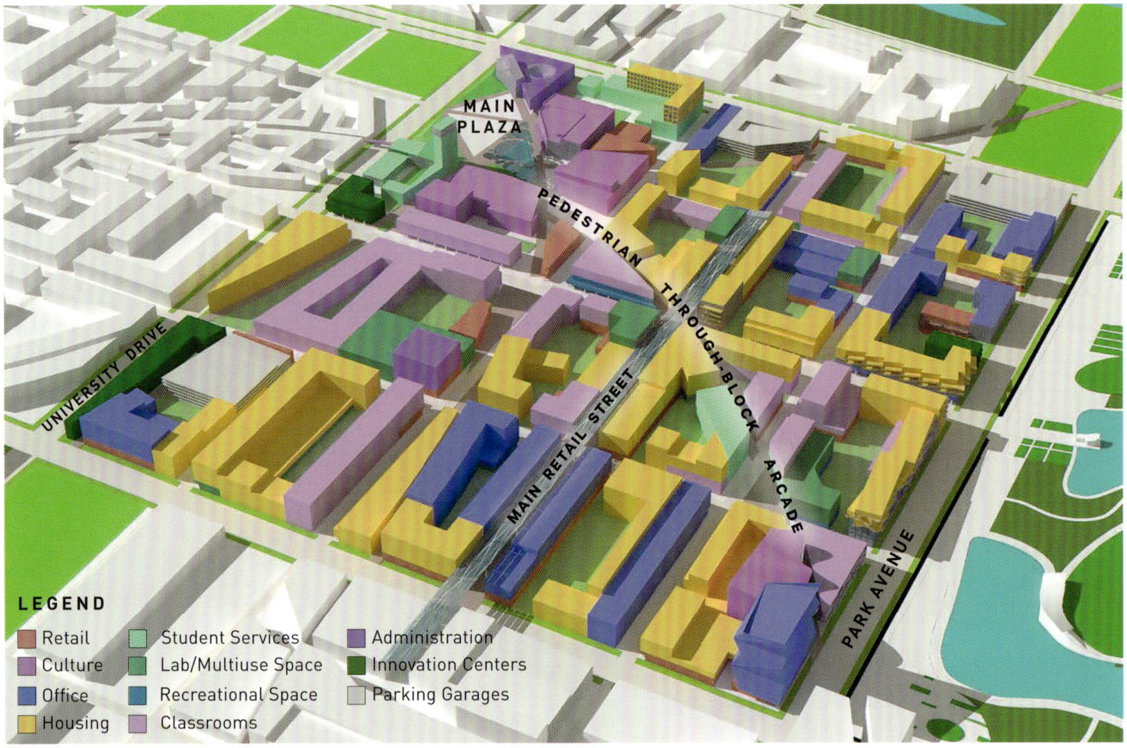

The Center

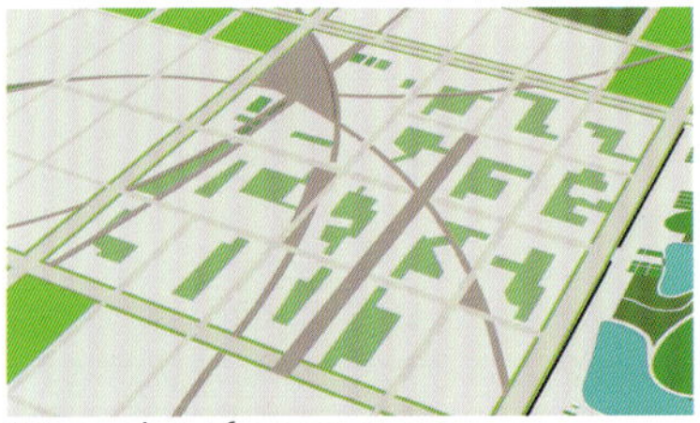

Hierarchy of open space

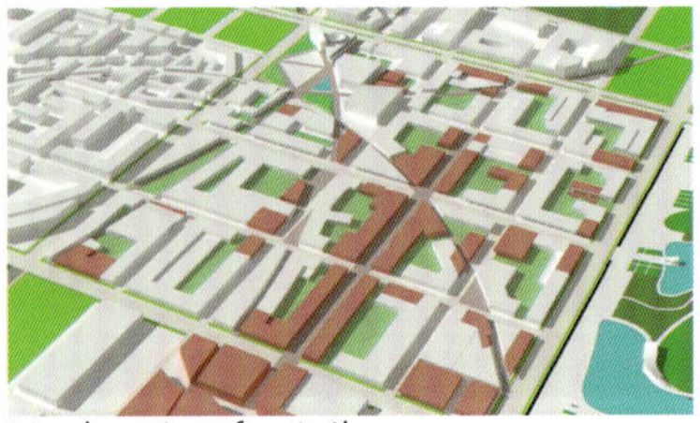

Lively mix of retail

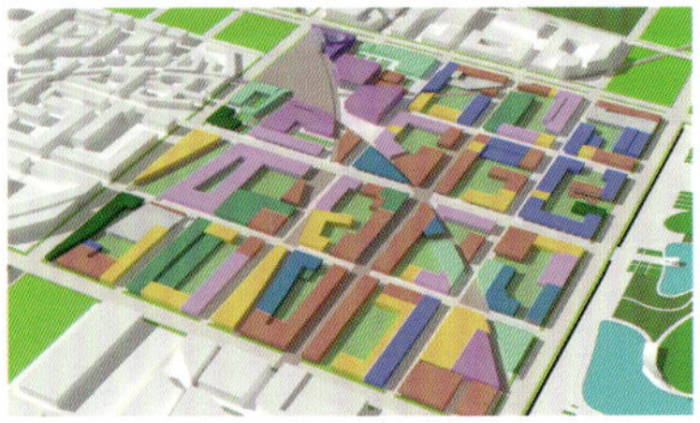

Active ground plane

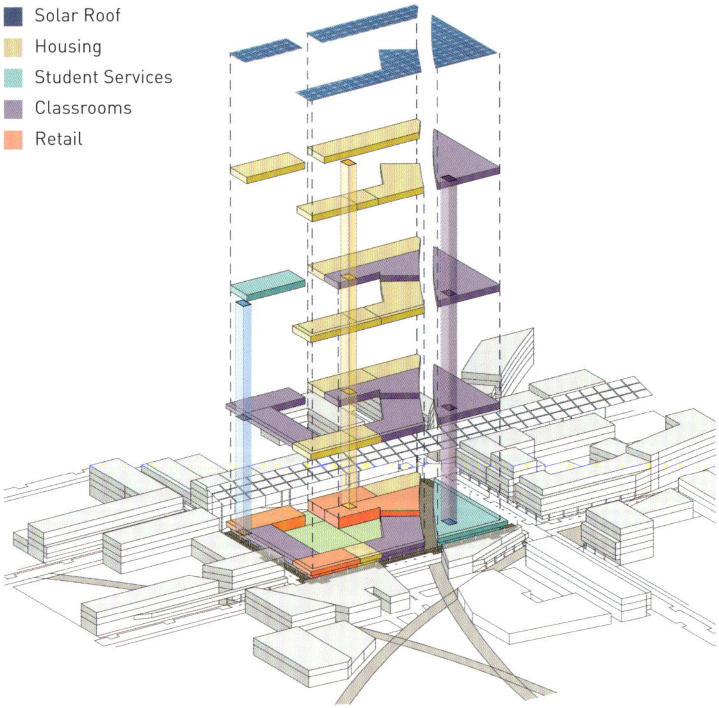

Vertically integrated blocks

Core land-use

- A multi-institutional education concept
- ± 9 million sq.ft. of prime office
- ± 6 million sq.ft. of creative industry R&D and logistics
- More than 12,000 new households

Engineering is a substantially different discipline than it was more than one hundred years ago when some of the UC Berkeley College of Engineering campus was first built. Today's College faculty and UC administration sought to reposition the campus to better address a changing curriculum that has moved from traditional disciplines like materials and civil engineering to computer and information-based sciences; and, to accommodate the transition from traditional teaching in single disciplines to a multidisciplinary and collaborative future in the sciences. While flexible academic facilities were an important part of that accommodation (including a new multidisciplinary research center building), a fundamental planning principle was to strengthen community through social interaction and to enhance the College's sense of place and identity.

Taking its cues from the 1906 John Galen Howard master plan for the overall Berkeley campus, the College of Engineering plan is organized around a linear pedestrian-oriented space that connects to Howard's cascade of open space "glades" that form the spine of the main campus. The plan identifies locations for infill projects around the redefined open space that promote interdisciplinary teaching and research, and whose ground floors define new

UC BERKELEY COLLEGE OF ENGINEERING
BERKELEY, CALIFORNIA, USA

UNIVERSITY OF CALIFORNIA
BERKELEY
0 300 600 900 FT
N

informal spaces for outdoor gatherings and social interaction among students and faculty of all disciplines. Central to the plan is a new Center for Information Technology Research in the Interest of Society building (CITRIS), now renamed Sutardja Dai Hall, which was designed as part of the planning and design process. This facility provides space for interdisciplinary research with connections to all colleges in the university as well as private research and engineering entities. The resulting campus precinct, its buildings and open space, support interdisciplinary research and teaching; promote the collaboration between private industry and the university; and adapt to changes in information infrastructure and the mobility of students and faculty.

Engineering building at UC Berkeley

GAYLEY ROAD
LA LOMA
LEROY
EAST TERRACE
UNIVERSITY WALK
DAVIS SOUTH REPLACEMENT
CITRIS II
THE GLADE
WEST TERRACE
NAVAL ARCHITECTURE
NEW CEE BUILDING
N
0
50
100 FT

UC Berkeley College of Engineering Campus

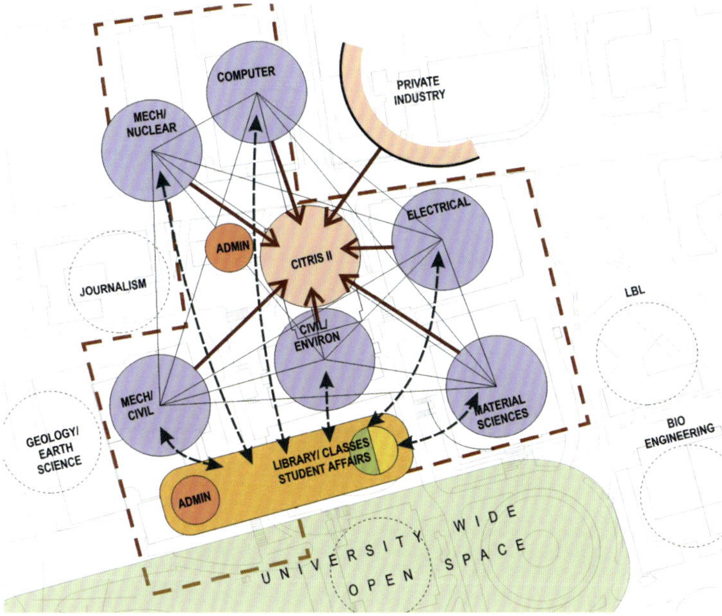

Concept diagram

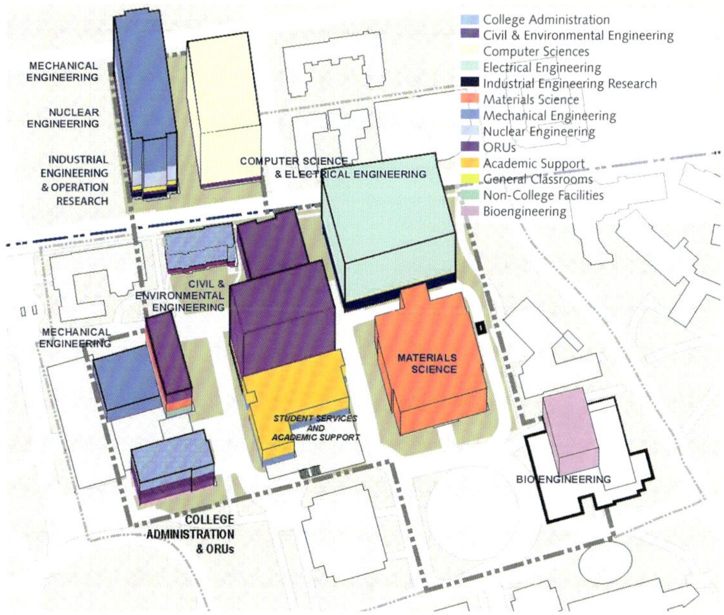

Engineering departments

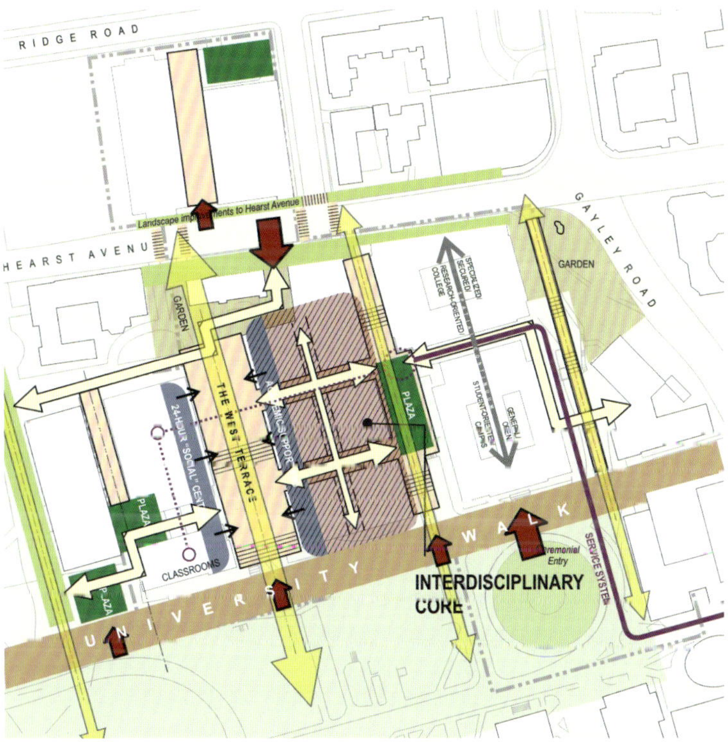

Interdisciplinary core

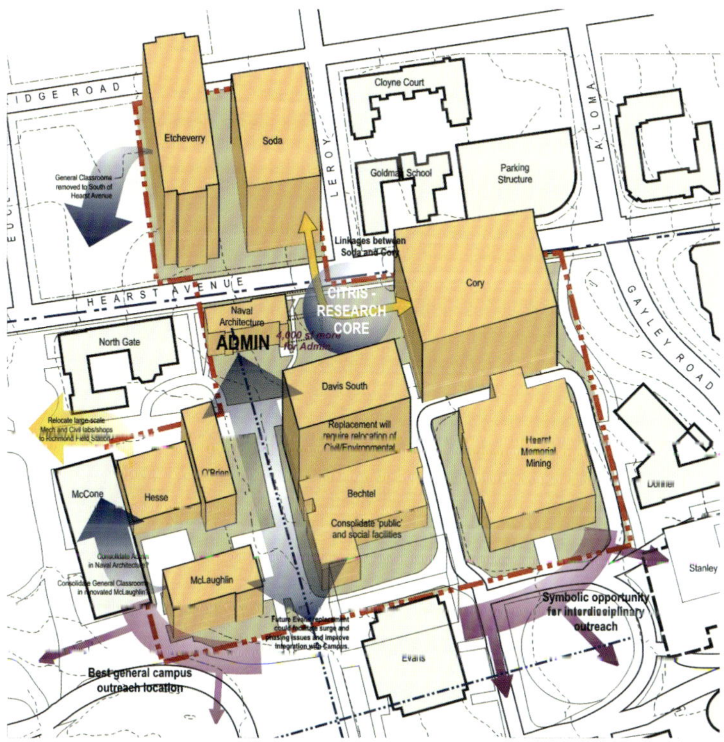

Opportunities

If the Houston project brought education to the city, UC Irvine Main Street brought the city to the campus. The urban design plan for Main Street breaks from the tradition of "town-gown" separation and brings urban uses onto campus where they are in close proximity and well-integrated into the academic, student-serving, and administrative areas. This was considered a breakthrough in campus planning because it mixed campus activities with the commercial activities of the village and reconceptualized the spatial connection between the two. By doing so, the urban space of the street repositions the center of campus to the main street and the plaza between it and the central park.

The UC Irvine campus is suburban both in location and design. Originally conceived in a garden-like setting, the campus is organized around a large circular park with academic areas clustered equally around it. Student housing is located between the academic areas with faculty housing at sites farther away from the park. In its original plan, the university campus was clearly separated from a nearby "village" that includes student serving retail and other civic uses, intentionally separating the "town" from

UC IRVINE MAIN STREET
IRVINE, CALIFORNIA, USA

AWARDS

- AIA National, Urban Design Award
- Progressive Architecture Design Award

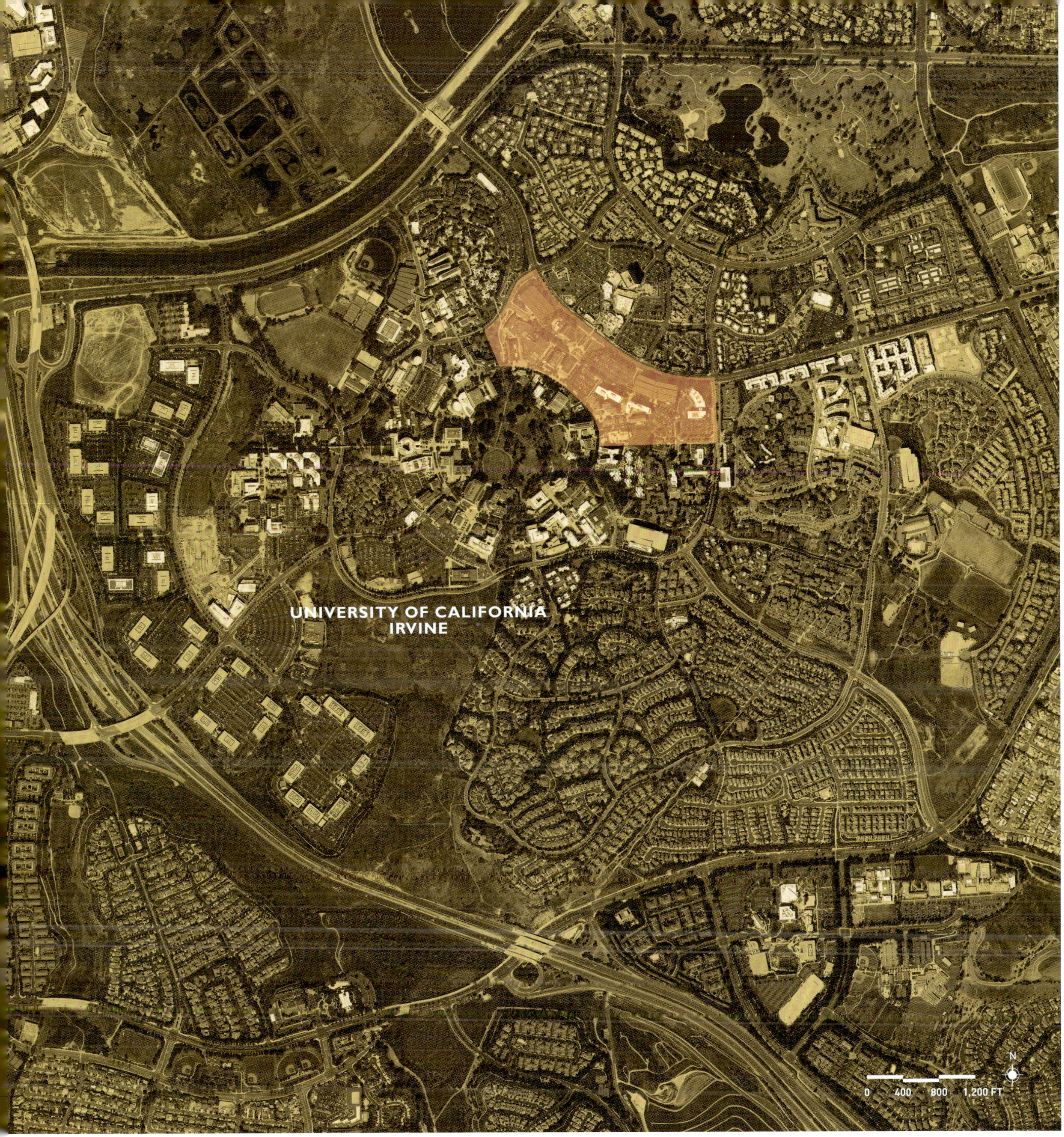
UNIVERSITY OF CALIFORNIA
IRVINE
N
0 400 800 1,200 FT

the "gown" in a traditional planning relationship. Ironically, the Main Street plan seeking to turn this about by establishing a connection between the two was proposed by the legacy firm of the planning group that developed the original plan.

The Main Street plan, organized into four conceptual zones, integrates the Main Street development with the campus's park-like background. Four zones provide transitional spaces and activities for the pedestrian: from the urban mixed-use Main Street to a series of landscaped semi-public courtyards to a set of academic buildings-in-the-park and finally to the bucolic central Aldrich Park itself. The Main Street creates a new sense of place through density and mix of uses, enclosed street edges, architectural scale, and massing relationships. The plan fulfills the daily needs of a burgeoning campus population and is easily accessible on foot or by bicycle.

A. STUDENT UNION - EXISTING
B. ADMINISTRATION - EXISTING
C. THEATER - PROPOSED
D. SOCIAL SCIENCE
S. SERVICE
1. STUDENT UNION EXPANSION
2. MAIN STREET RETAIL
3. PLAZA RETAIL
4. LIBRARY EXPANSION/ ADMINISTRATION
5. CULTURAL CENTER
(GALLERIES, ART SUPPLY, THEATER, CAFE)
6. UNIVERSITY COOP
(JR. DEPT, STORE, OFFICES, RESTAURANT)
7. UNIVERSITY GUEST HOUSE
(60 ROOMS, RESTAURANT, CONFERENCE)
8. OFFICE
P. PARKING

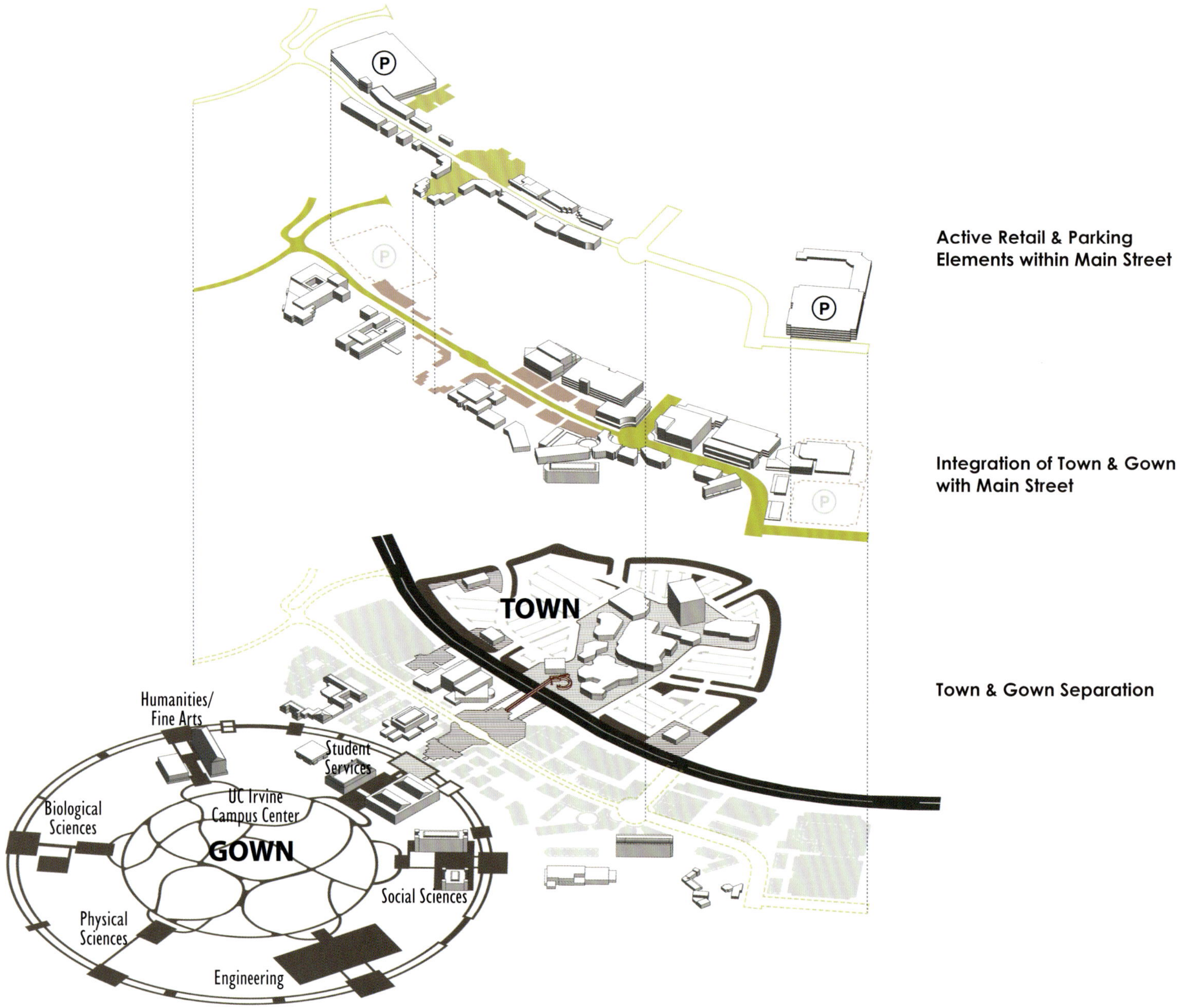

Town & Gown diagram

Figure ground

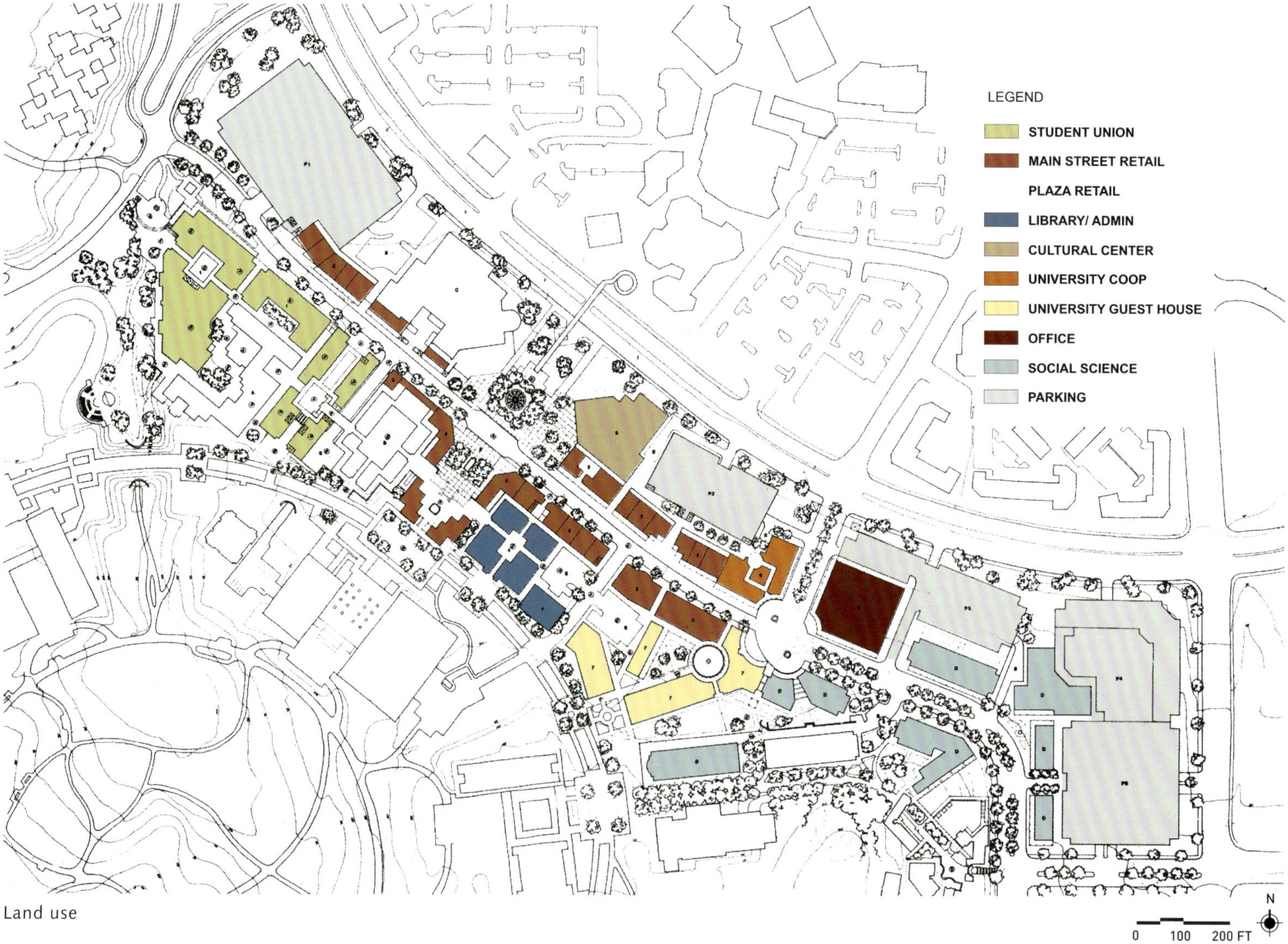

Land use

Physical models

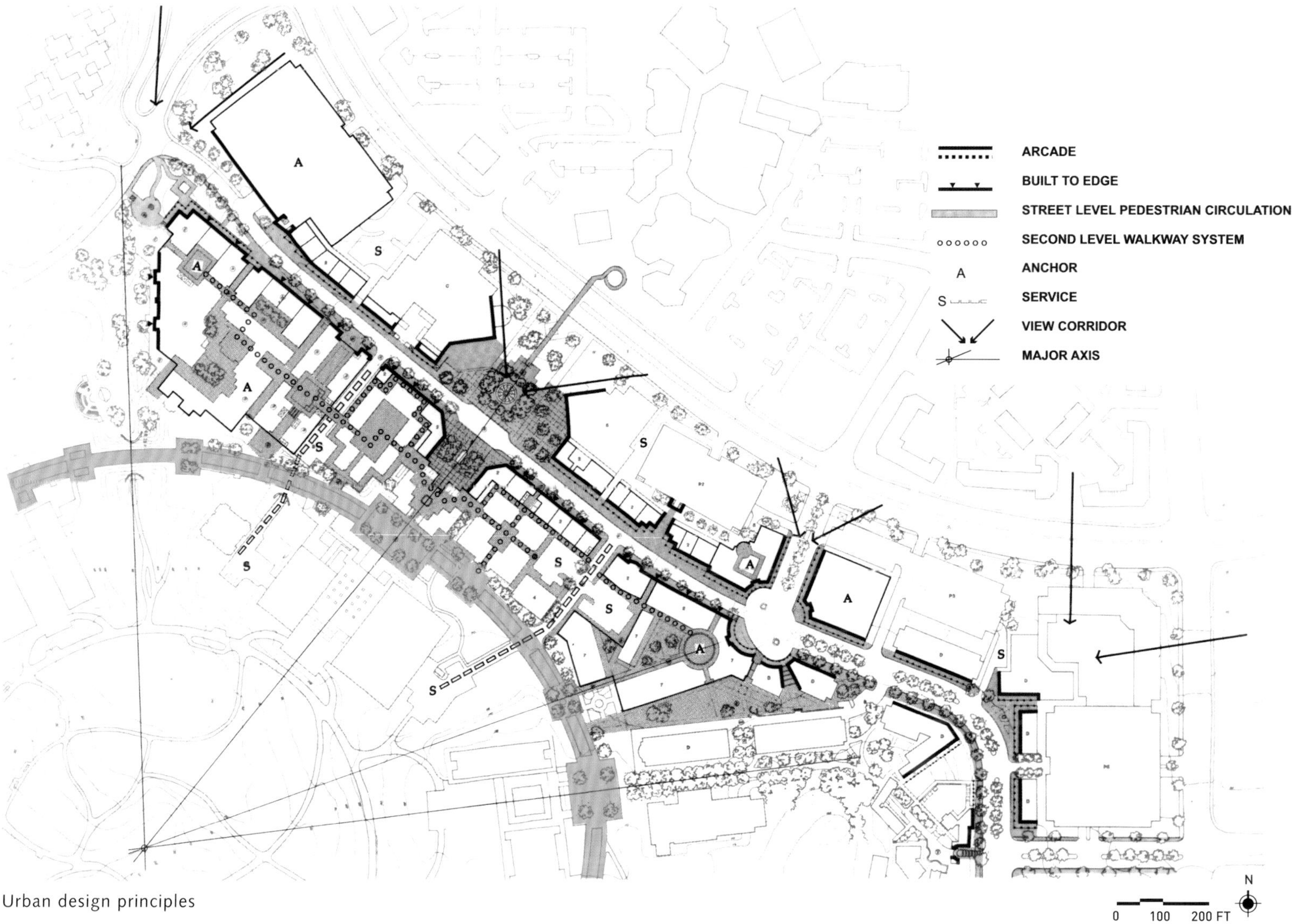

Urban design principles

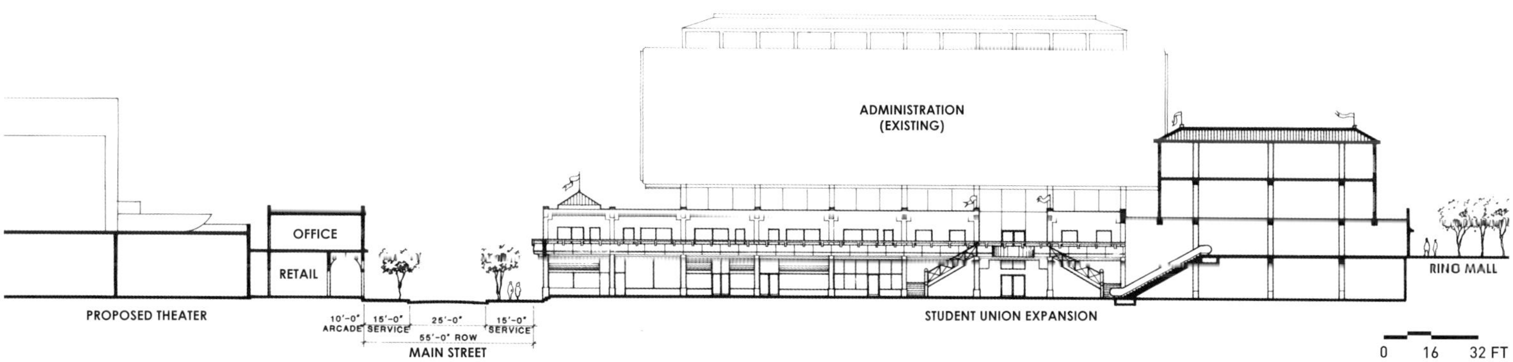

Section through student union expansion

What happens when an isolated natural setting is swallowed up by suburban sprawl? The Chadwick School was developed over 80 years ago as a campus immersed in the bucolic natural setting of the Palos Verdes peninsula. Surrounded by rolling hills and two canyons on the west and east, over time these were encroached upon by suburban residential neighborhoods. The school transitioned from a secluded boarding school to a commuter school and, having sold a large portion of its land holdings for financial reasons years earlier, the school's access was constrained such that those commuters must pass through the residential development that now occupies the land that was sold. The new residents were not pleased with the resulting traffic. The school had ironically created access issues and community resistance for campus use and expansion. With the vision to restore the school's original focus on environmental learning through its connection with nature, the master plan aimed to improve the instructional setting strengthening its connection with the site's natural features, as well as to address the issues of access.

CHADWICK SCHOOL
PALOS VERDES, CALIFORNIA, USA

PALOS VERDES PENINSULA
N
0 800 1,600 2,400 FT

The master plan reestablishes the relationship with the school's natural setting, so that the site becomes a laboratory for science, ecology, and environmental studies. The plan proposes construction of new studio-like classroom buildings of modular design whose flexibility promotes team teaching and ready adaptation to the site's topography. The small scale of each of the modular units also allows incremental development that can make best use of donor funds as they become available. Simplifying and minimizing vehicular movement is also a part of the plan. This improves pedestrian circulation and the integration of the campus with its natural setting. A menu of flexible development options will accommodate several alternative futures, including an alternative entry drive that avoids going through the adjoining neighborhood neutralizing regulatory restrictions on campus use.

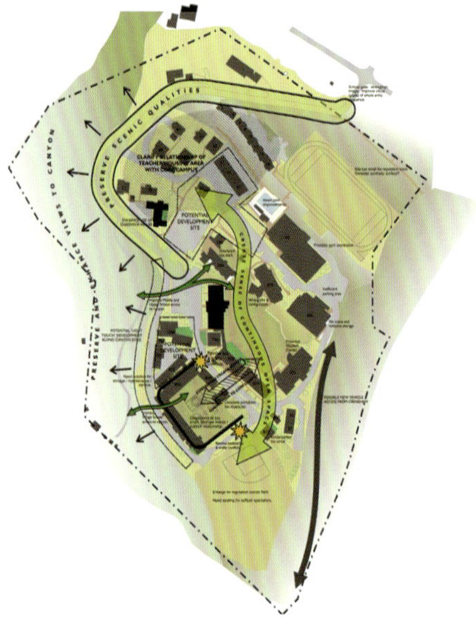

Opportunities and constraints

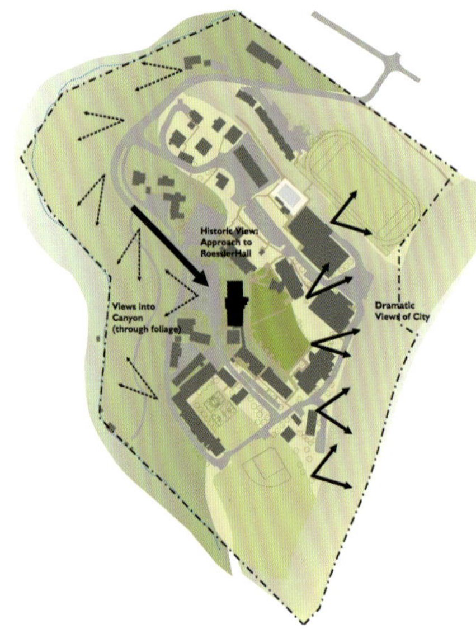

Preserve and enhance views

Water conservation

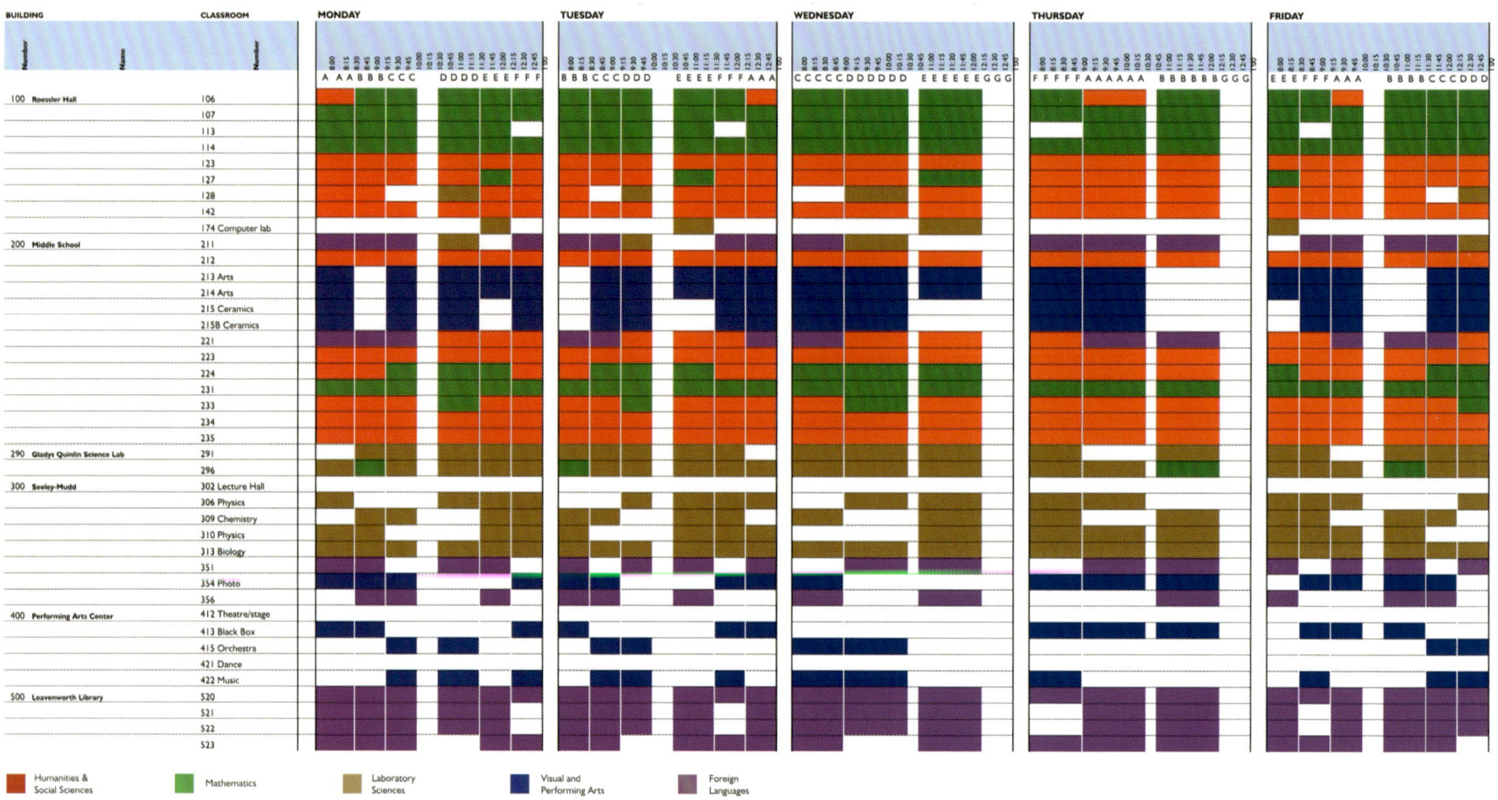

Classroom utilization

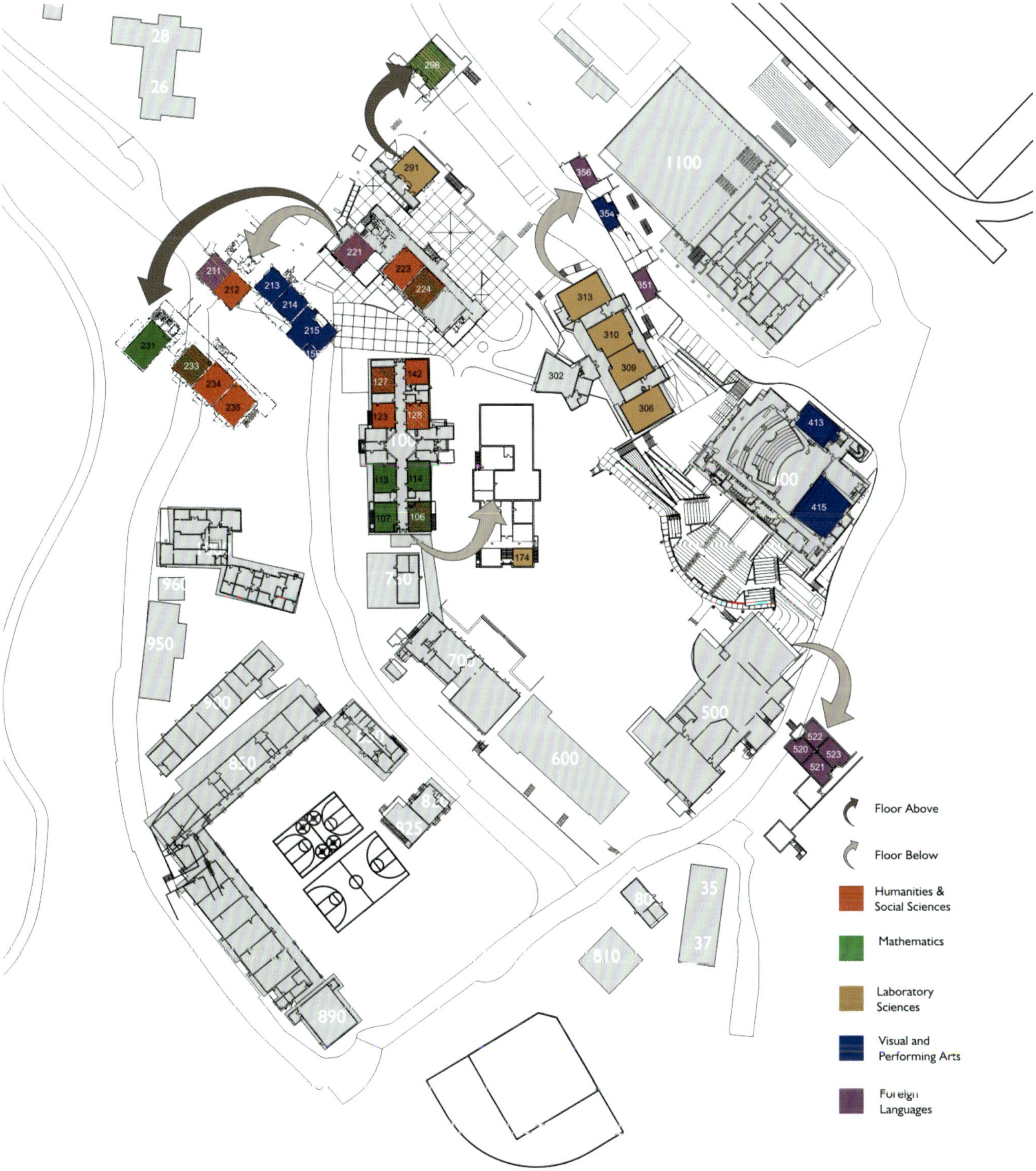

Classroom use analysis

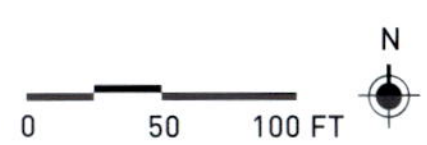

ALTERNATIVE SCHEMES

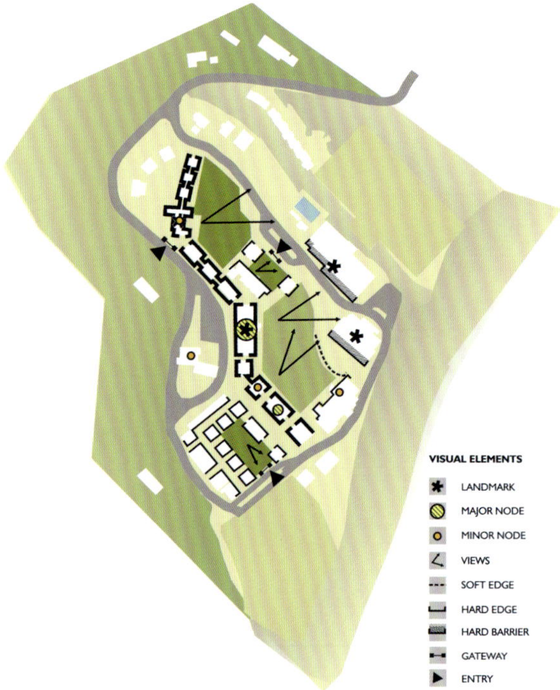

Scheme 1: Villages

Scheme 2: Community

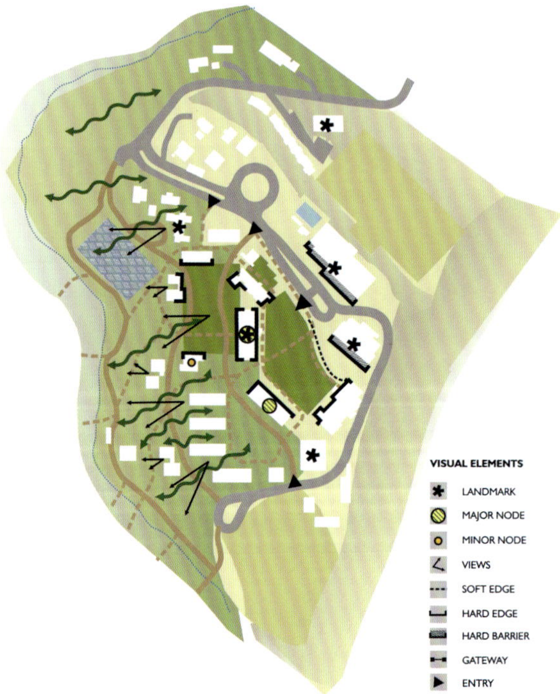

Scheme 3: Nature

Scheme 4: Home

Final master plan

A city's schools are among its most visible collective benefits, a resource shared across the population and the foundation of knowledge building in American social life. Ensuring equity across the subsets of the population is a significant challenge, however. In Los Angeles, existing public-school facilities have not kept up when compared with the newly constructed schools of the district that have a higher standard of maintenance, incorporate the latest school technologies and services, and accommodate new pedagogical models such as Small Learning Communities (SLC). Recognizing this disparity to be a critical issue, Los Angeles voters passed an $8 billion bond measure to modernize and upgrade existing Los Angeles Unified School District facilities to the same standards as the new schools. To determine the needs and what should be done, a series of school site Master Plans was prepared, beginning with a process that included a series of stakeholder meetings with school administration, teachers, and parents to discuss alternative concepts and establish a common vision.

The resulting master plans — for more than thirty school campus sites — offer a long-term vision for each individual school and provide a template from which the school district can evaluate which improvements are needed and how much they cost. Program factors included the evaluation of projected school attendance and classroom needs; identification of spaces and facilities that are obsolete and others in need of improvement or modernization; evaluation of historic campus layouts to understand the campus organizational structure; and, to the extent possible clarification of the spatial order of each campus. The individual school campus plans replaced aged portable classrooms with up-to-date facilities; retrofitted older buildings to remain; provided more efficient pedestrian circulation including improved disabled access; clarified the spatial order of campus layout, which had been compromised over years of incremental infill; and re-integrated school facilities with the surrounding community where shared use of the school site is needed for functions such as recreational uses or space for mobile health clinics. Each plan also incorporates principles of environmental sustainability, with attention to stormwater management, reduction of energy consumption, onsite alternative energy production, water consumption efficiency, waste treatment facilities, and heat island reduction.

LOS ANGELES UNIFIED SCHOOL DISTRICT CAMPUSES

LOS ANGELES, CALIFORNIA, USA

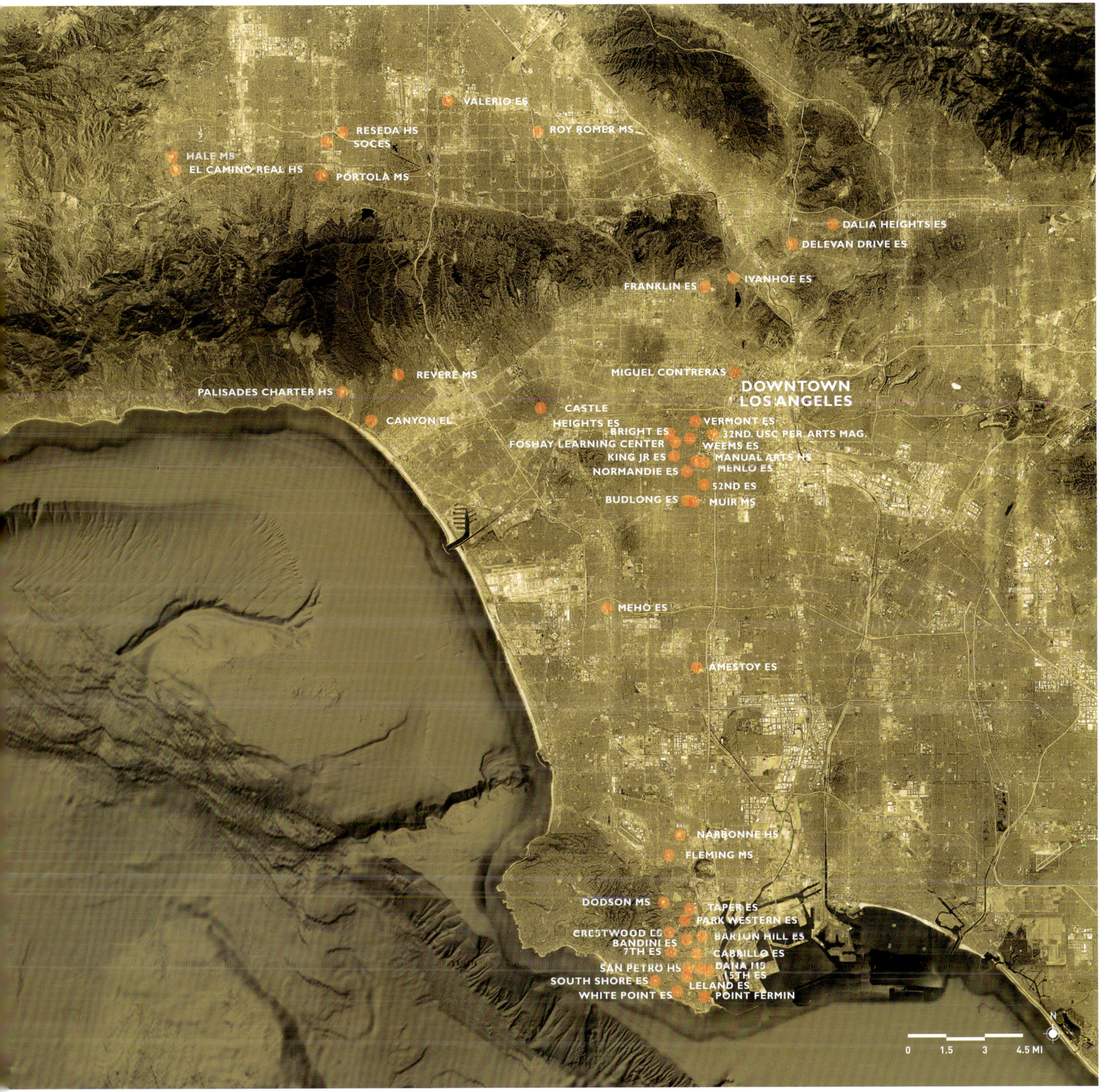
VALERIO ES
RESEDA HS
SOCES
ROY ROMER MS
HALE MS
EL CAMINO REAL HS
PORTOLA MS
DALIA HEIGHTS ES
DELEVAN DRIVE ES
FRANKLIN ES
IVANHOE ES
REVERE MS
PALISADES CHARTER HS
MIGUEL CONTRERAS
DOWNTOWN
LOS ANGELES
CASTLE
HEIGHTS ES
CANYON EL
VERMONT ES
BRIGHT ES
32ND. USC PER ARTS MAG.
FOSHAY LEARNING CENTER
WEEMS ES
KING JR ES
MANUAL ARTS HS
NORMANDIE ES
MENLO ES
52ND ES
BUDLONG ES
MUIR MS
MEHO ES
AMESTOY ES
NARBONNE HS
FLEMING MS
DODSON MS
TAPER ES
PARK WESTERN ES
CRESTWOOD ES
BARTON HILL ES
BANDINI ES
7TH ES
CABRILLO ES
SAN PEDRO HS
DANA MS
15TH ES
SOUTH SHORE ES
LELAND ES
WHITE POINT ES
POINT FERMIN
N
0
1.5
3
4.5 MI

1. San Pedro High School, 2. Dana Middle School

Portola Middle School

El Camino Real High School

Revere Middle School

Foshay Learning Center

Manual Arts High School

Leichman Special Education Center

Hale Charter Academy

Palisades Charter High School

Sherman Oaks Center for Enriched Studies (SOCES)

Narbonne High School

Reseda High School

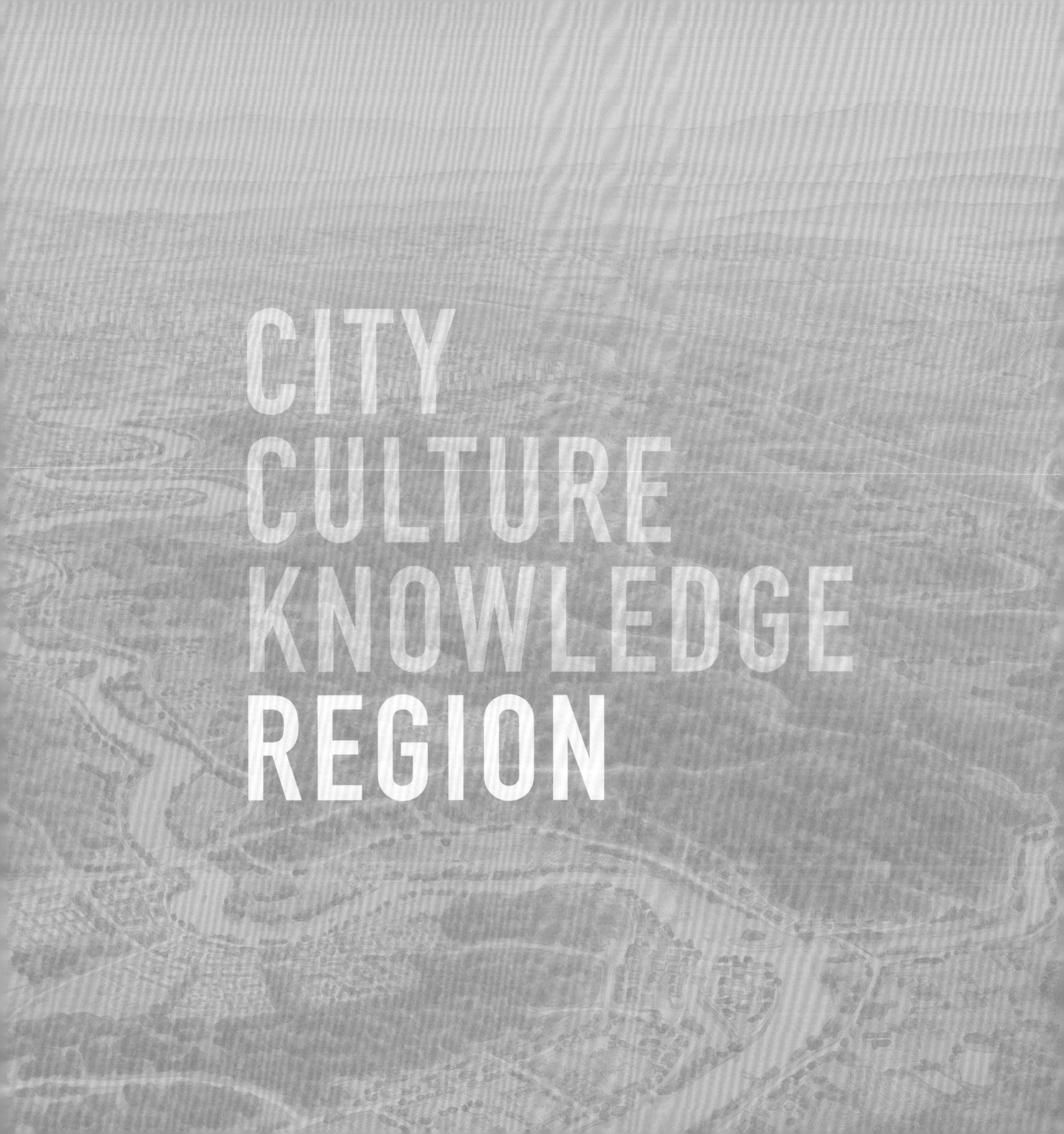

CITY CULTURE KNOWLEDGE REGION

In the Jinjiang River region of Sichuan Province, a critical water resource that has created affluence and placed Chengdu in a prominent position throughout China's long history, is now threatened by both planned and unplanned urbanization, pollution, and water diversion upstream. The agriculture rich and scenic Jinjiang River valley is within the rapidly expanding southern growth corridor of Chengdu. It is also a part of the ancient Dujiangyan irrigation system, built over 2,000 years ago and now classified as a UNESCO World Heritage Site. Water flows from the mountains to the west and is directed each year over a vast network of canals that cover a large alluvial plain of some of the most fertile soils in China, and then south through the city. However, earlier master plans by the City of Chengdu ignored this tremendous water resource by proposing to urbanize the valley, compromising this historical resource and natural regional asset. The new master plan sought solutions to accommodate future economic and population growth while protecting the agricultural and cultural resources of traditional family farming, a Sichuanese hallmark, within the great river's watershed.

The Jinjiang Corridor Master Plan challenges earlier city plans by reorienting city growth

JINJIANG RIVER CORRIDOR
CHENGDU, SICHUAN, CHINA

AWARDS

- AIA California Council, Urban Design Award
- AIA Los Angeles, Next LA Awards
- Architectural Record, China Awards

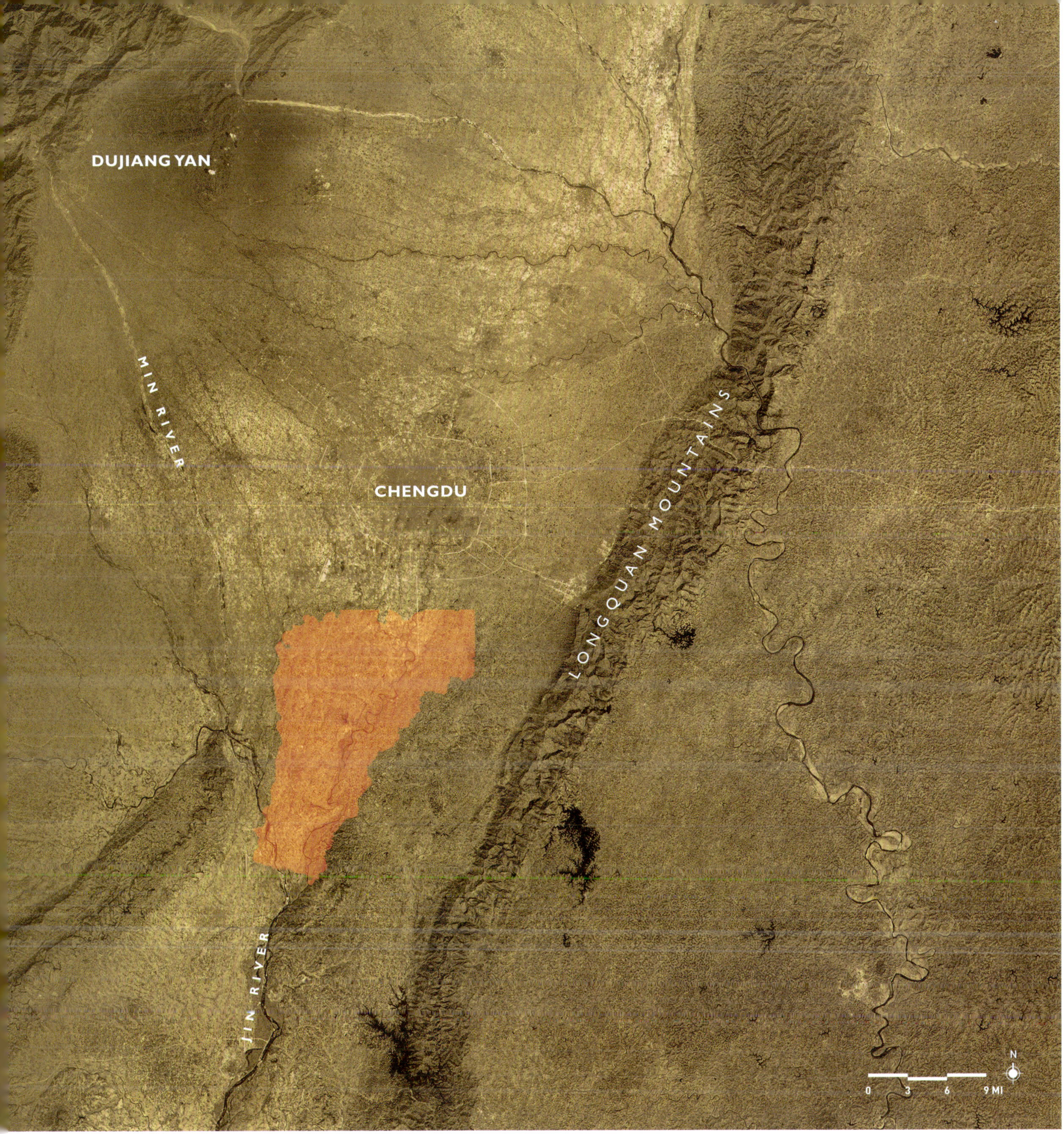
DUJIANG YAN
MIN RIVER
CHENGDU
LONGQUAN MOUNTAINS
JIN RIVER
N
0 3 6 9 MI

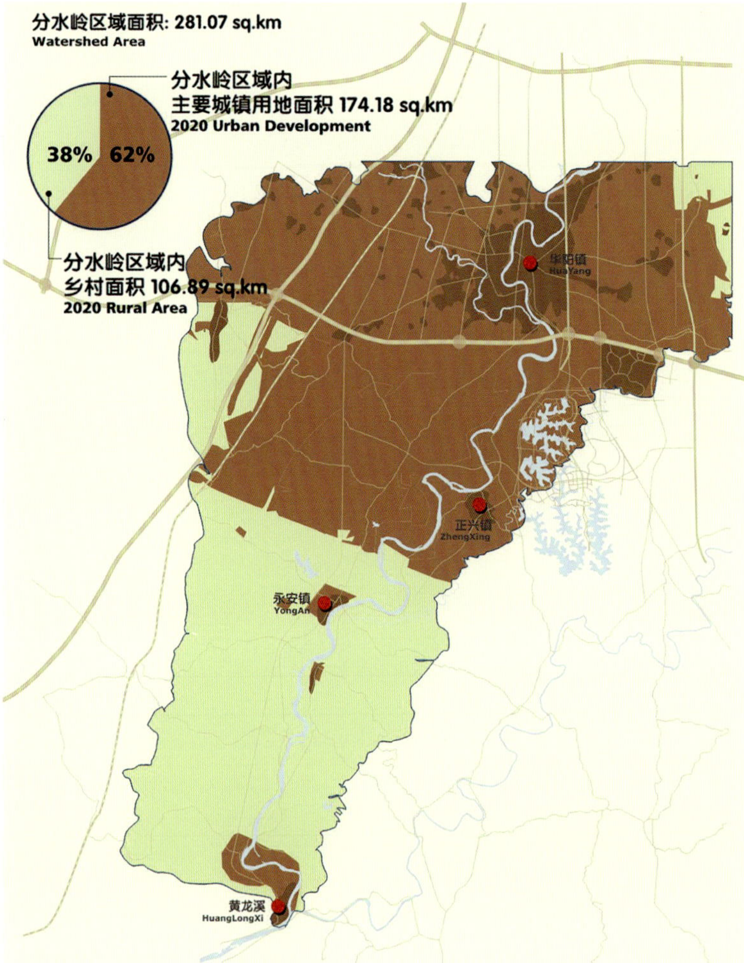

City's proposal for urban growth

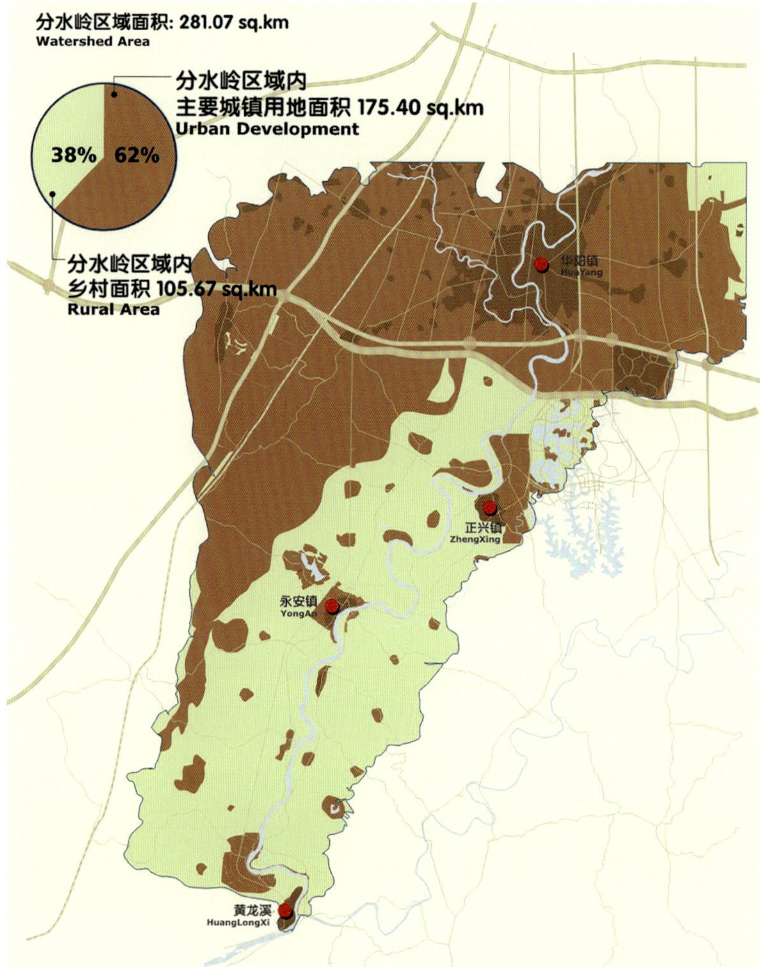

Proposed redirected urban growth corridor

away from the valley to a new growth vector to the west, conserving a broad riparian corridor for environmental enhancement and tourism. Redirecting urban infrastructure including rail, roads, and utilities, deflects urban growth away from the "protected" areas of the valley to more suitable land for development west of that area, so that conservation measures can be applied to the natural resources there. "Community Forest" is designated for some areas of the valley which, like in the United Kingdom, protects natural habitats from large scale urban development.

Agricultural and tourism land uses are proposed within the river corridor, forming a special economic relationship between rural and small urban settlements. The valley becomes a special asset for tourism with biking, swimming, hiking, and outdoor recreation. Appropriately scaled developments emphasizing the valley's heritage of small family farms is encouraged, including organic farming and celebration of the farm-to-table tradition that has made Sichuan cuisine famous worldwide.

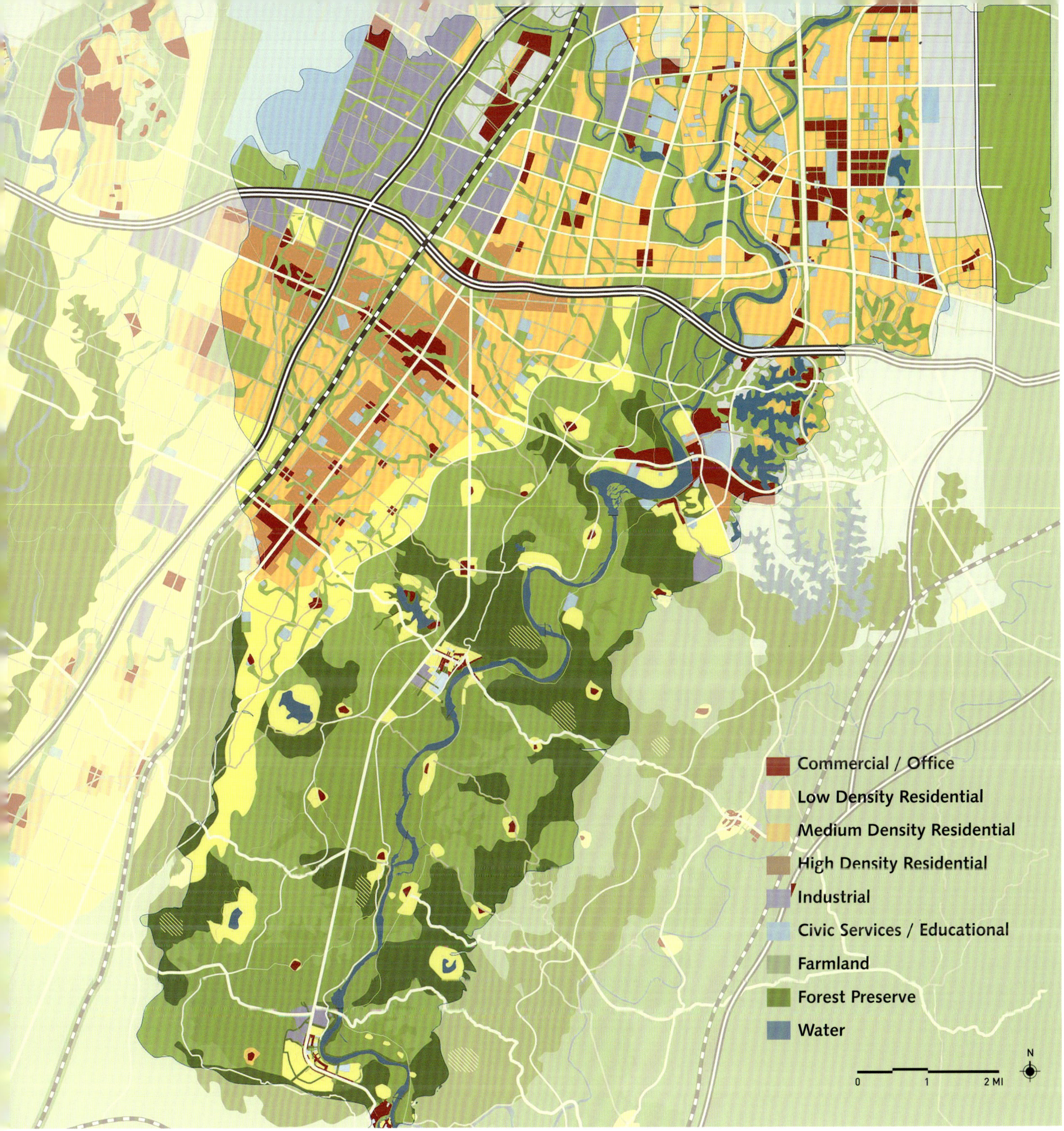
Commercial / Office
Low Density Residential
Medium Density Residential
High Density Residential
Industrial
Civic Services / Educational
Farmland
Forest Preserve
Water
0
1
2 MI
N

n Espinoza Associates

Watershed catchment areas

Eco infrastructure

Jin River

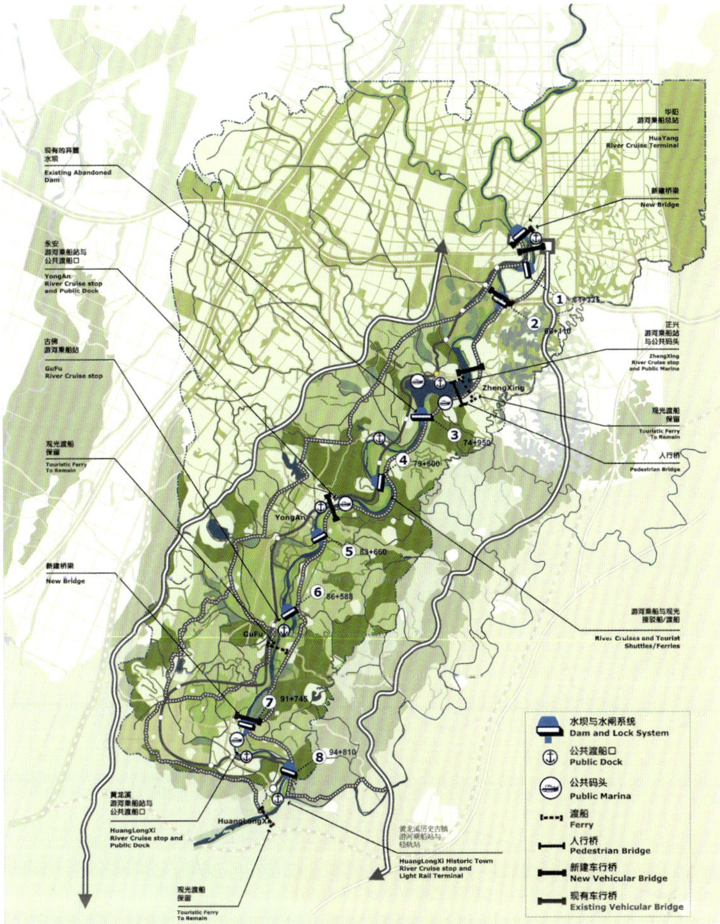

River navigation improvements

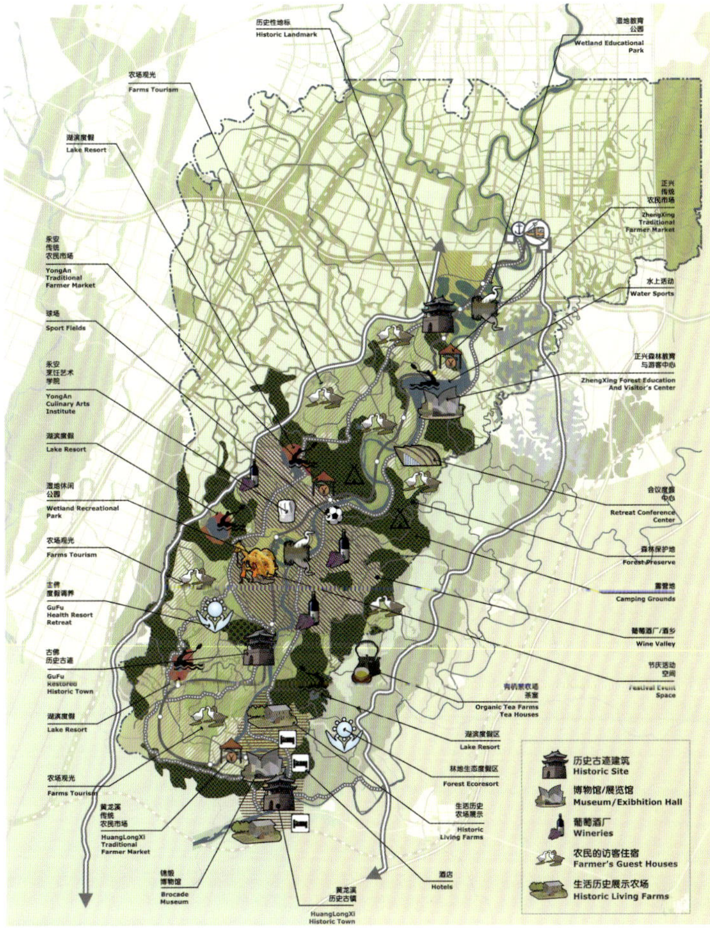

Tourism

Farming along the Jin River

Urban design and planning at its largest scale are a matter of balancing often competing interests, finding solutions that provide for common benefit for all parties and that mitigate against unintended consequences. When China broadened the focus of its international trade and development policy to emphasize development of its western region, the historic city of Chengdu, already the capital of Sichuan Province, was identified as its cultural, administrative, and economic capital. With this new prominence, Chengdu's urban growth became a national priority, particularly regarding the growth corridors radiating from the city center, often in conflict with existing agricultural and environmental resources. Located on the eastern edge of Chengdu's urban core and along the critical growth corridor between Chengdu and Chongqing, Long Quan Yi is an industrial area in need of revitalization with extensive agricultural land and scenic mountains. The primary hurdle for Chengdu's successful eastward expansion is this district, which is seen as a barrier to economically linking Chengdu and Chongqing.

The plan transforms Long Quan Yi from an industrial area into a prominent international trade center, elevating the position of Chengdu in world affairs by promoting and facilitating domestic and international business. The proposed center features a compact urban business district; a university; a research park, and the industrial base, located near each other and well connected by transportation and communication links. At the same time, the plan preserves agriculture and natural areas to create prosperous farming communities and high-quality tourism and recreational destinations. The plan calls for strategic reforestation in the Long Quan Mountains and establishes a comprehensive strategy to take advantage of adjacent Chengdu urban markets that would increase business opportunities for local farmers and preserve Chinese agricultural traditions and scenic beauty.

LONG QUAN YI DISTRICT
CHENGDU, SICHUAN, CHINA

AWARD

- First Place, International Design Competition

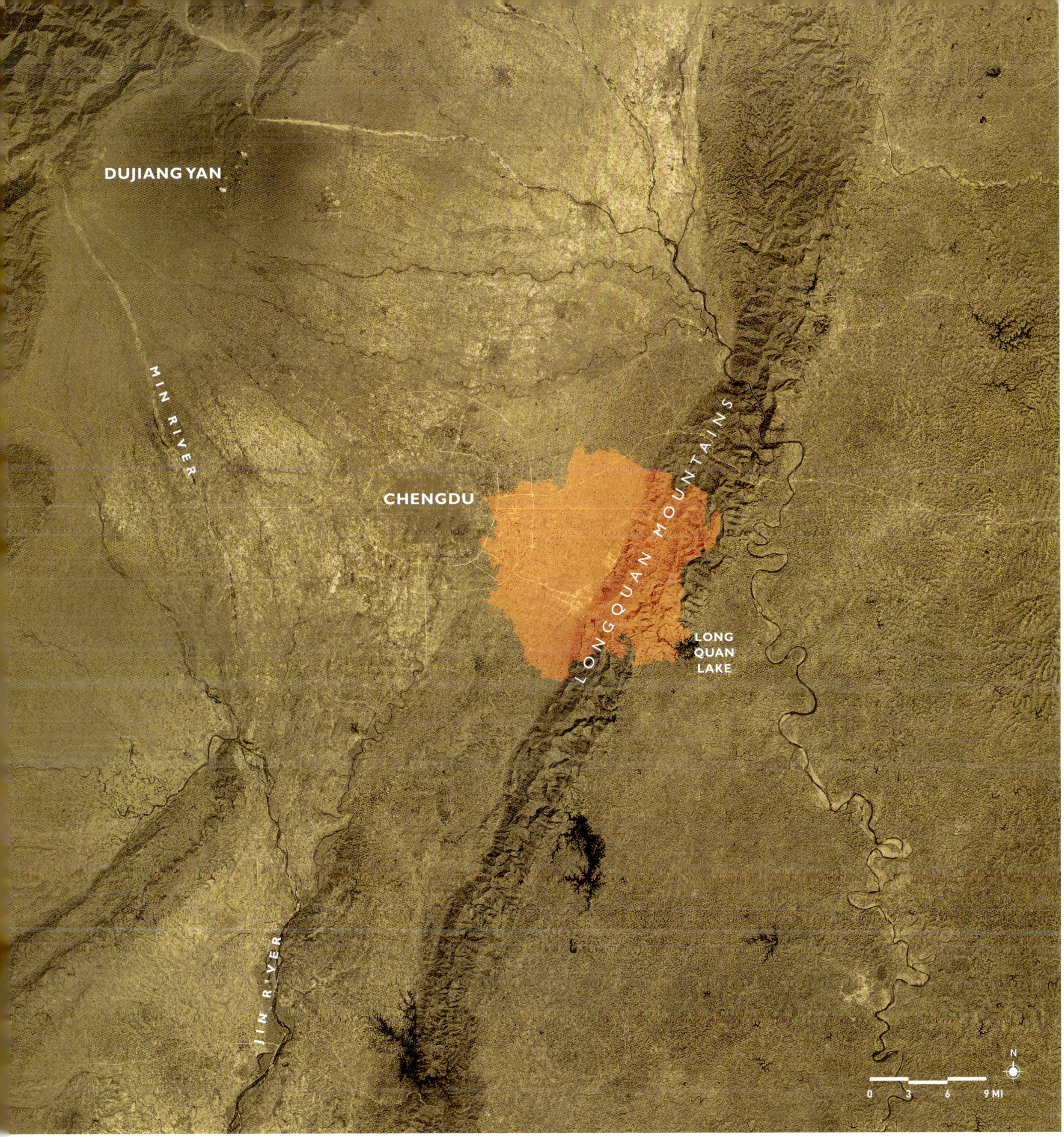
DUJIANG YAN
MIN RIVER
CHENGDU
LONGQUAN MOUNTAINS
LONG
QUAN
LAKE
JIN RIVER
N
0
3
6
9 MI

龙潭寺
保利
SHI LING
十陵街办
XI HE
西河镇
HONG HE
洪河
DA MIAN
大面街办
新兴
BA HE
TOWN
柏合镇
居住用地
RESIDENTIAL
公共服务设施用地
COMMERCE, HOUSING, MIXED-USE
制造工业用地
INDUSTRIAL/ MANUFACTURING
科研及开发用地
RESEARCH & DEVELOPMENT
机构用地
INSTITUTIONAL
水体
WATER
保护性绿地
PRESERVED OPEN SPACE
农业用地
AGRICULTURE

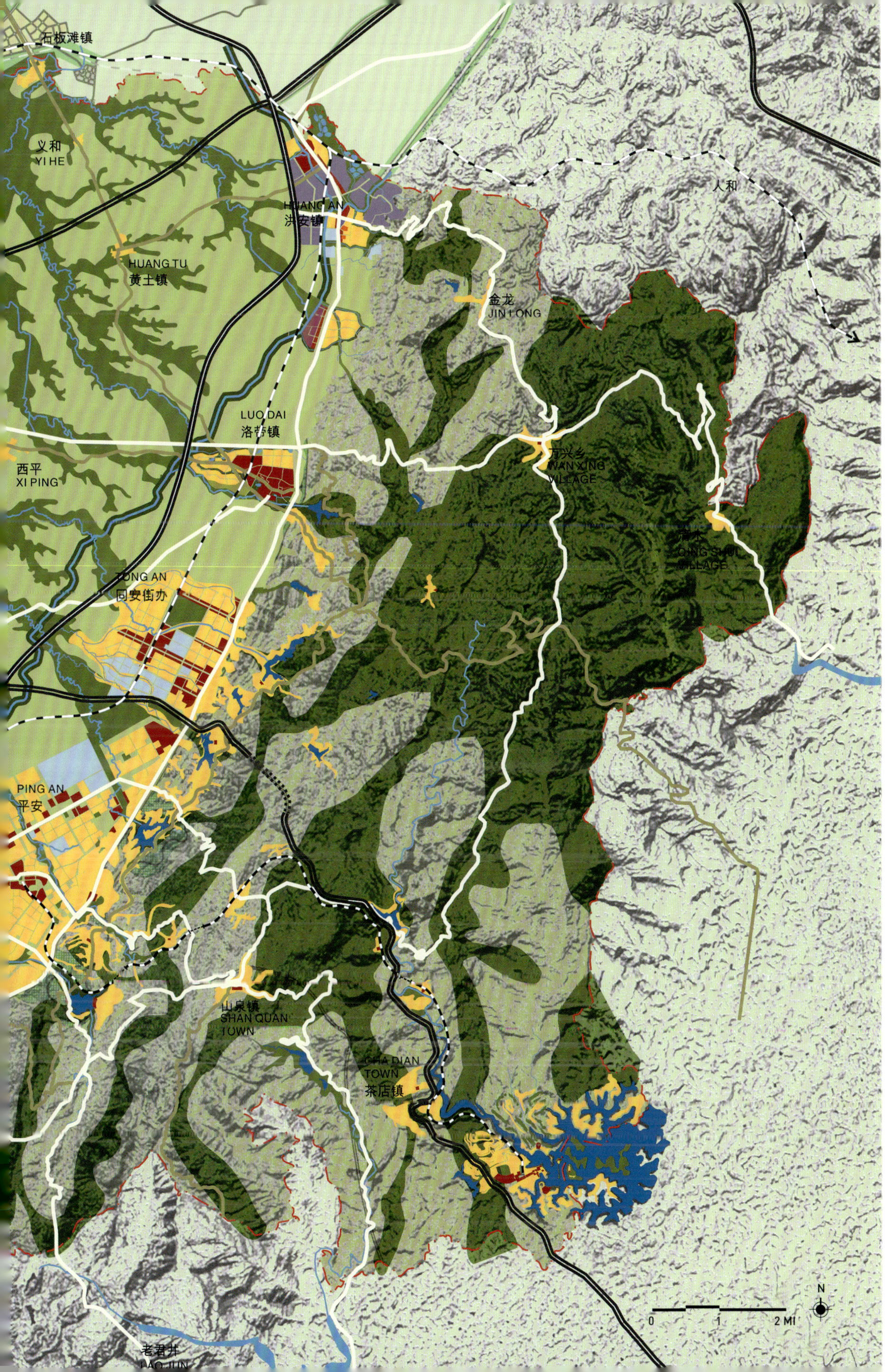
石板滩镇
义和
YI HE
洪安镇
HUANG TU
黄土镇
金龙
JIN LONG
人和
LUO DAI
洛带镇
西平
XI PING
万兴乡
WAN XING
VILLAGE
同安街办
PING AN
平安
山泉镇
SHAN QUAN
TOWN
TOWN
茶店镇
老君井
0
1
2 MI
N

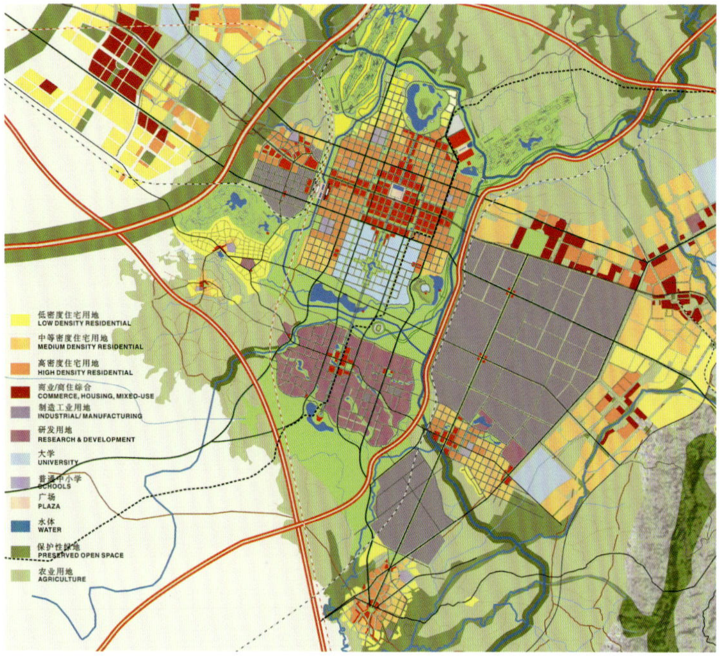

Proposed urban center land use

Proposed historic and cultural tourism

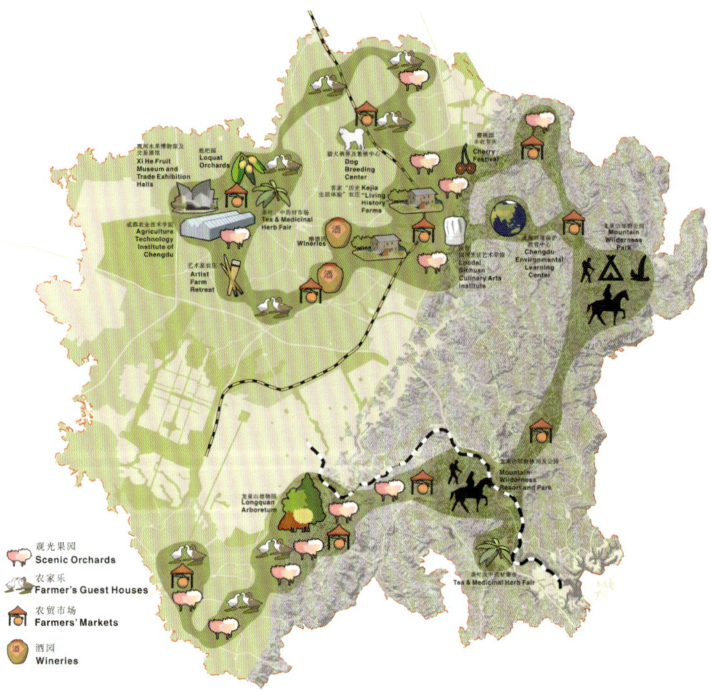

Proposed agricultural and ecological tourism

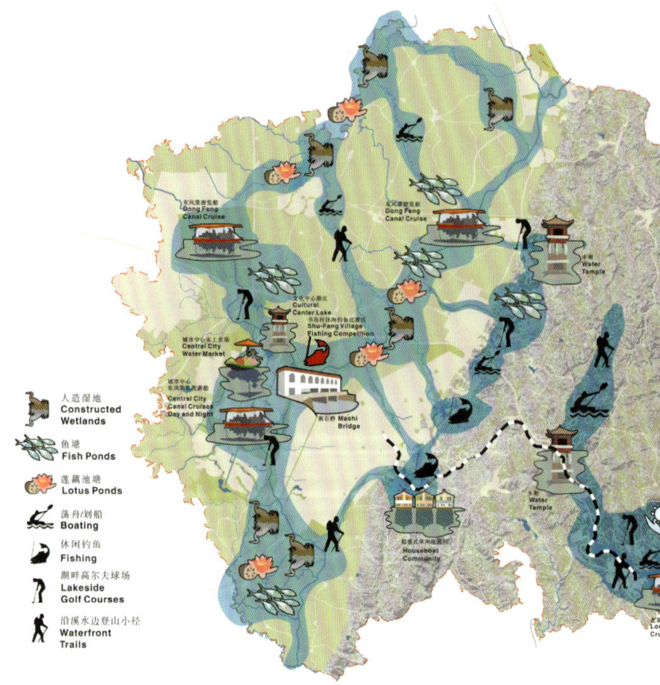

Proposed water recreation tourism

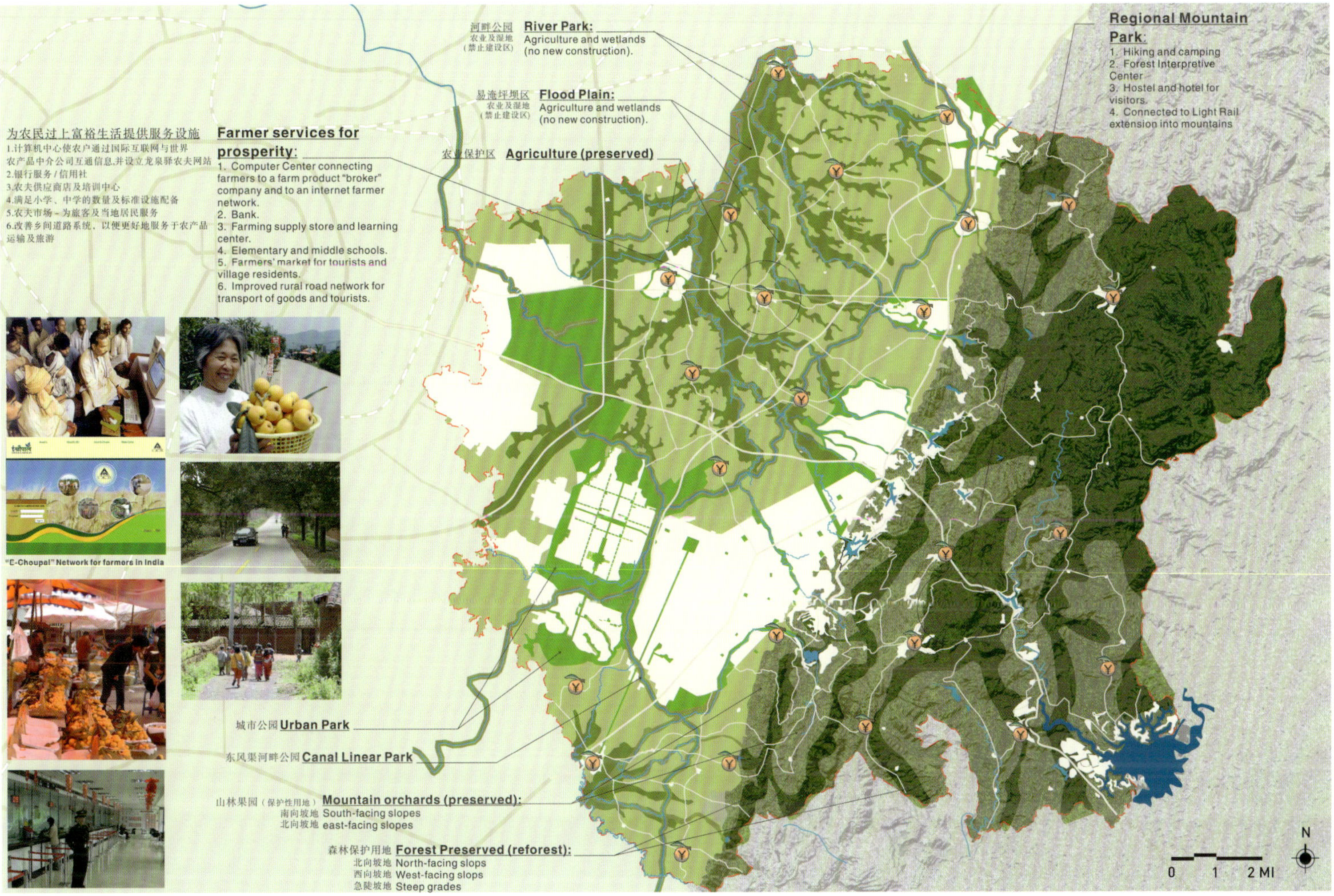

Proposed open space system

View of Long Quan Mountains

Planning to ensure the compatibility of natural resources with economic development is a persistent balancing act in China's growing economy. In a remote location in south-central China, in a setting of deep, steep-sided valleys of unique natural beauty and exceptional water quality, the 1,500-year-old Chinese whiskey industry exemplifies the conflict — and symbiotic relationship — between economic growth and resource preservation. Four hours south of Luzhou, a city on the Yangtze River, the 3,000 km^2 valley is formed by two watersheds of the Gulin and Chishui Rivers. It is said to be the only place in China where a unique bacterium grows that is critical for the whiskey distilleries located there, whose spirits are nationally and becoming internationally recognized. The exceptional water purity is attributed to the vast natural filtering karst limestone formations in the area; however, the recent discovery of high-quality coal within these formations puts that water quality at risk. The government's push to expand high quality coal production in the region, as well as a rapidly increasing urban populations, are recognized as potential hazards to the whiskey industry and natural qualities of the region.

The new regional plan undertaken to address these conflicting issues specifically protects the major watersheds essential to whiskey production, including the growing of sorghum fields, sorghum fermentation and distillation. Many of these same provisions also protect the scenic places and corridors in the region important for the future eco-tourism anticipated as the region becomes more accessible. The plan recognizes that smart water management is critical to future population growth particularly as Gulin City, in the heart of the valley, and smaller towns are expanded. The plan limits coal mining to low-impact locations and water runoff and debris and containment methods are proposed. Strategic goals and recommendations for long-term, mid-term and immediate development include land resources management guidelines, limited and concentrated urban growth areas that include a high-performance business center, a center for higher education, a primary medical center, a service center for the tourism industry, multi-modal transportation systems, and regional environmental guidelines for preservation and sustainability.

CHINESE WHISKEY VALLEY
LUZHOU, SICHUAN, CHINA

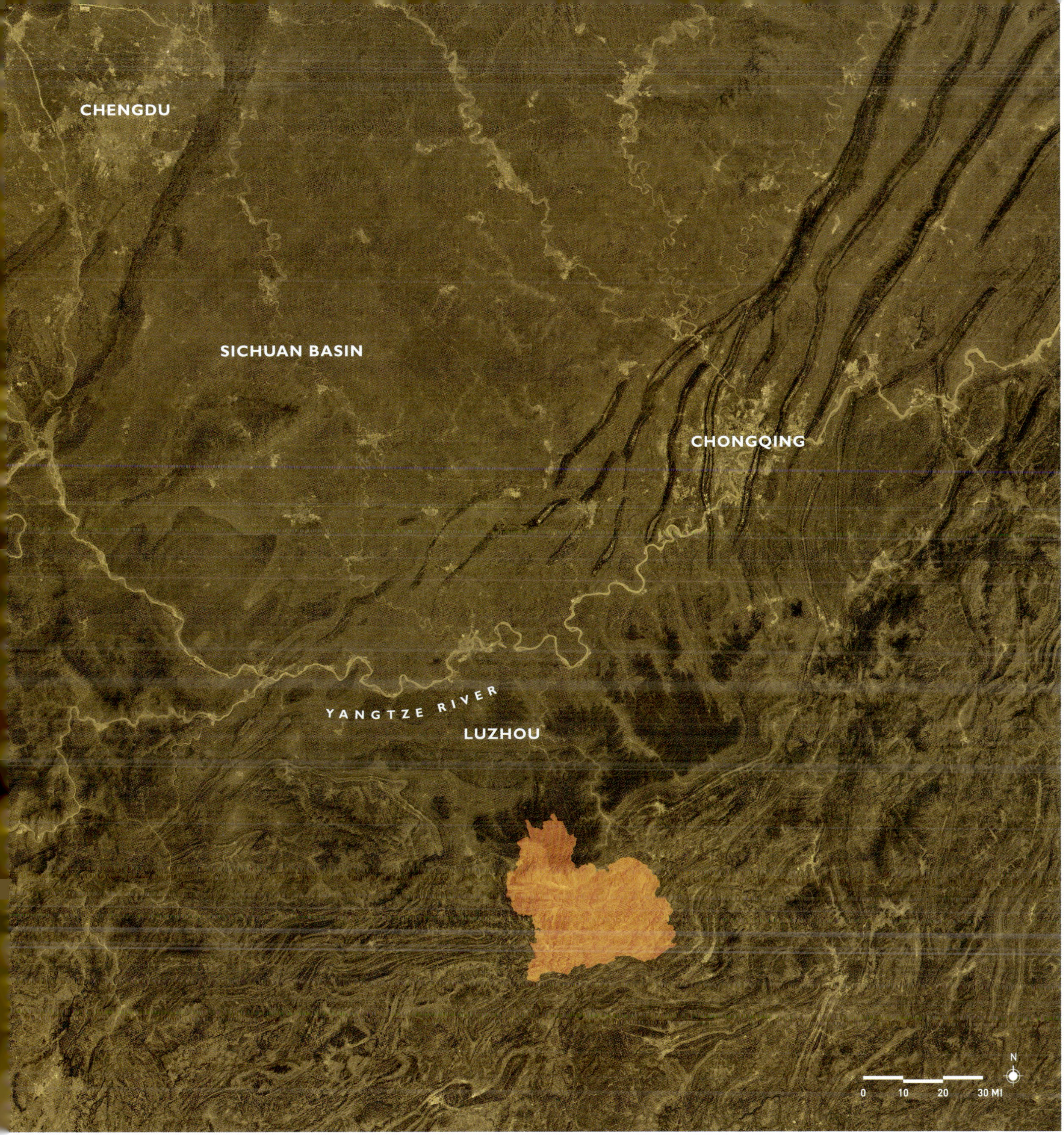
CHENGDU
SICHUAN BASIN
CHONGQING
YANGTZE RIVER
LUZHOU
N
0
10
20
30 MI

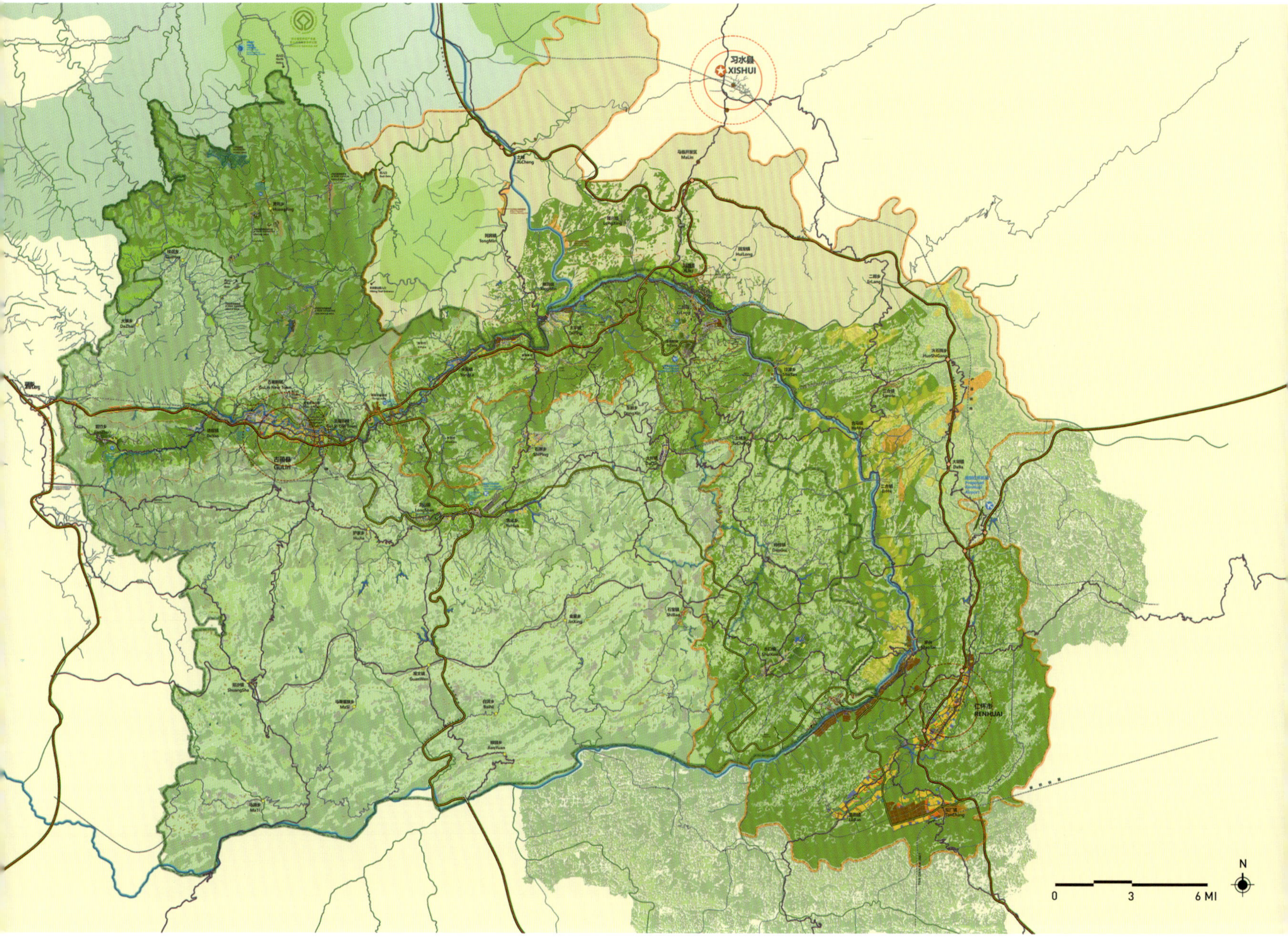

Gulin regional land use framework

Chi Shui River

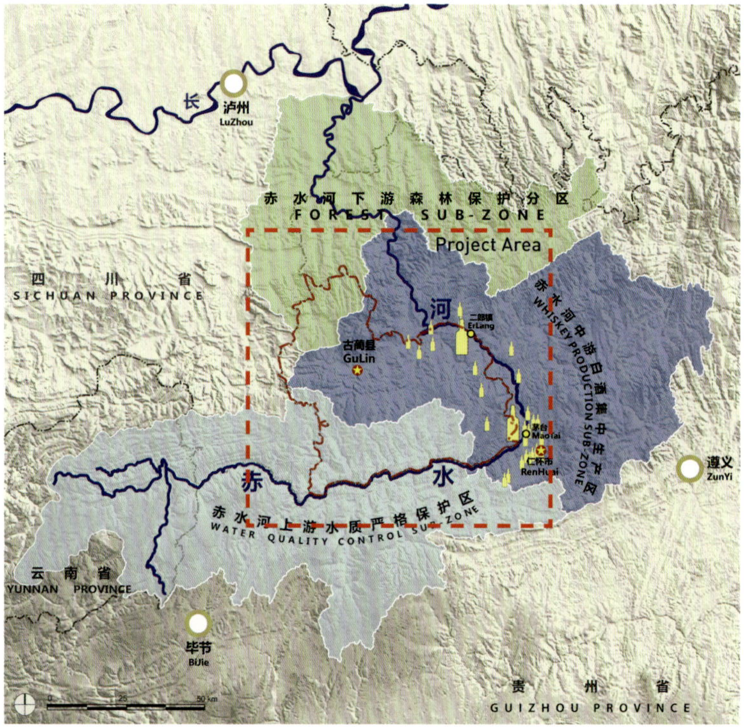

Water quality control zones — no coal mining permitted

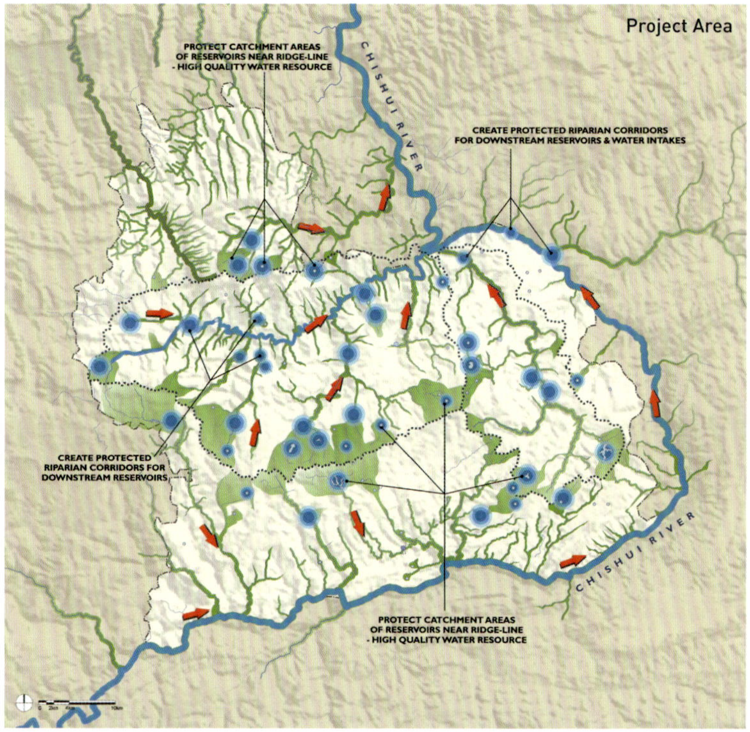

Proposed management of riparian corridors and reservoirs

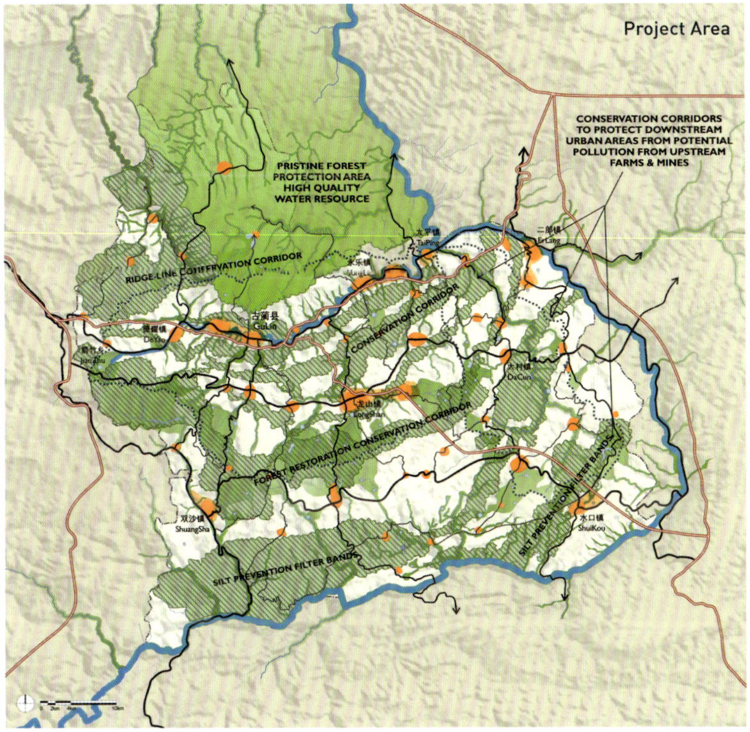

Conservation corridors to filter water runoff

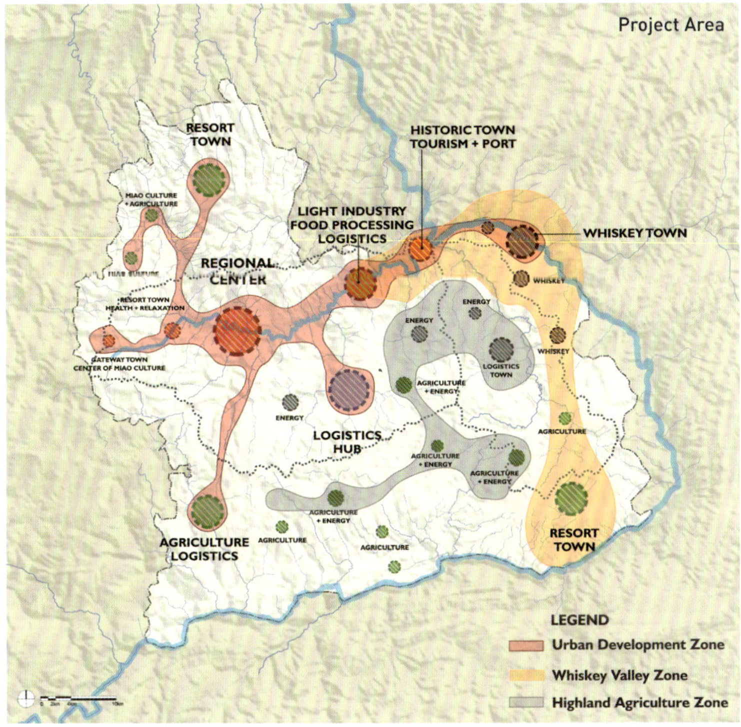

Economic centers concept

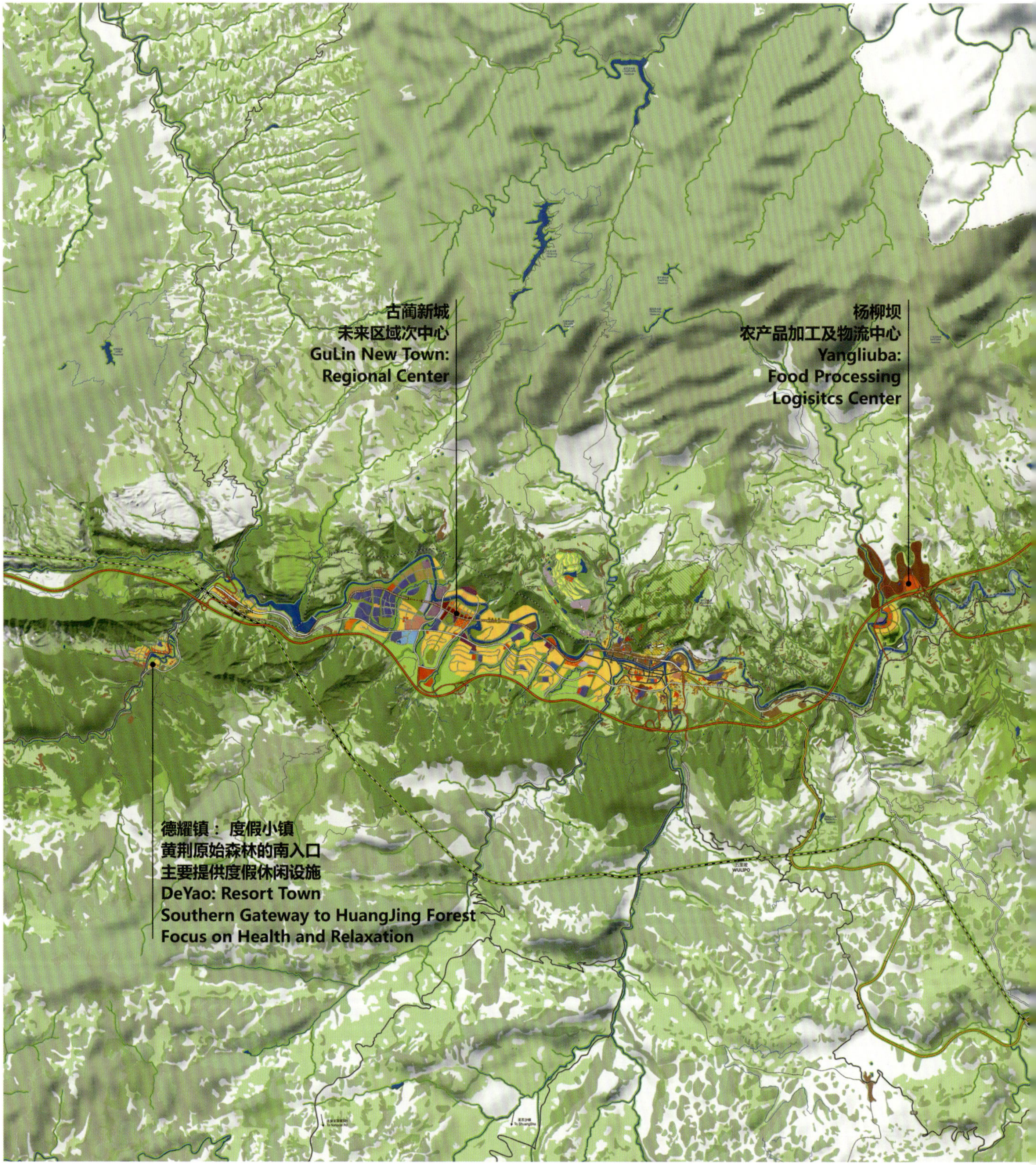
古蔺新城
未来区域次中心
GuLin New Town:
Regional Center
杨柳坝
农产品加工及物流中心
Yangliuba:
Food Processing
Logisitcs Center
德耀镇： 度假小镇
黄荆原始森林的南入口
主要提供度假休闲设施
DeYao: Resort Town
Southern Gateway to HuangJing Forest
Focus on Health and Relaxation

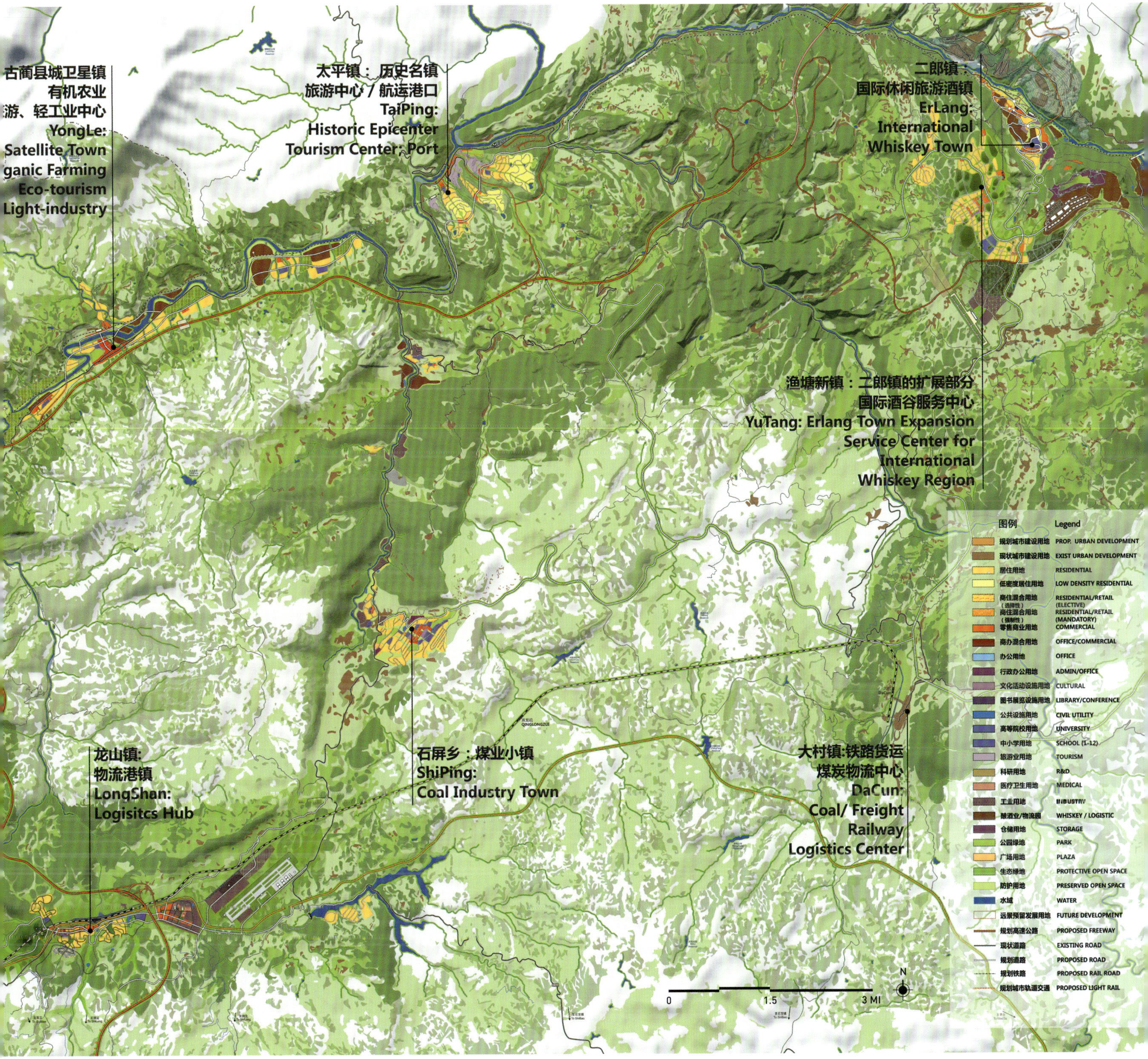
古蔺县城卫星镇
有机农业
游、轻工业中心
YongLe:
Satellite Town
ganic Farming
Eco-tourism
Light-industry
太平镇：历史名镇
旅游中心 / 航运港口
TaiPing:
Historic Epicenter
Tourism Center; Port
二郎镇：
国际休闲旅游酒镇
ErLang:
International
Whiskey Town
渔塘新镇：二郎镇的扩展部分
国际酒谷服务中心
YuTang: Erlang Town Expansion
Service Center for
International
Whiskey Region
石屏乡：煤业小镇
ShiPing:
Coal Industry Town
龙山镇:
物流港镇
LongShan:
Logisitcs Hub
大村镇:铁路货运
煤炭物流中心
DaCun:
Coal/ Freight
Railway
Logistics Center
图例
Legend
规划城市建设用地 PROP. URBAN DEVELOPMENT
现状城市建设用地 EXIST URBAN DEVELOPMENT
居住用地 RESIDENTIAL
低密度居住用地 LOW DENSITY RESIDENTIAL
商住混合用地（选择性） RESIDENTIAL/RETAIL (ELECTIVE)
商住混合用地（强制性） RESIDENTIAL/RETAIL (MANDATORY)
零售商业用地 COMMERCIAL
商办混合用地 OFFICE/COMMERCIAL
办公用地 OFFICE
行政办公用地 ADMIN/OFFICE
文化活动设施用地 CULTURAL
图书展览设施用地 LIBRARY/CONFERENCE
公共设施用地 CIVIL UTILITY
高等院校用地 UNIVERSITY
中小学用地 SCHOOL (1-12)
旅游业用地 TOURISM
科研用地 R&D
医疗卫生用地 MEDICAL
工业用地 INDUSTRY
酿酒业/物流园 WHISKEY / LOGISTIC
仓储用地 STORAGE
公园绿地 PARK
广场用地 PLAZA
生态绿地 PROTECTIVE OPEN SPACE
防护用地 PRESERVED OPEN SPACE
水域 WATER
远景预留发展用地 FUTURE DEVELOPMENT
规划高速公路 PROPOSED FREEWAY
现状道路 EXISTING ROAD
规划道路 PROPOSED ROAD
规划铁路 PROPOSED RAIL ROAD
规划城市轨道交通 PROPOSED LIGHT RAIL
0
1.5
3 MI
N

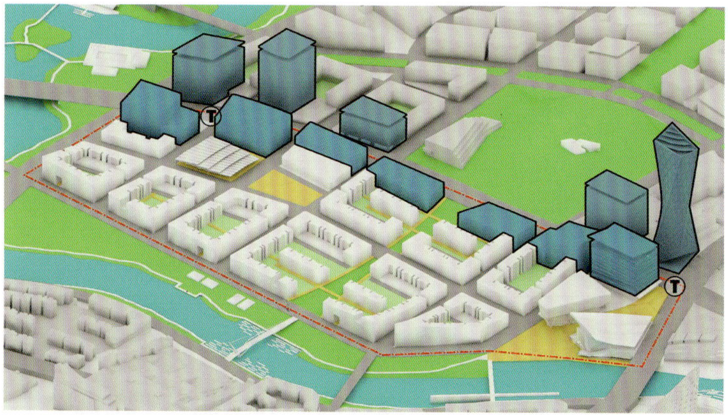

Commercial office

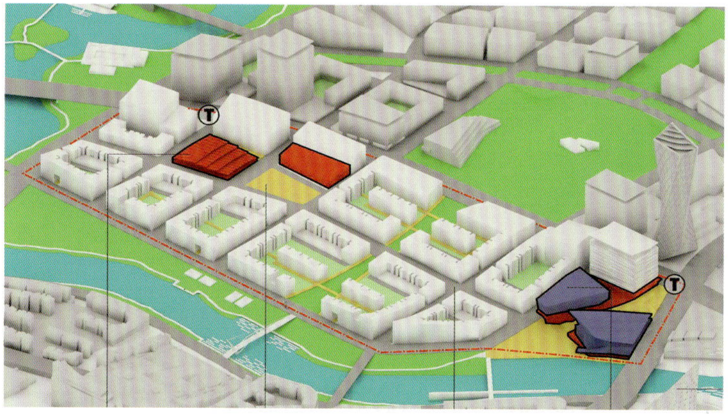

Commercial anchors

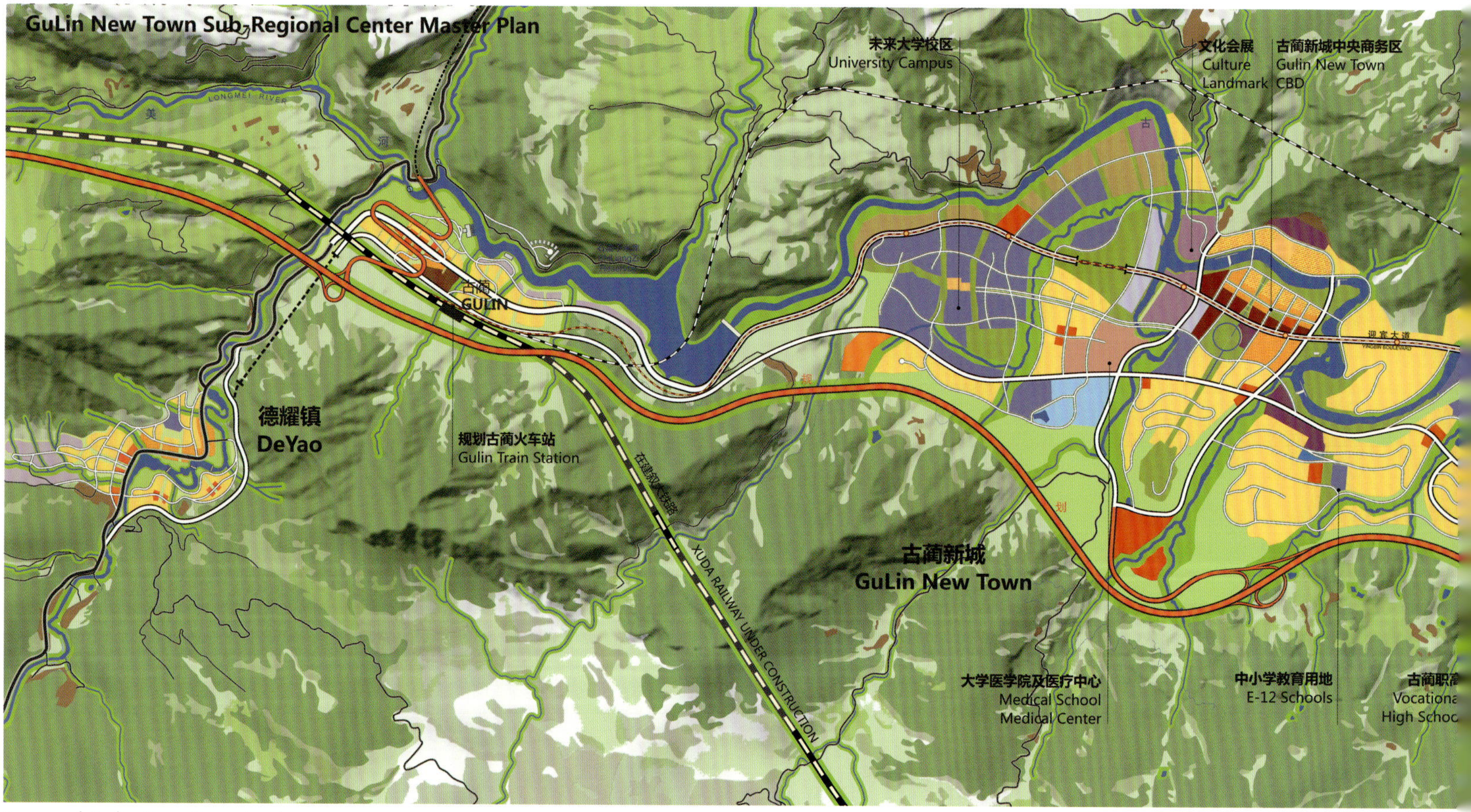

Proposed Gulin New Town land use plan

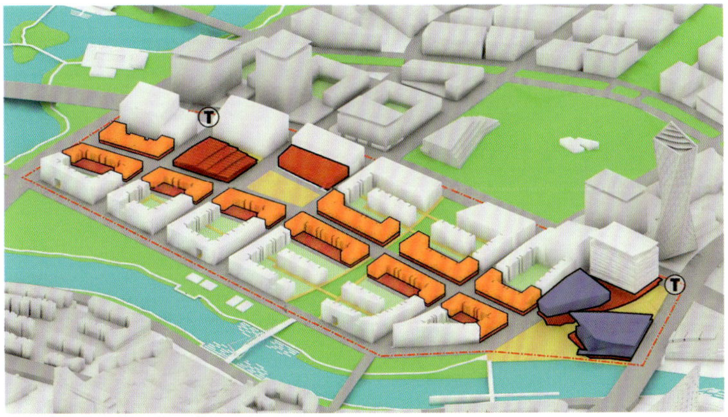

Mixed-use, residential and retail

Residential

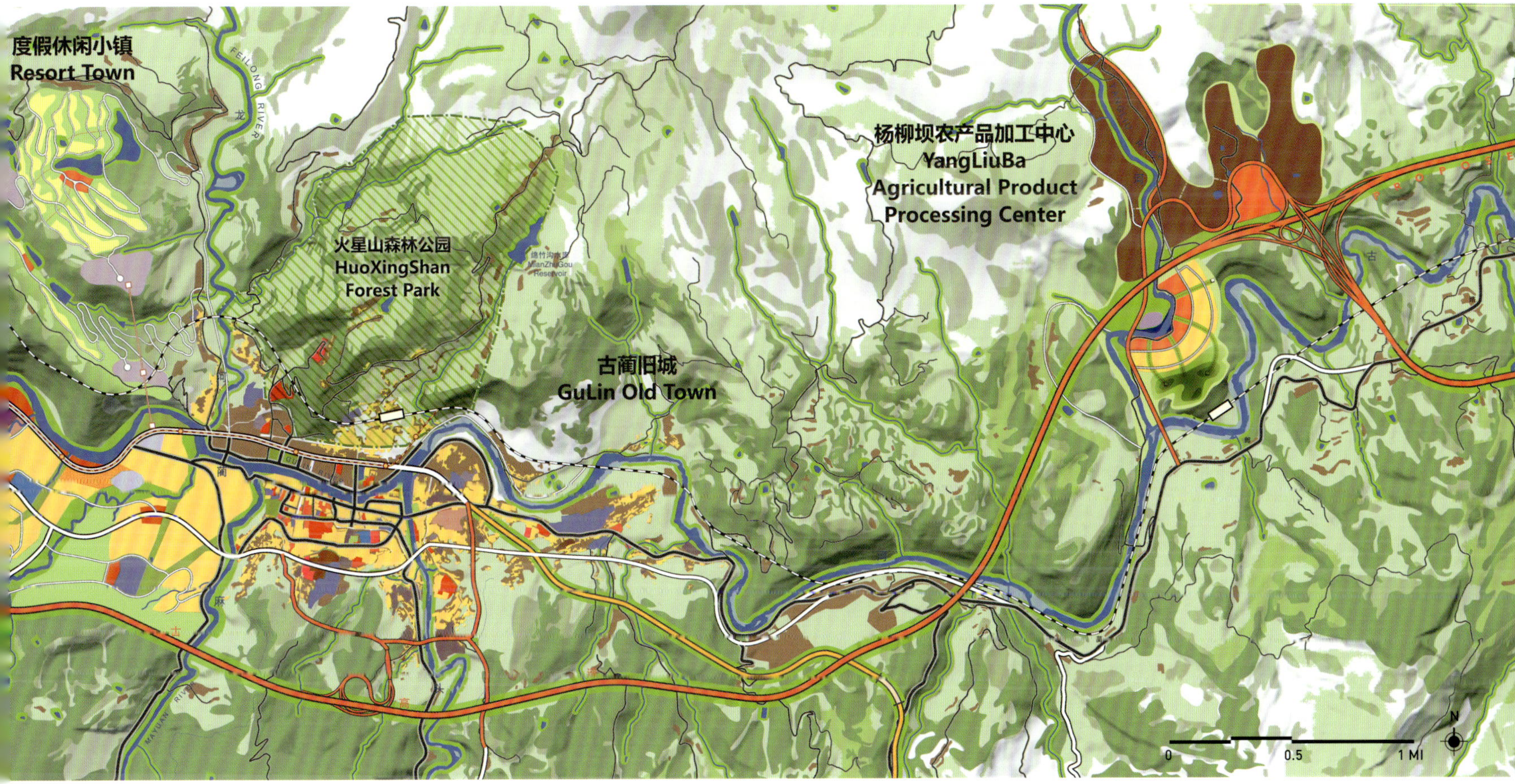

China's remarkable growth in economic output, population, and development is a global success story of the early twenty-first century. The City of Tianjin has participated substantially in this progress and is poised for even greater growth as one of China's primary urban regions—home to thriving industry, picturesque agriculture, and booming tourism. Not all this growth and development has been beneficial. Some policies have led to negative consequences including unguided sprawl that has consumed precious countryside while many areas of the region have been over-farmed, causing historic river water courses to be eliminated. In addition, public works have also altered waterways and degraded the natural environment. The Seven Mile Sea in Tianjin is an ancient seabed where over-farming and altered water courses have radically changed the natural ecology.

The master plan for Tianjin Seven Mile Sea proposes to counteract recent negative impacts of development on the delicate ecosystem, offering recommendations to officials in Tianjin regarding the future development of the region. The plan recommends to fully integrate restored wetlands with modest modernized farms, existing villages, and the development of ecologically sensitive new eco-towns. The plan proposes an archipelago of urbanized "islands"

TIANJIN ANCIENT WETLAND RESTORATION
TIANJIN, CHINA

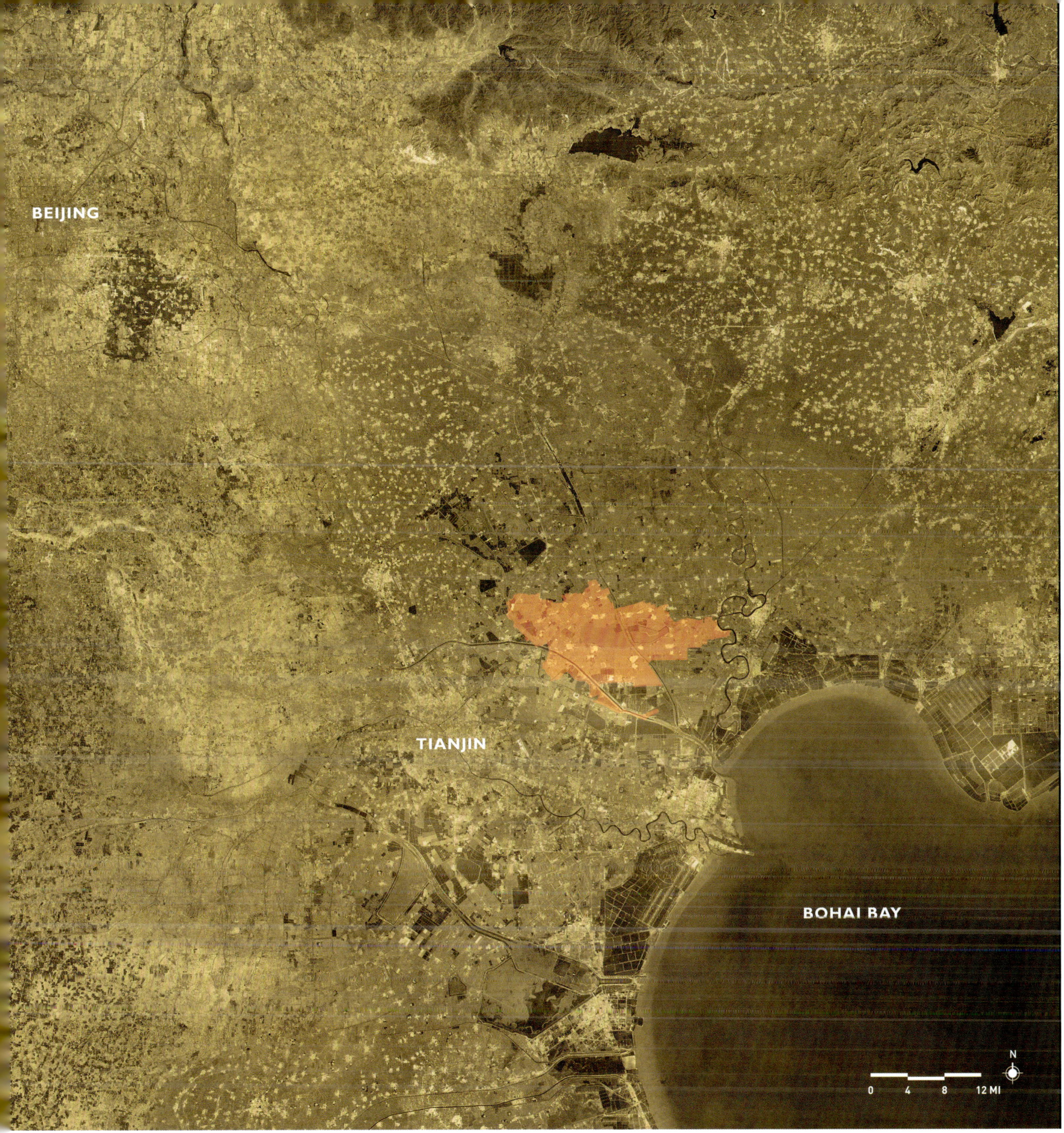
BEIJING
TIANJIN
BOHAI BAY
N
0 4 8 12 MI

蓟高速路南延线
Jinji Fwy S. Extension
津榆公路 JinYu Hwy
112 高速 Freeway
津京塘二号线
No.2 JingJin Tang Expwy
机场快速
Airport Expwy
往天津国际机场
To Tianjin International Airport

within a network of restored wetlands, defined by topography and hydrology. The watercourses and wetlands are prioritized and form the basis for organizing the plan. Farmlands are at a level above water flows and flood occasionally during rainy periods. Villages are located at a higher elevation, historically high enough to be protected from flooding. The low-lying farming zone surrounds and buffers the “islands” where the proposed eco-towns are located. The islands are linked together by a network of narrow bridges designed to allow water to flow freely below. The plan restores natural water flows from the mountains to the sea, while integrating farming and urban housing.

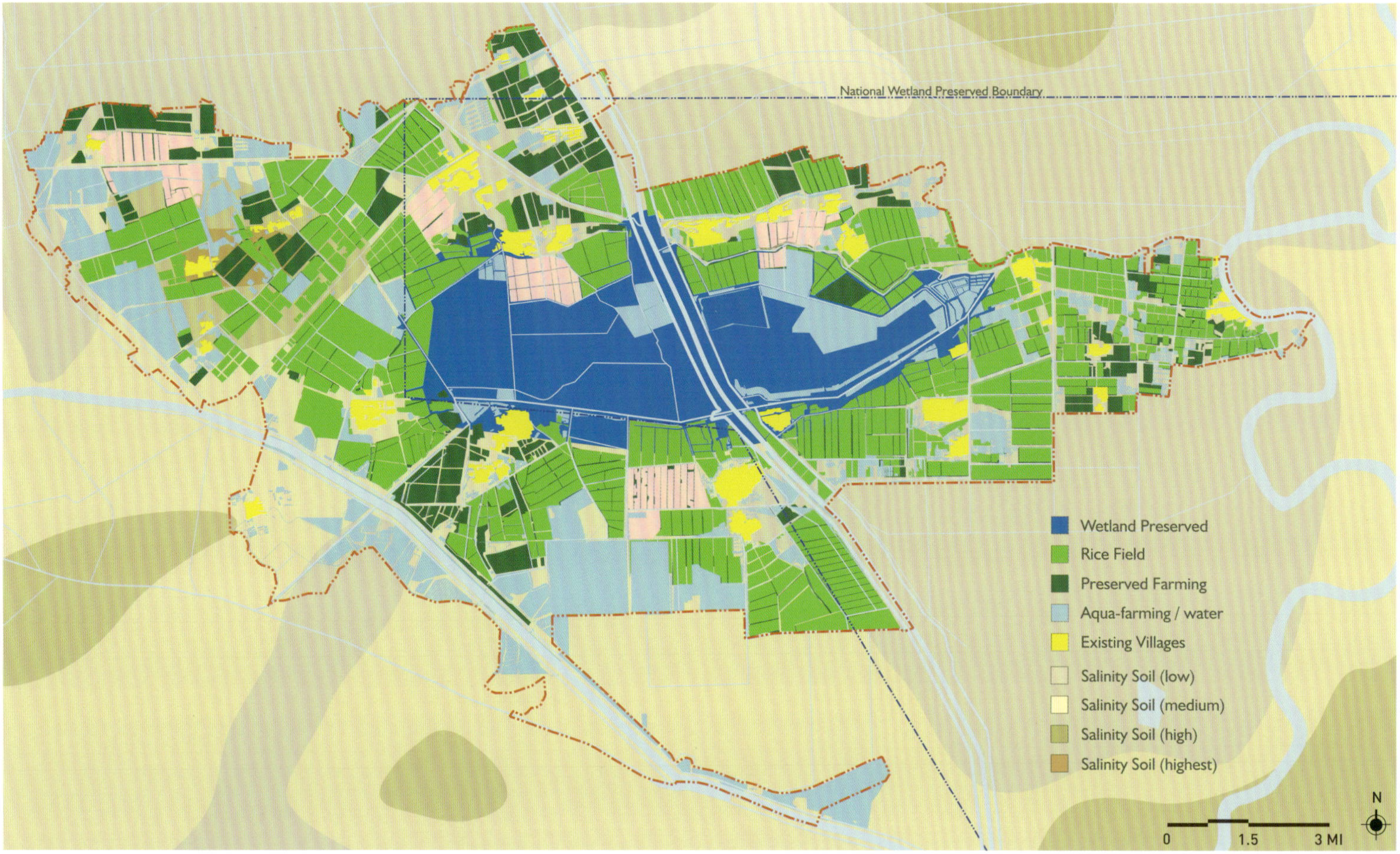

Existing agricultural conditions

Existing wetlands

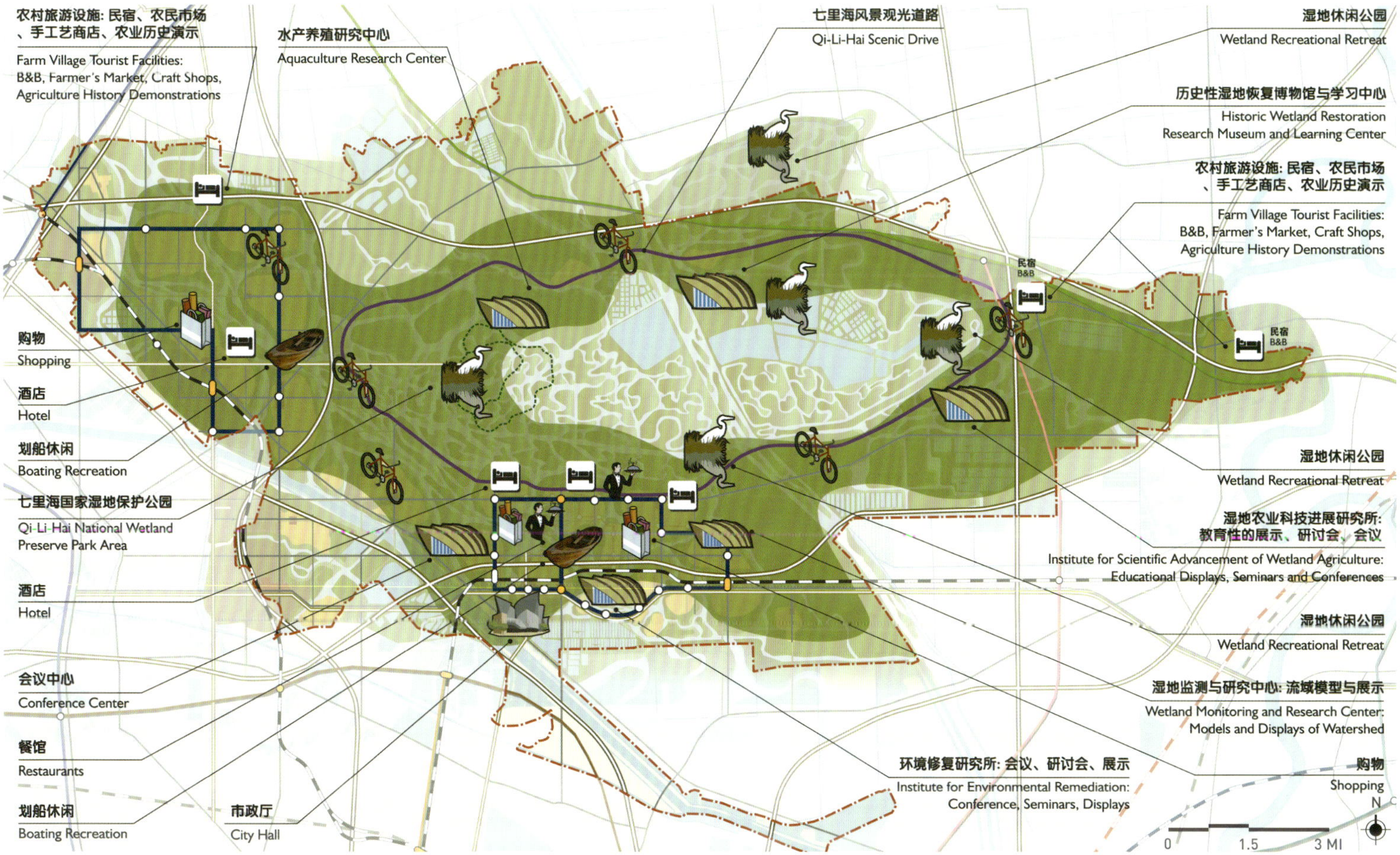

Proposed agro-tourism

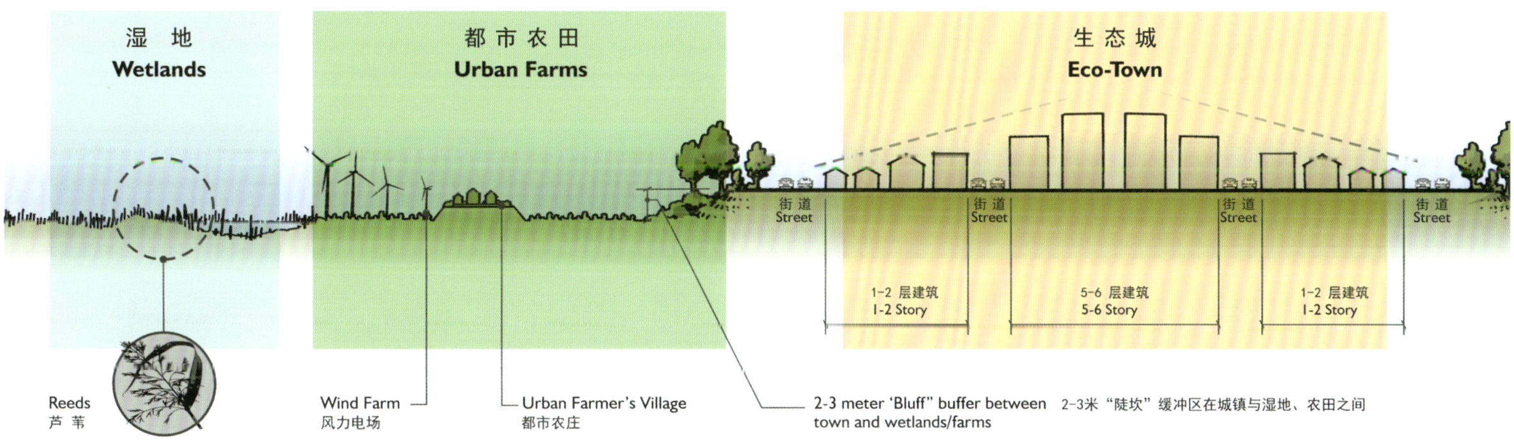

Proposed eco-town cross-sectional concept

For over two millennia Guangzhou has been a successful trading port located at the confluence of two regional growth corridors that extend south, one towards Macau on the west and the other on the east towards Hong Kong along the Pearl River delta. Guangzhou has sustained its leading position for commerce using a series of strategies that include the transformation from single centered city to multi-centered regional city; the formation of a new Central Business District; and the expansion of the westerly and easterly growth corridors. However, the government's original plan's easterly expansion policy of single use manufacturing and industrial uses conflicted with the area's current market demand for mixed-use commercial and residential projects. Thus, a new plan was needed to transform this area of large single use industrial blocks with wide service streets for truck access into new mixed developments organized as neighborhoods for housing and commercial retail along with smaller industrial districts providing a proper jobs-housing balance.

GUANGZHOU ECONOMIC DEVELOPMENT DISTRICT

GUANGZHOU, GUANGDONG, CHINA

AWARD

- First Place, International Design Competition

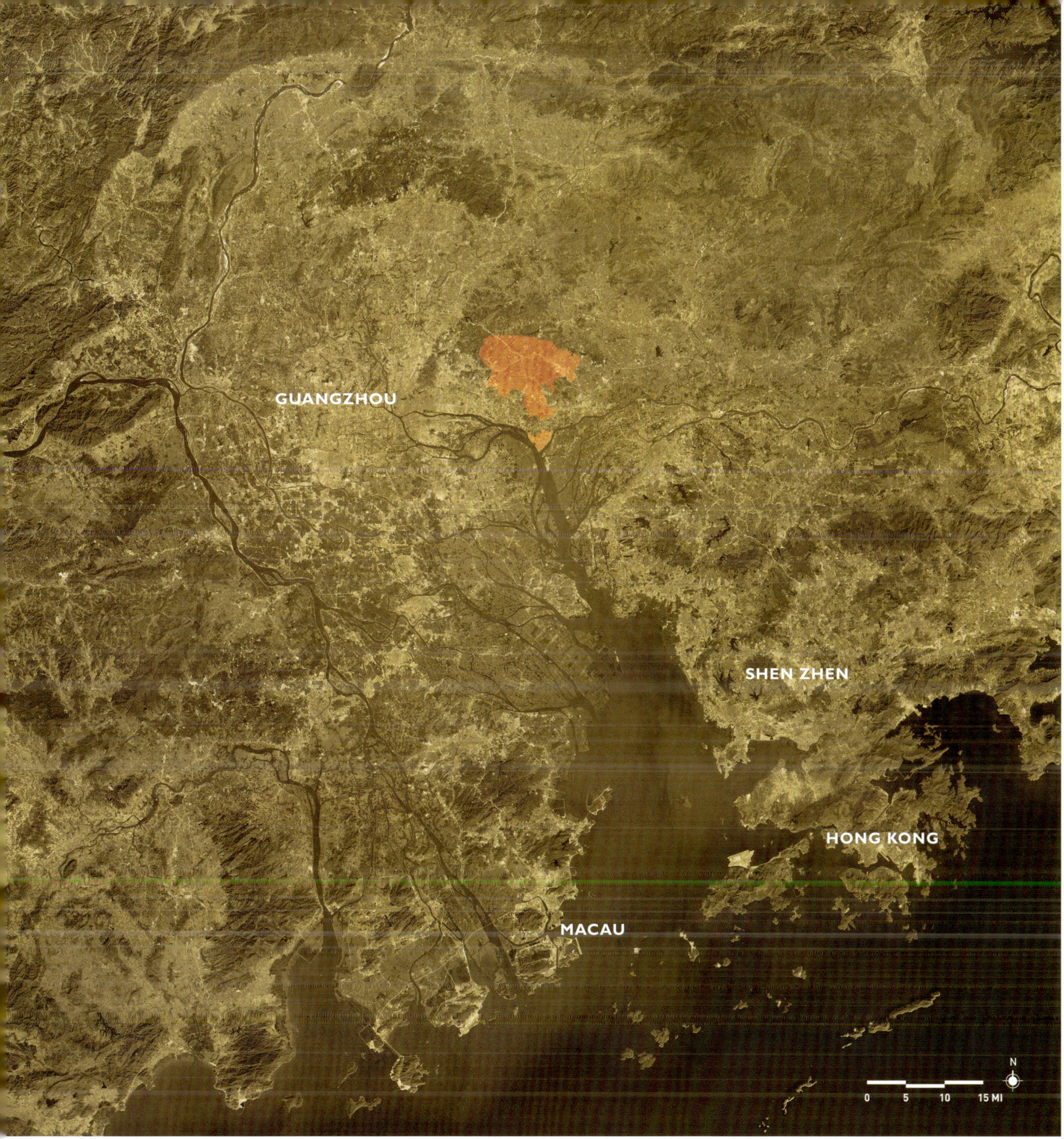
GUANGZHOU
SHEN ZHEN
HONG KONG
MACAU
N
0
5
10
15 MI

The new plan recognizes the importance of the Guangzhou Development Area encompassing 21,500 hectares through an eightfold strategy that extends the growth corridor of Guangzhou towards Hong Kong; encourages dense and mixed-use areas; realizes sustainable and resilient development; offers cultural land uses to enrich civic life; promotes innovation through university and industry collaboration; and achieves connectivity to natural settings by embracing the mountains and connecting to the river. The plan provides a new overall transportation framework that offers a high degree of mobility including various modes of public transit and a road system with redundant routes to minimize traffic congestion. It also identifies land development opportunities including a site for a new urban center, one of a number identified for the region. The overall site is stitched together with a comprehensive open space network offering new bike and pedestrian routes throughout, including trails that find their way into the surrounding mountains.

Regional concept diagram

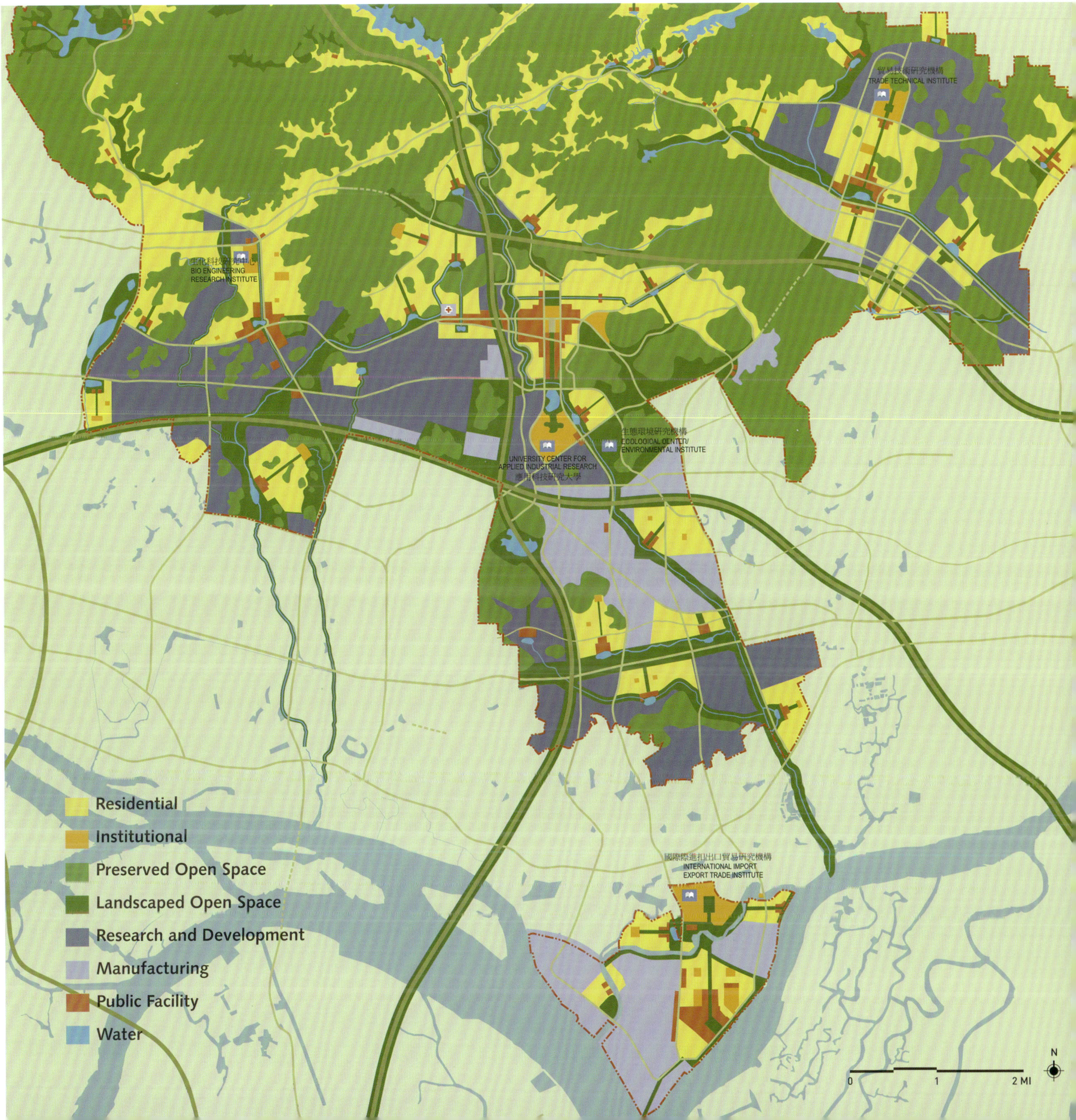

TRADE TECHNICAL INSTITUTE
BIO ENGINEERING
RESEARCH INSTITUTE
生態環境研究機構
ECOLOGICAL CENTER/
ENVIRONMENTAL INSTITUTE
UNIVERSITY CENTER FOR
APPLIED INDUSTRIAL RESEARCH
INTERNATIONAL IMPORT
EXPORT TRADE INSTITUTE
Residential
Institutional
Preserved Open Space
Landscaped Open Space
Research and Development
Manufacturing
Public Facility
Water
0
1
2 MI
N

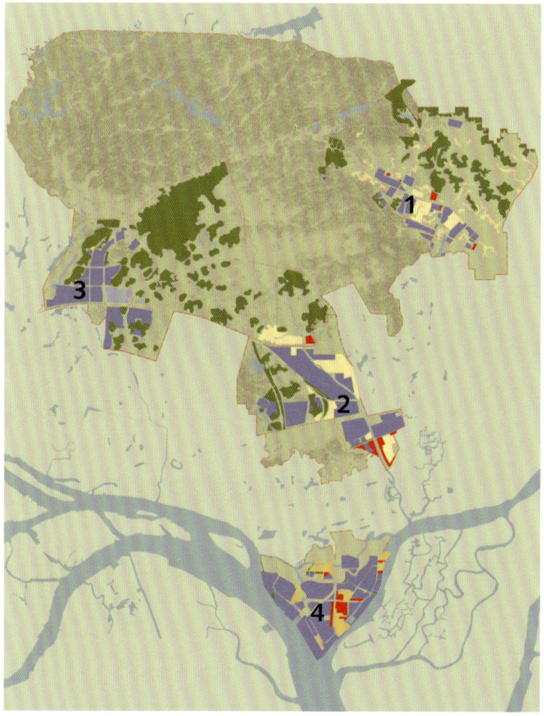

Existing land use

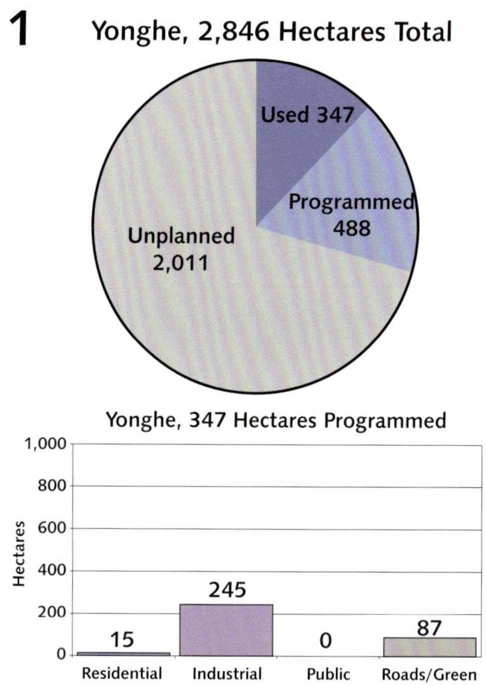

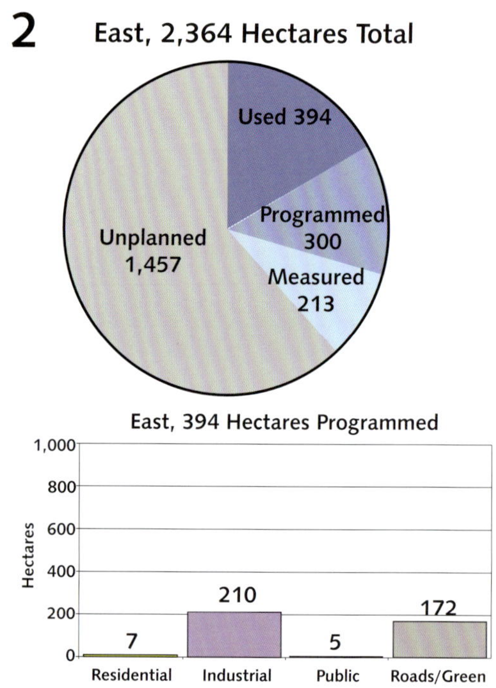

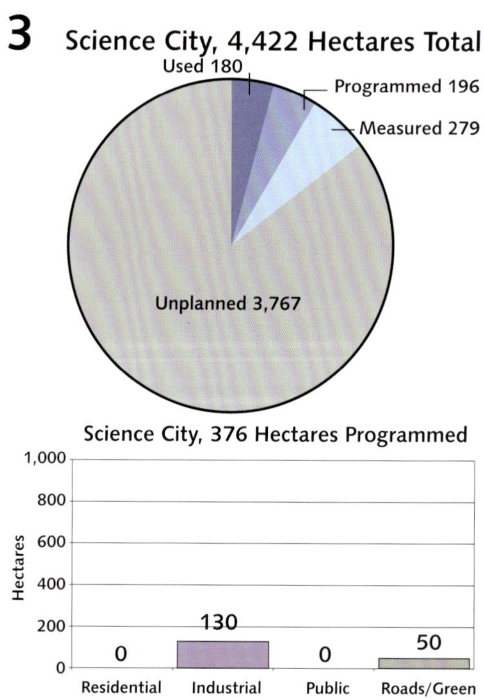

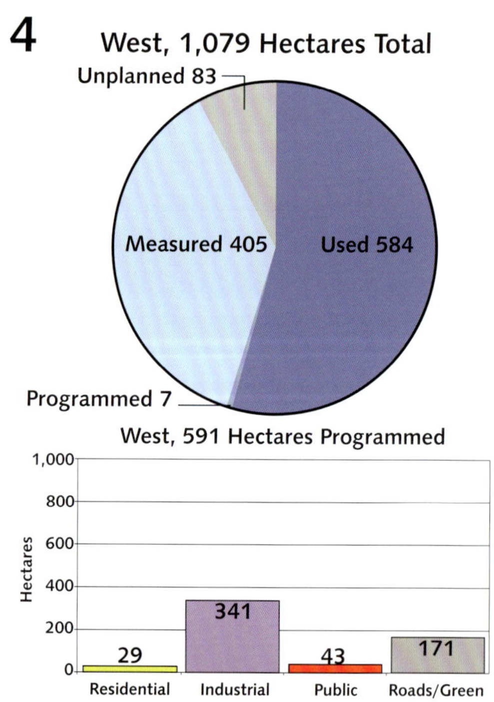

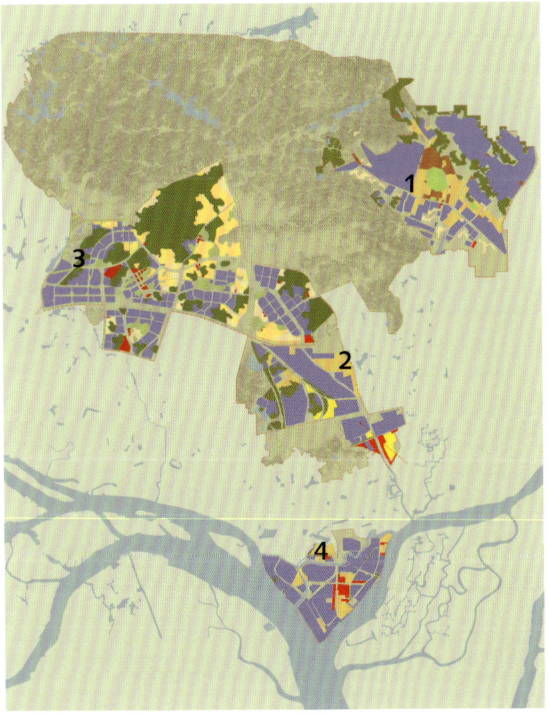

Proposed land use

1 Yonghe, 2,846 Hectares Total

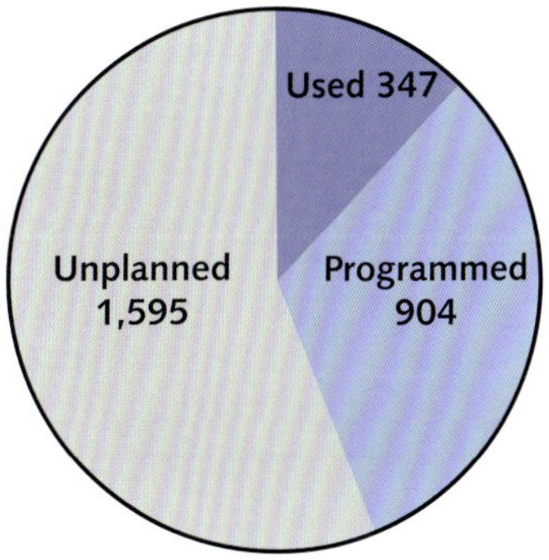

Yonghe, 1,251 Hectares Programmed

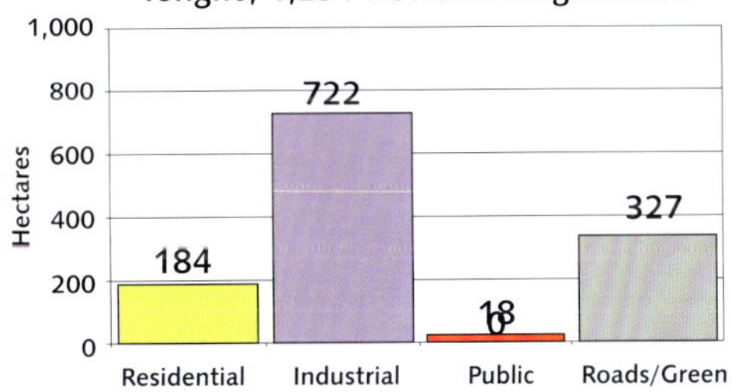

2 East, 2,364 Hectares Total

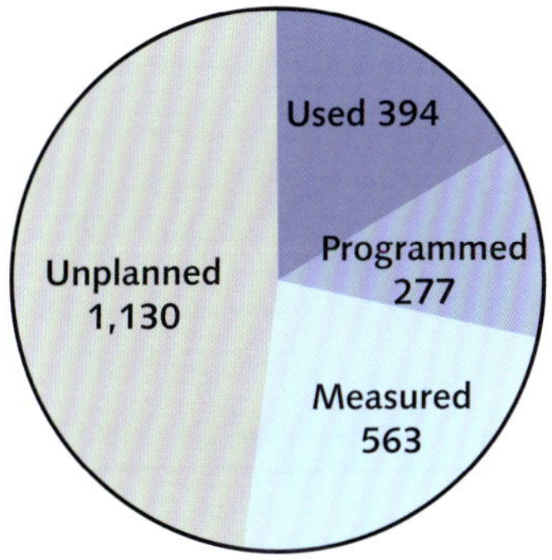

East, 671 Hectares Programmed

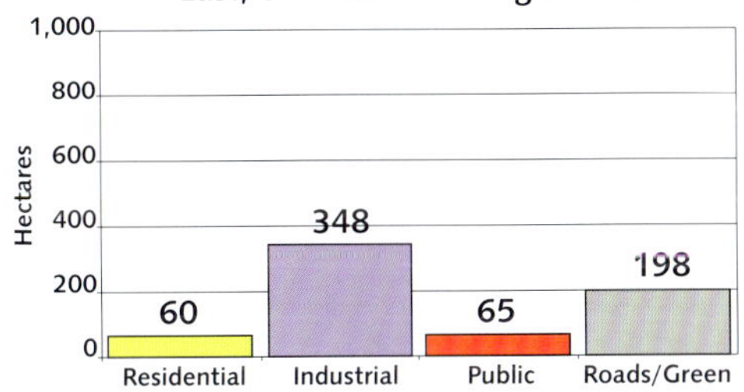

3 Science City, 4,422 Hectares Total

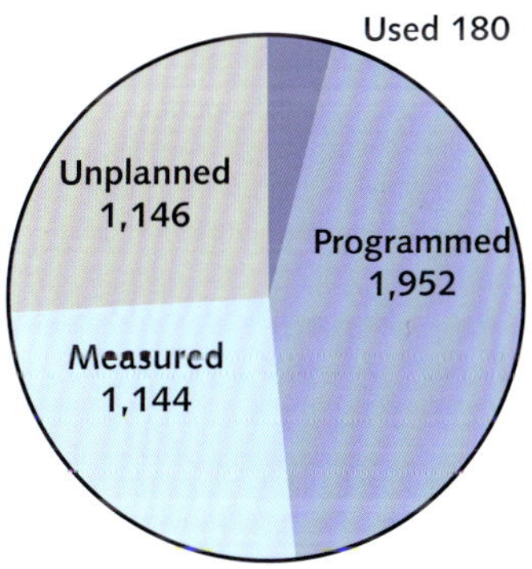

Science City, 2,132 Hectares Programmed

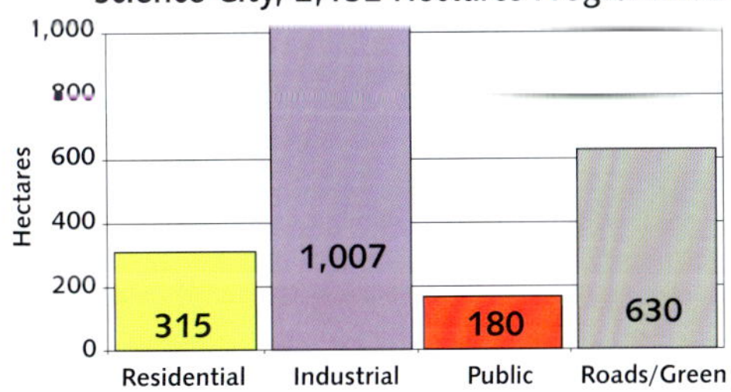

4 West, 1,079 Hectares Total

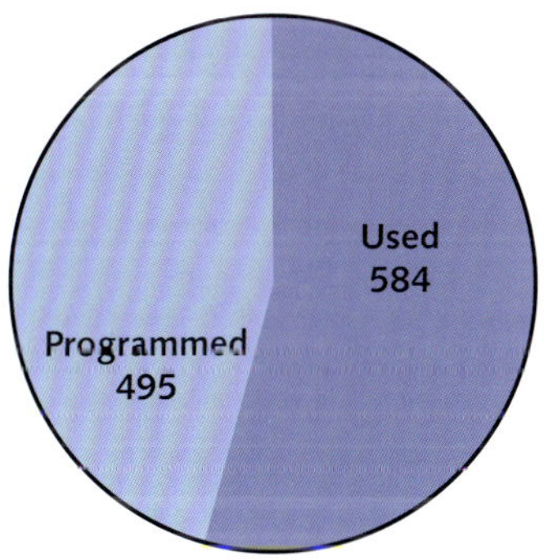

Science City, 2,132 Hectares Programmed

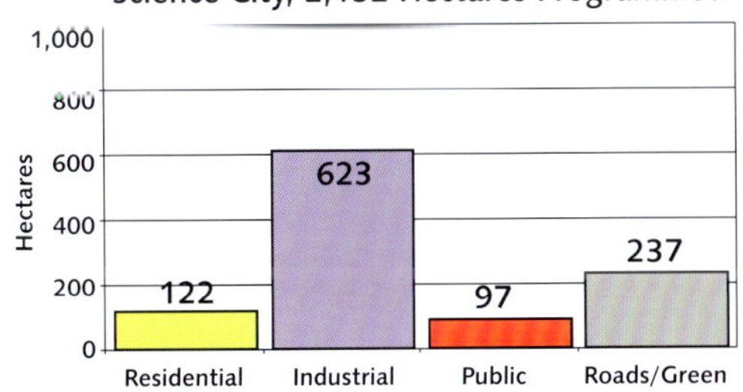

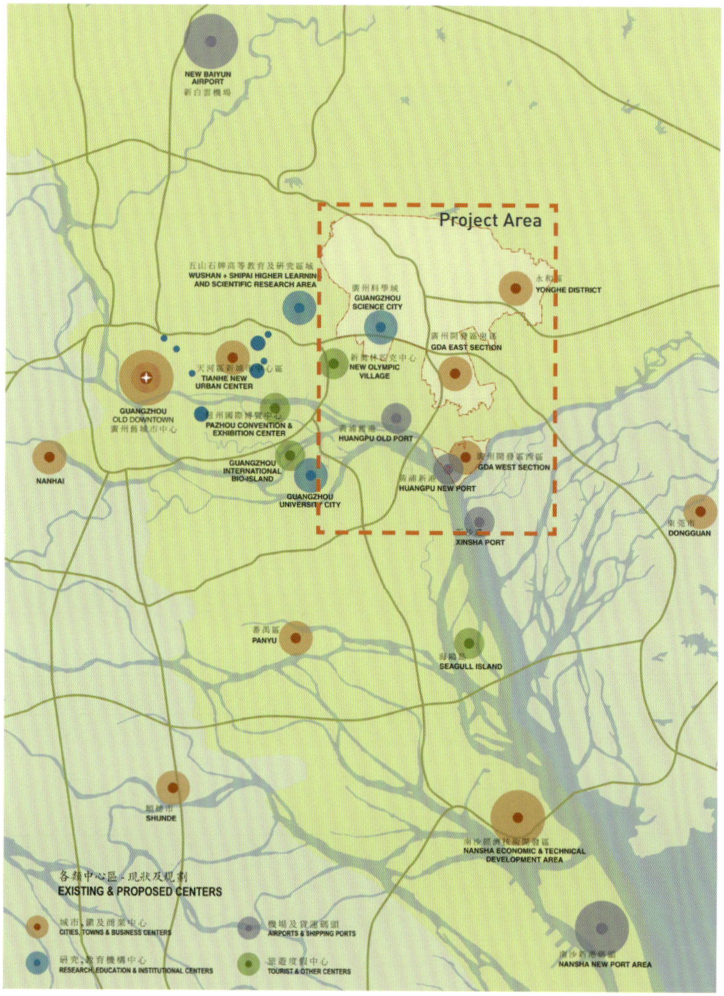

Existing and proposed regional centers

Development opportunity areas

Longtou Mountain

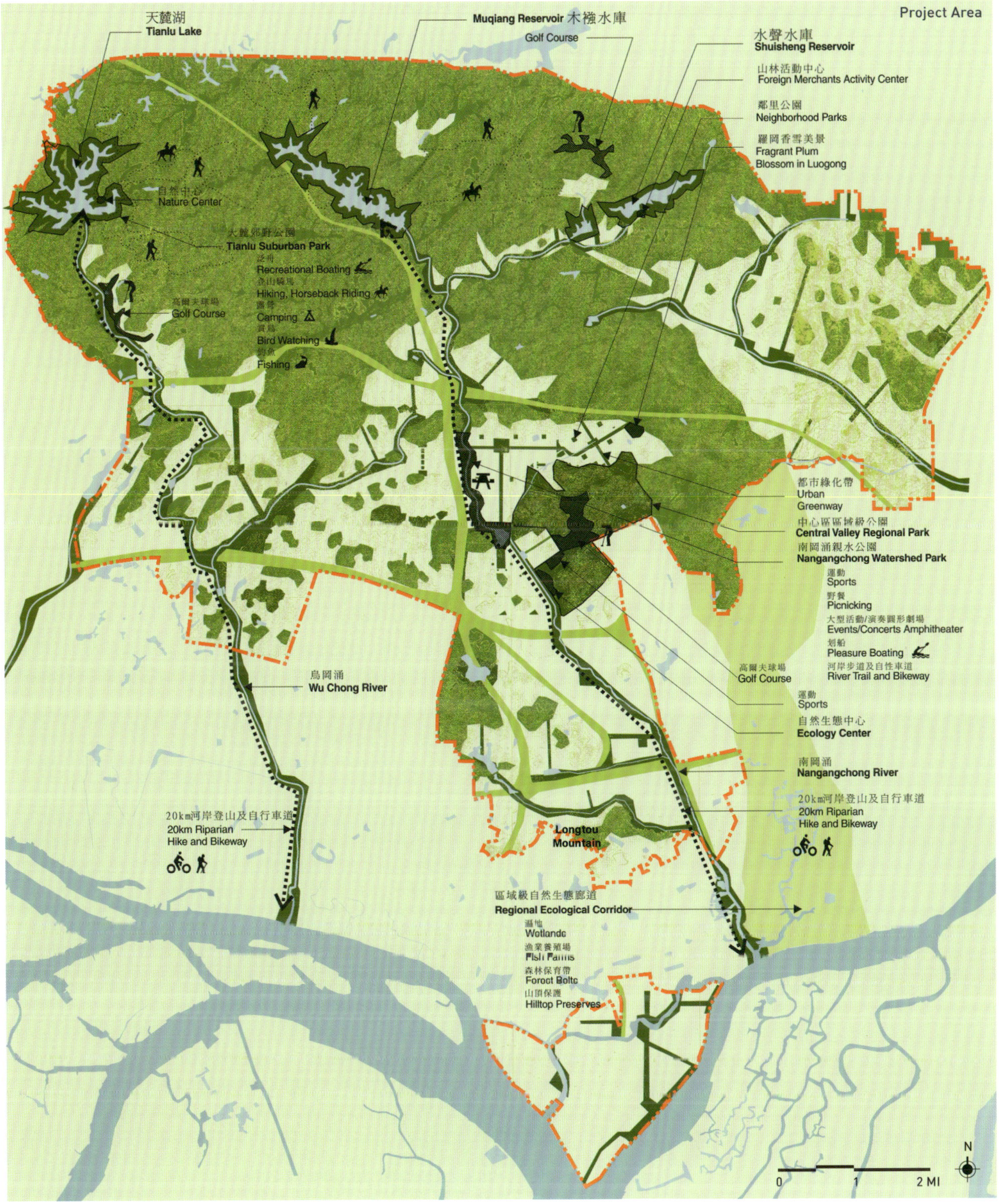

Open space plan

The Greenways Plan is "opportunistic," proposing a new set of urban scale organizing principles based on "found" features already present in the environment. The planned and unplanned development of Los Angeles illustrates the consequences of imbalance, what happens when current development elides the lessons and structures of the past, and how the use of "hidden" infrastructure can build quality of life for the future city's residents. Because of the rapid post-war growth of the Los Angeles region, particularly in single family detached homes and commercial districts, public parks and regionally connected public spaces were all too often neglected in favor of the privatization of land. Unlike some older American cities, Los Angeles never had a city beautiful or garden city movement foregrounding grand open spaces and parks as part of the city's infrastructure. Consequently, Los Angeles devotes approximately 4 percent of its surface area to public parks, unlike New York City where it is 17 percent, and Boston and San Francisco where it is 9 percent. These are remarkable statistics, given the perception of Los Angeles as a low density "garden city.' Indeed, the city has an abundance of gardens, but they are private gardens behind single family homes. Seeking common benefit, Los Angeles should strive to increase its usable public open

LA GREENWAYS
LOS ANGELES, CALIFORNIA, USA

AWARDS & EXHIBITS

- AIA Los Angeles, Urban Design Award
- Progressive Architecture, Award for Urban Design
- MOCA Exhibition, "Urban Revisions"

ANGELES NATIONAL FOREST
LOS ANGELES
0 2 4 6 MI
N

space, especially when the region is densifying along newly created public transit lines, and there is a deficit of open space.

The Greenways Plan uses residual and underutilized regional land resources—abandoned alignments of the old Red Car rail system, power line rights-of-way, and river and flood control channels, the region's "grid" road system—historical land resources largely forgotten in planning for the city's growth. The Greenways Plan links these land resources in a network more than 400 miles long, through new bikeways, jogging trails, and parks. It connects existing town centers, schools, libraries, post offices, and senior centers and where greenways intersect new transit lines provides sites for urban infill and intensification. Aspects of the Greenways Plan were adopted and incorporated into the official City of Los Angeles General Plan Framework; collateral and joint development on the new Metro transit lines and station areas has begun to yield public open space benefits anticipated by the plan.

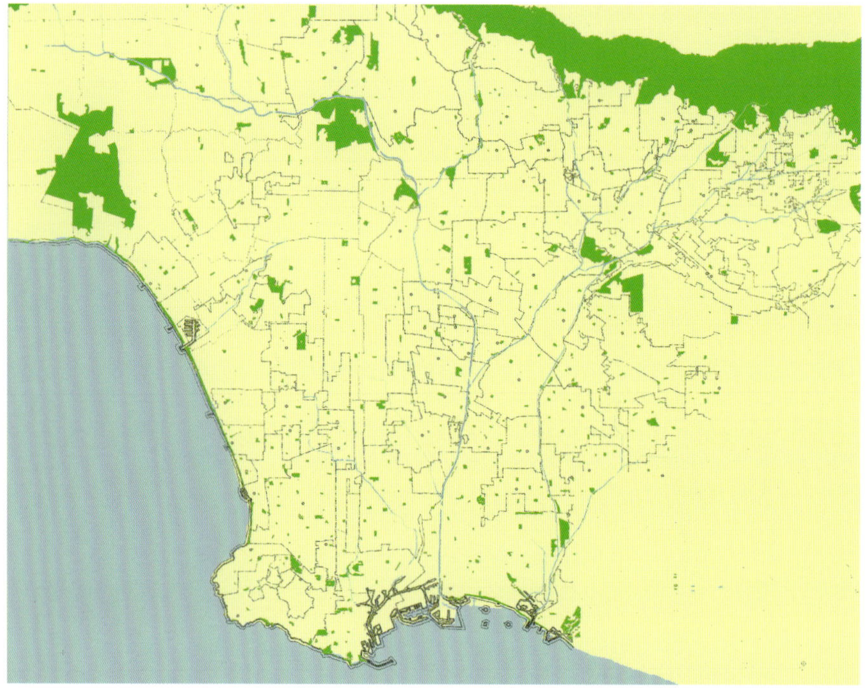

Existing open space

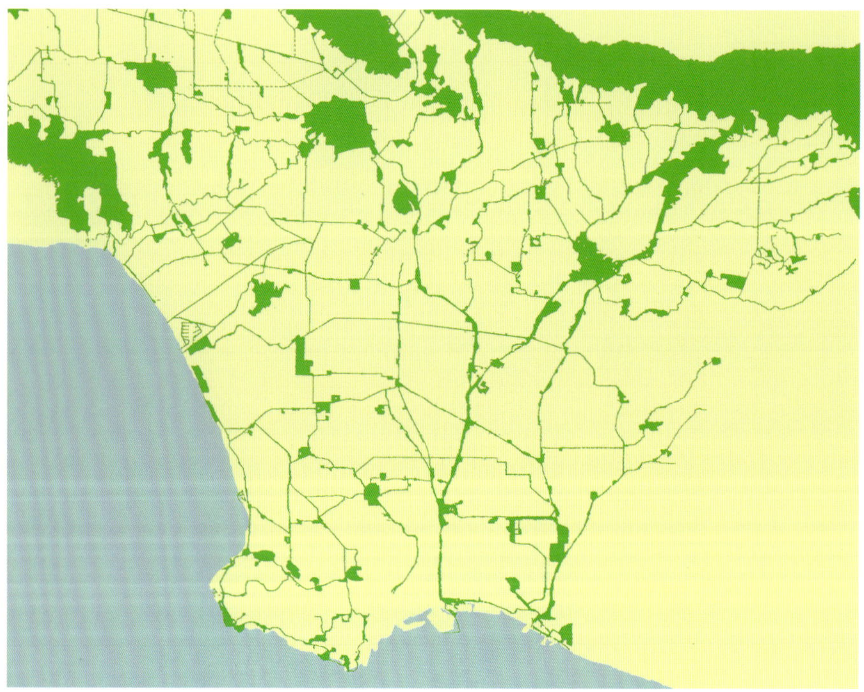

Proposed greenways

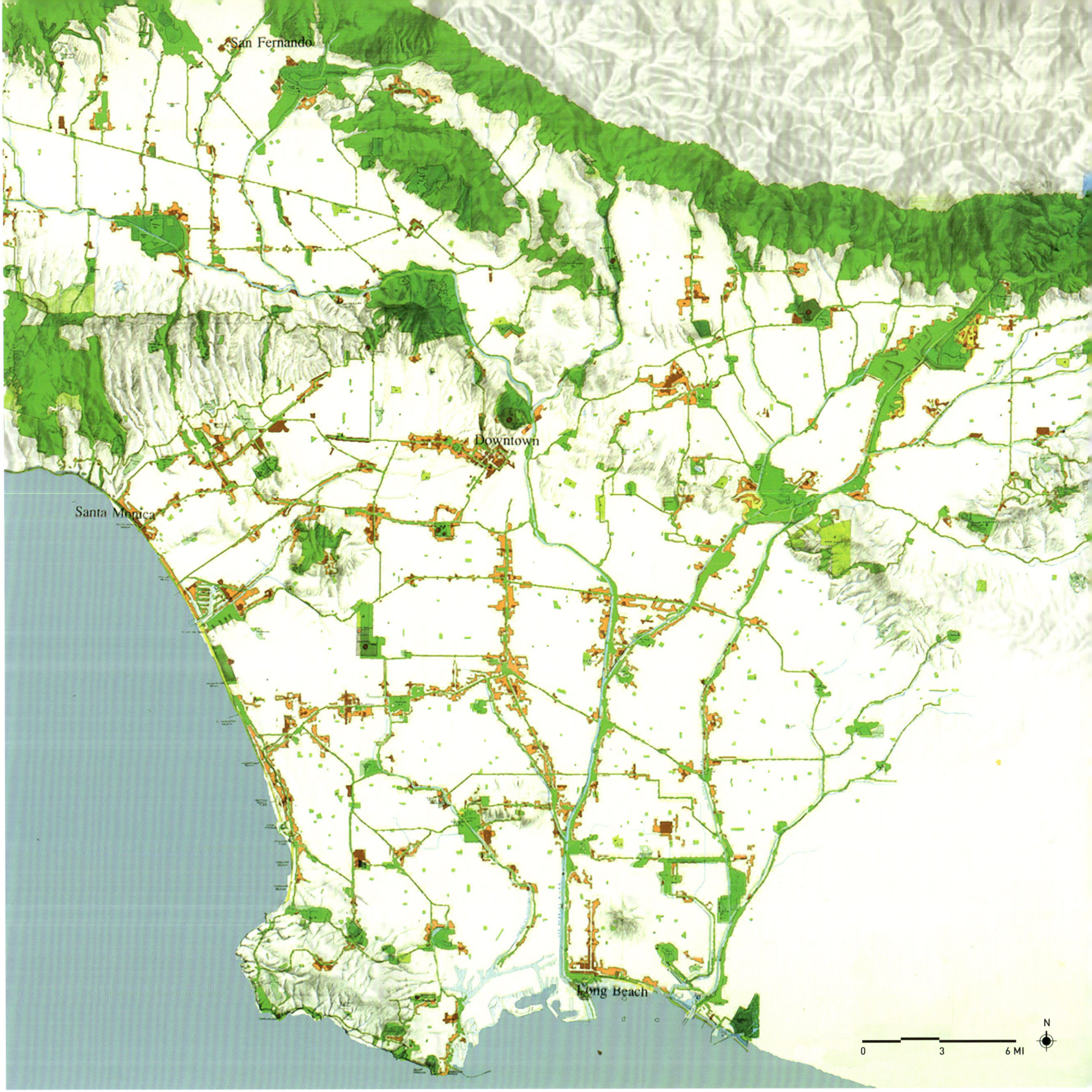

Greenways developments

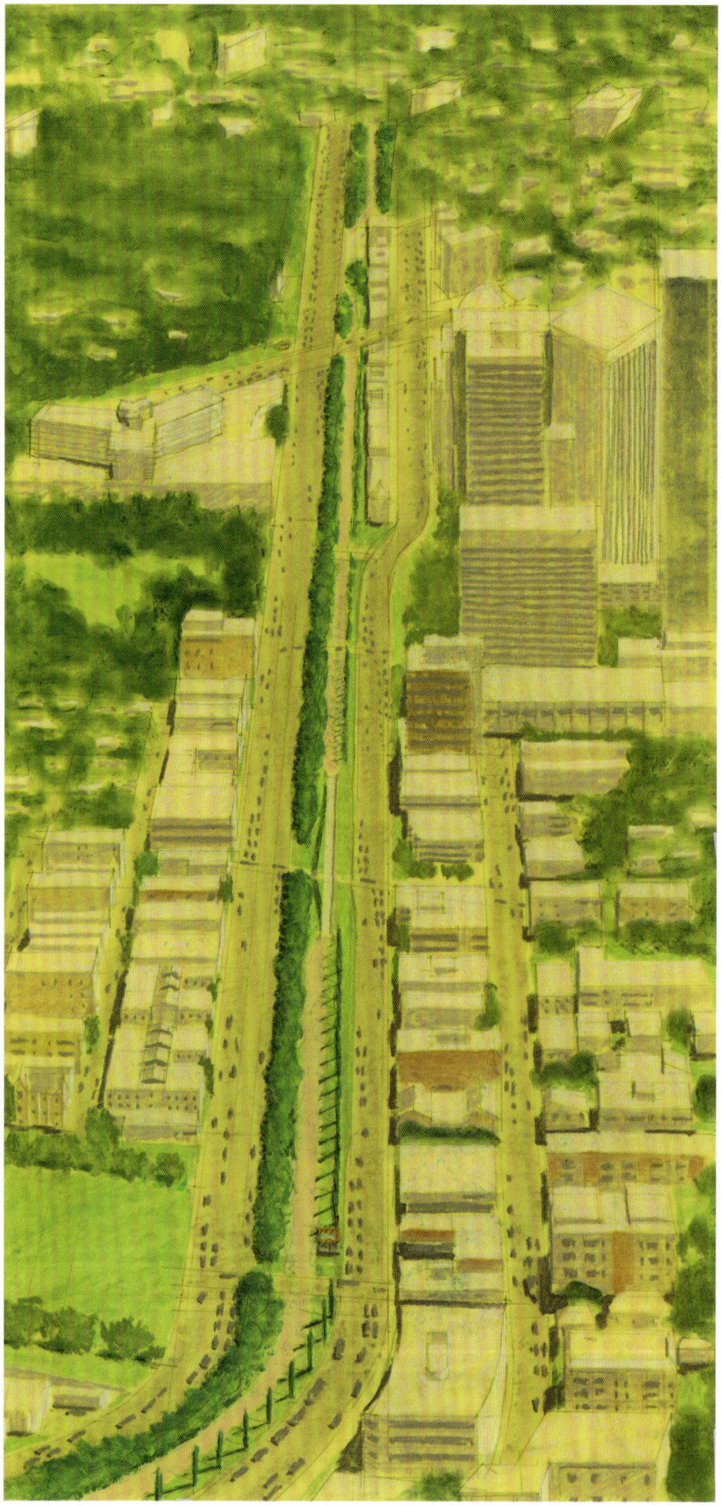
Santa Monica Blvd. looking east

LA River at Griffith Park looking east

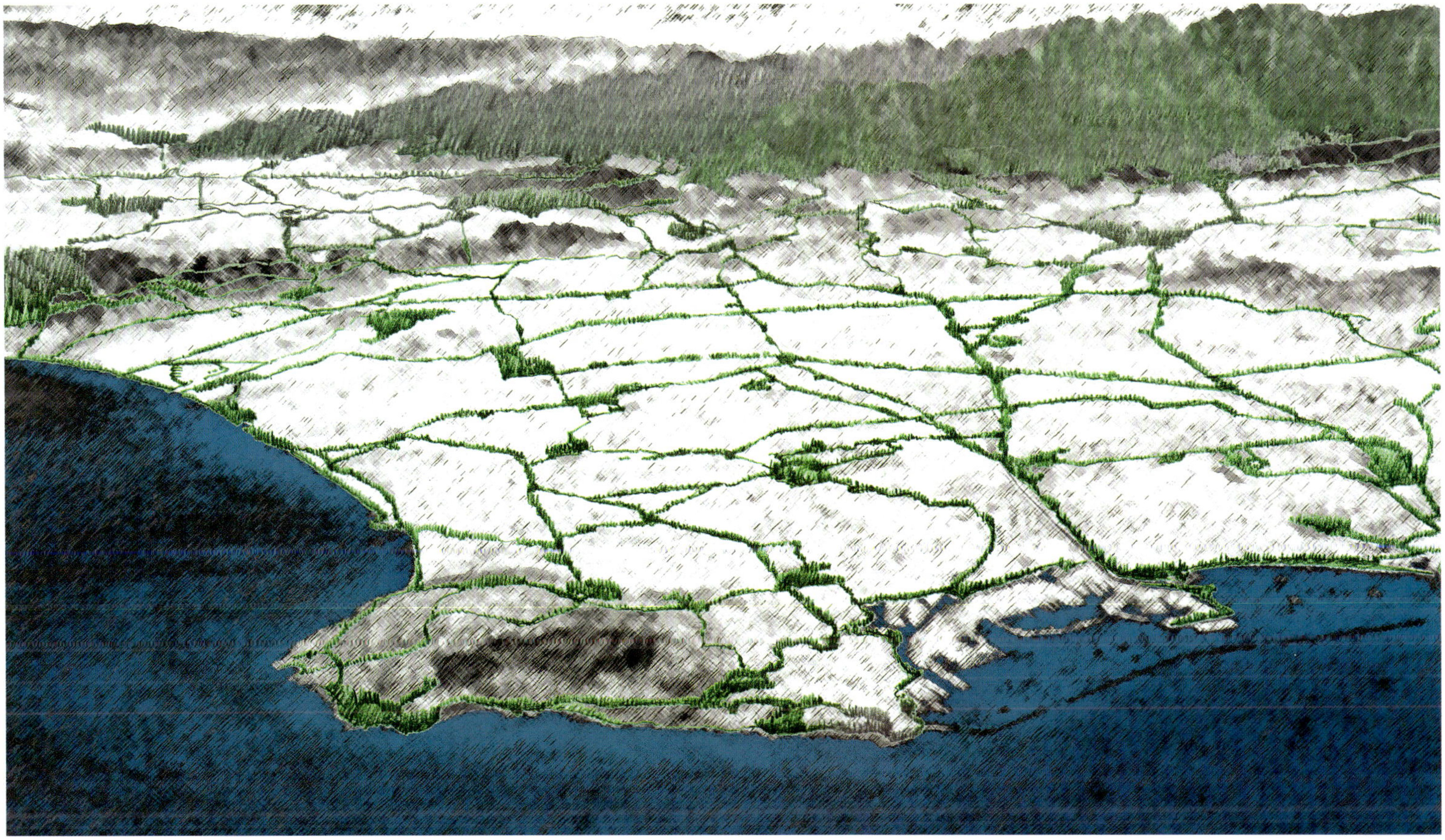

LA Greenways concept

MOCA Urban Revisions exhibit

LA River cross-section

Johnson Fain Studio
Los Angeles, California

APPENDIX

ACKNOWLEDGMENTS

At the outset, I would like to recognize the important contributions of Johnson Fain's many team members and project leaders who work collaboratively to originate ideas, develop concepts, and present them to the diverse and imaginative clientele our office serves. Without these dedicated collaborators and our visionary clients, the work represented in this monograph would not have been possible. In addition, I am deeply indebted to my colleagues Juan Carlos Begazo and David Alpaugh, principals of the office, who have been responsible for many of the projects described and illustrated in this publication. They have spent innumerable hours shaping the monograph, following the lead of Trina Gunther, a brilliant researcher in our office whose early visions for an urban design monograph on our work provided the foundation for the current publication. I am also grateful to Adrinee Bodakian, Shuangdi Dou, and Chunyan Zhang in our office for locating and clearing the rights to current photography of our projects and also for developing early layouts, to mention just a few of the tasks involved in the book-making process. The editing of the writings was skillfully done by Denise Bratton, who also worked with Trina Gunther and myself to develop texts on our urban design and planning projects at an earlier stage. Finally, the imagination behind the overall ensemble has been our book designer Kurt Hauser who, in collaboration with Gordon Goff and Jake Anderson of Oro Editions, has brought this book project to life.

I would like to recognize my partner Scott Johnson, who encouraged me to assemble this book. Scott recently authored a second monograph about the architectural and interiors work of our office and saw the need for a complementary edition about our urban design and planning projects to represent the breadth of work since the inception of the office in 1988. Johnson Fain, Inc. evolved from our legacy firm, William L. Pereira & Associates, founded in 1959. In 1969, half of Pereira & Associates became an ESOP for financial reasons, and in 1981, six months after I joined the office in June 1980, Pereira sold his remaining share to seven principals.

I had just returned from the East Coast at the time, having worked earlier in New York City at the Office of Midtown Planning and Development (OMPD) under Jaquelin T. Robertson, on the Fifth Avenue Special Purpose Zoning District and Madison Avenue Mall projects. OMPD was part of the Urban Design Group created by Mayor John V. Lindsay. In and out of a fellowship to study new towns in England and France and during graduate studies at the Harvard Graduate School of Design (GSD), I worked for the Boston Redevelopment Authority (BRA) and later for the New Communities Development Corporation at the Department of Housing and Urban Development (HUD) in Washington, D.C., before returning to Los Angeles. I was introduced to Pereira, who offered me a position in his office.

Scott Johnson had been a classmate of mine at the GSD, where we shared the same design studio. After the GSD, Scott moved to New York City to work for Philip Johnson, becoming one of his senior designers of the iconic tall buildings that have reshaped the skylines of many prominent cities throughout the United States, including Houston, Dallas, San Francisco, and New York City. In 1983, Scott was recruited by Roy Schmidt, then president of Pereira & Associates. We corresponded prior to his accepting the position. During Scott's first years in the Pereira office, he designed the Fox Plaza tower in Century City, which became a very important project in the transition of our office.

William Pereira passed away in late 1985, and by early 1986, both Scott and I had been offered partnership in the office. With the economy in a slump and the office in need of work, we made several demands on the principals, all of which were accepted, and by mid-1988, we became partners of Pereira Associates and afterward, renamed the office Johnson Fain and Pereira Associates. We bought out the ESOP in 1989, and in 1996, we renamed the firm Johnson Fain Partners. The office finally became Johnson Fain, Inc. at the end of 2002 and remains so today.

I would like to mention a number of individuals who over the years have contributed enormously to the success of Johnson Fain. Larry Ball, who along with managing many successful architectural projects also represented the office in other capacities, including assuming the role of principal in charge of our office in Guam during the 1990s and leading a team to Beijing in 1999, which resulted in an invitation to compete for the design of the Beijing Central Business District. Srini Rao and Steve Levine, who accompanied Larry on the trip, were instrumental in winning the competition that led to twenty years of work in China. Steve should also be recognized for his work on Highway 111 and the Amgen campus. As much of our work is research-based, it's important to recognize Mark Gershen, who early on coined the Johnson Fain motto, "We leave no stone unturned," and Katherine Rinne, whose research on the Hawaiian Islands led to the naming of Kapolei, an early Johnson Fain urban design and planning project for a Secondary Urban Center of the Hawaiian Islands. Katherine also discovered the location of the original well of the Native American Cahuilla Indians in the City of Indian Wells for our Highway 111 project. Trina Gunther's inquisitive mind and investigative skills led our team to many innovative ideas for the Chadwick School, LA Rivertown, Long Quan Yi District, and JinJiang River Corridor projects. Chunyan Zhang spent countless late-night hours communicating with our counterparts in Asia and organized multiple China projects. Robert Shaffer was important for his work on many of these projects, but in particular for his work on the First Americans Museum project. Bob worked with me through that entire twenty-five-year journey, from site selection to the project close-out in 2021. One of my fondest memories was working with Dan Janotta and Jen Spangler, both of whom Scott Johnson assigned to that project at different times. Dan worked with me during the conceptual phase, and Jen later, during design development. Both are enormously talented and work well with other team members. Kersu Dalal began his career working on the First Americans Museum, and came to assume leadership for a number of other Johnson Fain urban design projects. His creative mind and attention to details assured us that our projects are in good hands. Work by Mehr Wani and John Jackson is always excellent — well-researched and clearly presented. Design concepts for the YMCA Piers project were beautifully executed by Arnold Swanborn. Perhaps one of the most memorable presentations was made by Evan Jenkins, who skillfully explained the ideas behind the Knowledge City project to one of our most discerning clients.

In the following pages we gratefully acknowledge all the Johnson Fain team members who have had a role in realizing the projects presented in this publication: "Project Leaders," those key individuals who were directly responsible for each project presented here, and "Project Team" members who have worked on projects in the office are listed comprehensively, and in the pages devoted to "Project Data," our collaborating design and engineering firms, consultants of all stripes, agencies, and of course our clients, project by project. We have made every effort to be inclusive in these lists and regret any unintentional oversights.

William H. Fain, Jr.

PROJECT LEADERS

CITY

Mission Bay: William Fain, Juan Carlos Begazo

Beijing Central Business District: William Fain, Larry Ball, Srini Rao, Steve Levine, Juan Carlos Begazo, Neil Kritzinger

Jiangwan New Town: William Fain, Srini Rao, Robert Shaffer

Jiading New Town: William Fain, Juan Carlos Begazo, Daniel Janotta, Chunyan Zhang

Wadala Central Business District: William Fain, Juan Carlos Begazo, Kersu Dalal, Mehr Wani, Trina Gunther

Luxe Lakes Eco-City: William Fain, Robert Shaffer, Mehr Wani, Chunyan Zhang

Henderson West: William Fain, David Alpaugh, John Jackson, Shareefa Abdulsalam

Westfield Promenade: William Fain, Scott Johnson, Juan Carlos Begazo, Greg Verabian, Brian Knight

HemisFair Park Redevelopment: William Fain, David Alpaugh, Kersu Dalal, Trina Gunther, John Jackson

Playa Vista Phase II: William Fain, David Alpaugh, Juan Carlos Begazo, Kersu Dalal

LA Rivertown: William Fain, David Alpaugh, Juan Carlos Begazo, Kersu Dalal, Trina Gunther

Culver City Transit Oriented Development: William Fain, David Alpaugh, Trina Gunther, John Jackson, Mehr Wani

Highway 111: William Fain, Steve Levine, Katherine Rinne, Mark Gershen

CULTURE

First Americans Museum: William Fain, Scott Johnson, Robert Shaffer, Dan Janotta, Jen Spangler, Juan Carlos Begazo, Kersu Dalal, Larry Ball, Douglas Gardner, David Alpaugh, Suma Spina, Craig Lawrence

YMCA Piers: William Fain, Juan Carlos Begazo, Arnold Swanborn

West LA VA Campus: William Fain, David Alpaugh, Kersu Dalal, John Jackson, Mehr Wani

Disney ABC Studios: William Fain, Juan Carlos Begazo, David Alpaugh, Trina Gunther

DreamWorks SKG Studios: William Fain, David Alpaugh, Juan Carlos Begazo

KNOWLEDGE

Amgen: William Fain, Juan Carlos Begazo, David Alpaugh, Steve Levine, Larry Ball, Robert Shaffer, Trina Gunther

Genentech: William Fain, David Alpaugh, Dan Janotta, Abhijeet Mankar

Jet Propulsion Laboratory (JPL): William Fain, David Alpaugh, Srini Rao, Mark Gershen

Knowledge City: William Fain, David Alpaugh, Juan Carlos Begazo, Kersu Dalal, John Jackson, Evan Jenkins

UC Berkeley College of Engineering: William Fain, Scott Johnson, David Alpaugh, Larry Ball, Robert Shaffer, Mehr Wani, Greg Verabian, Patricia Shigetomi

UC Irvine Main Street: William Fain, Juan Carlos Begazo, Mark Gershen, Katherine Rinne

Chadwick School: William Fain, David Alpaugh, Trina Gunther

Los Angeles Unified School District Campuses: Juan Carlos Begazo, Jeffrey Levy

REGION

JinJiang River Corridor: William Fain, Robert Shaffer, Trina Gunther, Chunyan Zhang

Long Quan Yi District: William Fain, Robert Shaffer, Kersu Dalal, Trina Gunther, Chunyan Zhang

Chinese Whiskey Valley: William Fain, Robert Shaffer, Chunyan Zhang, John Jackson, Kersu Dalal, Trina Gunther, Mehr Wani, Mark Gershen

Tianjin Ancient Wetland Restoration: William Fain, Robert Shaffer, Larry Ball, Chunyan Zhang

Guangzhou Economic Development District: Robert Shaffer, Trina Gunther, Chunyan Zhang

LA Greenways: William Fain, Robert Shaffer, Pat Dawe, Katherine Rinne, Mark Gershen

JOHNSON FAIN TEAM

Shareefa Abdulsalam
Bridget Ackeifi
Gevo Aelian
Marcella Aguilar
Kiyoshi Akuzawa
Nelson Almendarez
David Alpaugh
Eric Altizer
Morteza Alvani
Kristen Anderson
Paul Anvar
Lauri Arneson
Demetrios Avraamides
Christian Baker
Maria Baldenegro
Larry Ball
Angela Barker
Yasaman Barmaki
Jocelyn Basseporte
Juan Carlos Begazo
Caroline Bell
Adrinee Bodakian
James Brakefield
Tom Brakefield
Sean Briski
Paige Burke
Jessica Campion
Aron Carcamo
Adileni Caro
Jonathan Chang
Helen Chen
Sherry Chen
Warren Chen
Shih-Pu Nora Chen
Helen Cheuk
Max Chirkov
Karon Choi
Hyeyoon Chung
Steve Chung
Becky Cohen
Tricia Converse
Matthew Conway
Joanne Costello
Arlene Cuevas
Weiyan Dai
Kersu Dalal
Patrick Dawe
Philip De Cancio
Ryan Del Poso
Angel De Romana
Margie Dianco
James (JED) Donaldson
Nastasja Dorandi
Shuangdi Dou
Lori East
Kristine Edinchikyan
Natalie Egnatchik
William H. Fain Jr.
Edwin Fang
Mary Faria
Feryal Farahzad
Carol Fisher
Dana Fisher
Christopher Flacke
Peter Flores
Jack Fong
Christina Fujii
Marc Futterman
Garine Gabrielian
Renata Ganis
Shanoa Garcia
Douglas Gardner
Mark Gershen
Linet Ghukasyan
Eric Giragosian
Todd Gish
John Gralewski
Barbara Gray
Nick Guarna
Trina Gunther
Junichi Harada
Amira Hersi
Vera Hetcel
Sapeer Hillel
Megumi Hironaka
Alexandra Holguin
India Howllet
Jeanette Hsu
Joy Huang
Po Yuan Huang
Adriana Jackson
James Jackson
John Jackson
Daniel Janotta
Jelena Jegdic
Evan Jenkins
Kristina Johnson
Scott Johnson
Neil Kaplanis
Oleksandra Kazymirska
Gregory Keating
Aris Keshishian
Celine Khachatourian
Saba Khalili
Esra Kilickan
Caroline Kim
Paul Kim
Brian Knight
Anne Koshalek
Neil Kritzinger
Gunilla Kronvall
Dana Ladd
Amber Langlois
Craig Lawrence
Byungha Lee
Edward Lee
Grace Lee
Jaewon Lee
Leni Lee
Stephen E. Levine
Jeffrey Levy
Li Li
Xue Lin
Lauren MacColl
Kavita Mahabaleshwark
Hung Mak
Ethan Manaster
Abhijeet Mankar
Nicholas Martinez
Kristel Marquez
Michael McCarthy
Gigi McGee
Richelle Leviste-Medina
Rouland Medina
Alexis Melnicki
Jillian Miller
Lex Moloney
Akira Nakano
Daniel Nay
Thomas Nohr
Ron Oster
Mark Owen
Carlo Paganuzzi
Andrew Palmer
Margie Parentela
David Park
Darnell Park
Tigran Parsamyan
Hui-Yi Paterson
Andrea Pavia
Luc Peltier
Sixto Pena
Layton Petersen
Chinh Pham
Alejandro Pijuan
Corey Pope
Isabel Portillo
Lorenz Quinley
Harold Ramirez
Raymond Rangel
Srinivas Rao
Shahrzad Razi
Ian Remulla
Elizabeth Rendon
Stacey Rigley
Katherine Rinne
Arnold Rivera
Chris Roades
Cheaseon Roh
Francois Ruel
Taylor Sanderson
Joey Sandoval
Zlatan Sehovic
Alexander Sexsmith
Robert Shaffer
Keerthi Shekar
Aman Sheth
Ritsuko Shibutani
Patricia Shigetomi
Juan Silva
Jillian Skelton
Dana Smith
Julia Smith
John Son
Boram Song
Leticia SooHoo
Jenifer A. Spangler
Suma Spina
Tom Stallman
Elsa Su
Meng Sun
Matthew Sunseri
Chang Suo
Arnold Swanborn
Bahareh Tabatabaei
Crystal Tan
Scott Taylor
Travis Taylor
Lek Thanavatik
Priyanka Thatte
Bradley Thomas
Todd Thongeiam
Brian Tichenor
Larry Tighe
Hung Ting
Joshua Treiber
Kevin Tyrell
Donna Vaccarino
Gregory Verabian
Robert Villagomez
Nicole Villamin
Dorian Viniegra
Denis Vitoreli
Viviana Vivero
Loann Vu
Li-Hsin Wang
Wenlan Wang
Yang Wang
Mehr Wani
Quincy Wargo
Aran Weng
Bobby White
Allen Wong
Eeechin Wong
Li Wu
Kevin Yan
Esther Yang
Jui-Ni Yang
Jenny Yee
Christian Yen
Vivian Yeung
Sean Yun
Holly Zeiler
Hraztan Zeitlian
Chunyan Zhang

PROJECT SPONSORS

Alexandria Real Estate Equities
American Indian Cultural Center Foundation
Amgen
Atlas Capital Group
BaoDing City FuRui Landscape Co.
Barker Pacific Group
*Beijing CBD Administrative Committee
Bel-Air Country Club
BioMarin Pharmaceutical Inc.
Boeing Realty
Booth Estate
Brook Partners, Inc.
Byron Winery
C.C.A. Limited
California Institute of Technology
Catellus Development Corporation
CBRE
CBS Television City
Century City Realty LLC
Cesar Chavez Foundation
Chadwick School
Chateau Western Royal Spring Co.
Chengdu BRC Group
Chengdu Jin Tang LanGuang HeJun Property Development Co.
Chengdu LongQuan Yi District Government
Chengdu ShuangLiu Urban Planning Administration Bureau
Chengdu Wide Horizon Investment
China Foods Limited
Christ Catholic Cathedral Corporation
City National Bank
City of Beverly Hills
City of Culver City
City of Fullerton
City of Indian Wells
City of Irvine
City of Long Beach
City of Los Angeles
Commonwealth Partners
Concourse Federal Group
Conexant
Constellation Place, LLC
Country of Saudi Arabia
Country of Qatar
County of Los Angeles
County of Solano
Curtis School
Cushman & Wakefield
Co-You Corporation
DanDong JinDi YingDa Real Estate Development Co.
Dandong Nan-Tian-Yuan Real Estate Company
Disney-ABC Television Group
Dotterweich Carlson Mehner Design Inc.
DreamEast Group Limited
DreamWorks SKG
E. & J. Gallo Winery
East Los Angeles College
Experian
Fairplex
Fangshan University
Fashion Institute of Design and Merchandising
Forest City Development
Forest City Residential West
Forest City Washington
Garden Lane Properties, LLC
Genentech
Gilead
GPI Companies
Guam Airport Authority
Guam Housing Corporation
Guangzhou Development District Design Competition Committee
Gulin District Municipal Government, Sichuan
HemisFair Park Area Redevelopment Corporation
Hillcrest Country Club
Hilton Hotels
Hines
IMT Capital
James Campbell Company
Jamison Properties
Jet Propulsion Laboratory
JMB Realty
JMI Realty
Jones Lang LaSalle
JSB Development
Kamehameha Schools
KB Home
KNBC/ Telemundo
Laguna Beach Company
LA Plaza de Cultura y Artes
LDC Advisors
Legacy Partners
Lennar
Le Plastrier Development Consulting,
Lincoln Property Company
LNR
Lockheed Corporation
Long Quan Yi District Government, Chengdu
Los Altos Hills Estate
Los Angeles Area Chamber of Commerce
Los Angeles Center Studios
Los Angeles Community College District
Los Angeles Country Club
Los Angeles County Department of Public Works
Los Angeles County Metro
Los Angeles County Museum of Art
Los Angeles County Natural History Museum
Los Angeles Dodgers
Los Angeles Times
Los Angeles Unified School District
Los Angeles World Airports
LuoJiang City Government
MacFarlane Partners
Mack Urban
Maguire Thomas Partners
Marlborough School
Marriott
MCA / Universal
McCourt Group
MDI-Miyama Development International
Microsoft
Mills Development Corporation
Mitsui Fudosan America
Mumbai Metropolitan Region Development Authority
Native American Cultural and Educational Authority
NBC / Universal
NEOM
Nestle USA
Newhall Land & Farming
New Urban West
Nolan Capital, Inc.

Norton Air Force Base
Ohio State University
Omninet - The Broadway Company
Opus One Winery
Otis Art Institute
Pacific Earth Resources
Pao Chi Development Co.
Pao Huei Construction Company
Paramount Studios
Pepperdine University
Pierce College
Playa Capital Company
PT. Farpoint Realty Indonesia
Pueblo Nuevo Development
QingDao MingHe Construction & Estate Development Co.
Rand Corporation
Reality SF
Republic Metropolitan
Rising Realty Partners
Robert Mondavi Winery
Roman Catholic Diocese of Orange
Sandstone Properties, Inc.
San Jose Redevelopment Agency
Sauvage Real Estate
Shanghai Chia Chun Real Estate Corporation
Shanghai City Planning and Land Resource Bureau
Shanghai Jiading District Government
Shanghai Municipal Investment Group
Shanghai SongJiang District Government
Shanghai Shen-Di Group Company
Sheraton Hotels
Shuangliu District Municipal Planning Bureau, Chengdu
Sichuan LangJiu (Whiskey) Group
Silverstein Properties, Inc.
South Coast Plaza
Stadco
Stanford Research Institute
Stanford University
State of California
State of Oklahoma
SunAmerica
SunCal Companies
Sunkist

The Clarett Group
The Chadwick School
The Los Angeles Country Club
The Lundquist Institute
The Mills Corporation
The Ratkovich Company
The Staubach Company
Thomas Safran & Associates
Tianjin Real Estate Development & Management Group
Ticketmaster
Tishman International
Toyota Motor Sales USA
Trammell Crow Company
Twentieth Century Fox
Twenty-First Century Insurance
Twinwood USA
Unibail-Rodamco-Westfield
Union Bank
United States General Services Administration
Universal Studios
University of California, Berkeley
University of California, Irvine
University of California Los Angeles
University of California Riverside
University of California San Diego
University of California Santa Barbara
University of Southern California
University of Southern California Keck School of Medicine
Unocal
Urban Partners
US Department of Energy
Venus Over Manhattan
Veterans Advocacy
Vista Canyon, LLC
Walt Disney Imagineering
Walter J. Company
Warner Bros.
Wells Real Estate Fund
Welltower
Whittier College
William Morris Rodeo
YMCA San Francisco
Young Nak Church

PROJECT DATA

CITY

Mission Bay
San Francisco, California, USA

- AIA National, Honor Award for Regional and Urban Design

Master Plan and Design Standards & Guidelines
Planning and Urban Design Dates: 1996–1998
Site Area: 303 acres
Program: University of California San Francisco Mission Bay campus, Bio-Tech research, private Bio-Tech research and development, hospital, residential, retail, hotel, public school, public library, fire and police stations, community facilities, and public open space
Client: Catellus Development Corporation
Landscape Architect: Laurie Olin, OLIN Studio
Civil Engineer: KCA Engineers, Inc.
Traffic Engineer: Wilbur Smith Associates, Inc.
Public Workshops Consultant: SMWM

Central Business District
Beijing, China

- First Place, International Design Competition

Conceptual Master Plan and Urban Design
International Design Competition: 2000–2001
Site Area: 990 acres
Program: HQ office, services, retail, cultural, civic, and other public amenities, residential, and public open space
Client: Beijing CBD Administrative Committee

Jiangwan New Town
Shanghai, China

- First Place, International Design Competition

Conceptual Master Plan and Urban Design
International Design Competition: 2001
Site Area: 2,500 acres
Program: Mixed-use residential neighborhood, university, research and development, schools, other public amenities, wetland restoration, lakes, and public open space
Client: Shanghai Municipal Investment Group

Jiading New Town
Shanghai, China
Central Business District Master Plan
International Design Competition: 2011
Site Area: 104 acres
Program: Commercial offices, services, retail, conference center and hotel, cultural and civic amenities, residential, and public open space
Client: Shanghai City Planning and Land Resource Bureau and Shanghai Jiading District Government

Wadala Central Business District
Mumbai, India

- First Place, International Design Competition

Central Business District Master Plan
International Design Competition: 2012
Site Area: 270 acres
Program: Commercial office, hotel, retail, cultural and civic, residential, and public open space
Client: Mumbai Metropolitan Region Development Authority
Landscape Architect: OLIN Studio
Environmental Planning & Engineering: ARUP
Associate Architect & Local Liason: DSP Design Associates

Luxe Lakes Eco-City
Chengdu, Sichuan, China
Programming and Master Plan
Planning and Urban Design Dates: 2005–2007
Site Area: 4,200 acres
Program: Low-impact urban development, residential, creative office, retail, colleges, school, cultural and civic uses, and public open space
Client: Chengdu Wide Horizon Investment
Landscape Architect: Famous Garden

Henderson West
Henderson, Nevada, USA
Master Plan and Urban Design
Planning and Urban Design Dates: 2016
Site Area: 103 acres
Program: Residential, offices, retail, and public Open Space
Client: Sauvage Real Estate, LLC
Landscape Architect: The Office of James Burnett
Civil Engineer: Slater Hanifan Group (SHG)
Real Estate Economics: RCLCO Fund Advisors
Planning Consultant: Richard T. Serfas, American Nevada Company

Westfield Promenade
Warner Center, Los Angeles, California, USA
Master Plan and Urban Design
Planning and Urban Design Dates: 2016–2020
Site Area: 35 acres
Program: Class A and creative offices, lifestyle retail, two hotels, an entertainment venue for athletic events and performances, residential, and public open space including a central park
Client: Westfield Group
Economics: HR&A Advisors, Inc.
Urban Designers: Johnson Fain
Architects: Johnson Fain | Togawa Smith Martin, Inc. | HKS Architects, Inc.
Landscape Architects: Burton Studio
Civil Engineer: INCLEDON Consulting Group
Transportation Consultant: Gibson Transportation Consulting, Inc
MEP Consultant (EIR): AMA Group, Consulting Engineers
Sustainability Consultant (EIR): GAIA Environmental Consulting
Parking Consultant: Choate Parking Consultants

HemisFair Park Redevelopment
San Antonio, Texas, USA
Redevelopment Framework and Master Plan
Planning and Urban Design Dates: 2010–2011
Site Area: 72 acres
Program: Residential, office, hotel, retail, cultural and civic uses, school, and public open space
Client: HemisFair Park Area Redevelopment Corporation
Landscape Architect: Cindy Sanders, OLIN Studio
Traffic, Transportation, Parking, Hydrology and Civil Engineer: Pape-Dawson Engineers, Inc.
Civil Engineer: RJ Rivera Associates, Inc.
Historic Preservation: William A. Dupont, FAIA
Economics, Finance & Feasibility: HR&A Advisors, Inc.
Market Overview: CBRE Group, Inc.
Sustainability Consultant: ARUP
Associate Architect: Jim Poteet, FAIA, Poteet Architects, LP

Playa Vista Phase II
Los Angeles, California, USA

- APA California, Planning Award
- APA Los Angeles, Planning Award

Urban Design Standards and Guidelines
Planning and Urban Design Dates: 2006
Site Area: 111 acres
Program: Residential, office, Playa Vista Town Center retail, and public open space
Client: Playa Capital Company, LLC
Landscape Architect: Meléndrez Landscape Architecture
Civil Engineer: Psomas
Traffic Engineer: Raju Associates, Inc.

LA Rivertown
Los Angeles, California, USA

- AIA California Council, Urban Design Award
- AIA Los Angeles, NEXT LA Award
- ASLA California Council, Urban Design Award

Urban Regeneration Master Planning and Urban Design Guidelines
Planning and Urban Design Dates: 2012
Site Area: 27 acres
Program: Residential, office, retail, cultural and civic, and public open space
Client: Young Nak Church and STADCO Broadway Company

Culver City Transit Oriented Development
Culver City, California, USA

• APA California, Planning Award

Transit Oriented Development Visioning Study
Planning and Urban Design Dates: 2016–2017
Study Area: Centered on the Metro Station with a one-mile radius, about a twenty-minute walk from the station
Program: Vision for the future of mobility in Culver City
Client: City of Culver City
Mobility Consultant: Steer Davies & Gleave, Ltd.
Transportation Engineer: KOA Corporation

Highway 111
Indian Wells, California, USA

• AIA National, Urban Design Award
• AIA Los Angeles, Urban Design Award
• Progressive Architecture, Urban Design Award

Urban Design and Specific Plan
Planning and Urban Design Dates: 1988–1991
Site Area: 446 acres along 3.5 miles of highway corridor
Program: Establish development controls and urban design standards, determining criteria for land uses, circulation improvements and landscape features as part of an integrated design
Client: City of Indian Wells
Planning Team Coordination and Zoning: The Planning Associates Group, Inc.
Environmental Impact Review Consultant: UltraSystems Environment, Inc.
Traffic Engineer: Weston Pringle & Associates, Linscott Law & Greenspan
Civil Engineer: Haver & Associates LLC
Housing Consultant: Castaneda & Associates, Inc.
Planning Consultant: Cotton Vreeland Associates, Inc.
Consulting Architect: Jonathan Barnett, FAIA, AICP
Plant Consultant: Eric Johnson

CULTURE

First Americans Museum
Oklahoma City, Oklahoma, USA

• AIA Next LA, Honor Award
• AIA Oklahoma City Chapter Merit Award
• AIA Los Angeles, Design Award
• National EPA Phoenix Award, Excellence in Brownfield Development
• ULI, Americas Award for Excellence

Cultural Center & Museum Master Plan and Architectural Design
Master Planning and Architectural Design Dates: 1997–2021
Site Area: 280 acres
Program: Cultural center and museum, lodge and meeting center, specialty retail, artists' village, foundry, indoor/outdoor ceremonial area, interpretive landscaping, dance grounds, and outdoor amphitheater
Client: American Indian Cultural Center Foundation
Institutional Planning: Lord Cultural Resources, Inc.
Museum Exhibit Planning and Design: Ralph Applebaum Associates
Indigenous Peoples History Consultant: Don L. Fixico, Ph.D., University of Arizona
Landscape Architect: Hargreaves Jones
Engineering: ARUP, Nabih Youssef Associates, Stantec
Civil Engineer: The Benham Group
Local Architect: Hornbeek Blatt Architects
Art Direction Consultant: Rick Carter
Economics: Harrison Price Company
Agency Representative: Architectural Design Group (ADG), Inc.
Lighting Design: David Weiner Design
Earned Income Consultant for Cultural Institutions: Manask & Associates
Interpretive exhibit planning and design: Andrew Merriell & Associates, LLC
Museum development and facility planning: Exhibition Associates
Museum Retail Consultant: Shelley Stephens + Associates

YMCA Piers
San Francisco Piers 27, 29, and 31, California, USA
Urban Waterfront Redevelopment
Planning and Urban Design Dates: 2001–2002
Site Area: 23 acres
Program: Maritime-related office, recreational enterprises, retail, restaurants and cafes, sports courts, maritime and outdoor oriented public open space
Client: YMCA San Francisco and Mills Development Corporation
Landscape Architect: SWA Group
Civil & Traffic Engineer: Korve Engineering, Inc.
Associate Architect: Michael Willis, FAIA; D'Agostino Izzo Quirk (D'AIQ) Architects, Inc.
Historical Architect: TreanorHL
Maritime Consultant: TranSystems Corporation
Legal: Kay & Merkle, LLP
Structural Engineer: KL&A, Inc. of California; McNamara Salvia
MEP Consultant: Flack + Kurtz Consulting Engineers
Parking Consultant: Walker Parking Consultants/Engineers

West LA Veterans Administration Campus
Los Angeles, California, USA

• APA California, Urban Design Award
• APA Los Angeles, Planning Award

Campus Master Plan and Urban Design
Planning and Urban Design Dates: 2015–2016
Site Area: 388 acres
Program: Permanent supportive housing, hospital, services, amenities, administrative office, and public open space
Client: Veterans Advocacy Associates (VAA)
Legal 1: Munger, Tolles & Olson (MTO), LLP
Legal 2: Public Counsel
Legal 3: ACLU of Southern California
Environmental Site Assessment: Geosyntec Consultants, Inc.
Cost Consultant: Jones Lang LaSalle (JLL), Inc.

Disney ABC Studios
Santa Clarita, California, USA
Film/Television Studio Master Planning and Urban Design
Planning and Urban Design Dates: 2008–2012
Site Area: 56 acres
Program: Production offices, studio offices, sound stages, talent support space, production support, back lot, studio mills, and commissary
Client: Disney-ABC Television Group
Landscape Architect: Laurie Olin, OLIN Studio
Sound Stage Consultant: Scott Carter

Dreamworks SKG Studio
Los Angeles, California, USA
Film/Television Studio Master Plan
Planning and Urban Design Dates: 1995–1996
Site Area: 100 acres
Program: Production offices, studio offices, sound stages, talent support space, production support, back lot, studio mills, and commissary
Client: Dreamworks SKG
Urban Design Consultant: Jonathan Barnett, FAIA, AICP
Landscape Architect: Laurie Olin, OLIN Studio
Art Direction Consultant: Rick Carter

KNOWLEDGE

Amgen
Thousand Oaks, California, USA
Bio-Tech Campus Planning & Urban Design
Planning and Urban Design Dates: 1995–present
Site Area: 120 acres
Program: Research laboratories, administrative offices, food services, product manufacturing, facilities, warehousing, childcare, athletic facilities and other amenities, arts programs, and open space
Client: Amgen
Landscape Architect: Meléndrez Design Partners, Mia Lehrer + Associates
Civil Engineer: Crosby Mead Benton & Associates
Traffic Engineer: Crain & Associates, Inc.
Lighting: Horton Lees Brogden Lighting Design
Fountain Consultant: STO Design Group, Inc.
Signage & Graphics: Sussman/Prejza & Company, Inc.

Genentech
South San Francisco, California, USA
Bio-Tech Campus Planning & Urban Design
Planning and Urban Design Dates: 2003–2012
Site Area: 98 acres
Program: Research laboratories, administrative offices, food service, athletic facilities and other amenities, and open space
Client: Genentech, Inc.

Jet Propulsion Laboratory (JPL)
Pasadena, California, USA
Science and Technology Campus Master Planning
Planning and Urban Design Date: 2003
Site Area: 130 acres
Program: Research laboratories, administrative offices, food services and other amenities, and open space
Client: Jet Propulsion Laboratory
Landscape Architect: Mia Lehrer + Associates
Civil Engineer: Crosby Mead Benton & Associates
Traffic Engineer: Linscott Law Greenspan, Engineers (LLG)

Knowledge City
Houston, Texas, USA

- AIA Los Angeles, NEXT LA Award

New Town Master Planning and Environmental Resource Master Planning
Planning and Urban Design Dates: 2012–2016
Site Area: 15,000 acres
Program: New town development, nature conservation, urban forestry, and agriculture
Client: Twinwood U.S., Inc.
Development Economics: RCLCO Fund Advisors
Marketing and Positioning: Cecilian Worldwide
Landscape Architect: Hargreaves Jones
Civil Engineering and Hydrology: Sherwood Design Engineers: LJA Engineers
Agricultural Consultant: Daron Joffe, Farmer D Consulting

University of California Berkeley, College of Engineering
Berkeley, California, USA
College Facilities Master Plan
Planning and Urban Design Dates: 2001–2002
Site Area: 10 acres
Program: laboratories, offices, auditorium, cafe food service, conference rooms, and classrooms
Client: University of California Berkeley (UCB)
Landscape Architect: Ken Kay Associates

University of California Irvine, Main Street
Irvine, California, USA

- AIA National, Urban Design Award
- Progressive Architecture Design Award

University Campus Master Planning and Urban Design
Planning and Urban Design Dates: 1986–1987
Site Area: 35 acres
Program: library and administration, cultural center, university guest house, commercial, retail, parking
Client: University of California Irvine (UCI)
Landscape Architect: SWA Group
Civil Engineer: RBF Consulting, LLC
Traffic Engineer: Kunzman Associates
Transportation Engineer: University of California Irvine Institute of Transportation Studies

Chadwick School
Palos Verdes Peninsula, California, USA
School Campus Master Planning and Programming
Planning and Urban Design Dates: 2007–2008
Site Area: 55 acres
Program: Village school facility, student center, media center, faculty and staff housing, teaching pavilions, and studio classrooms
Client: Chadwick School

Los Angeles Unified School District Campuses
Los Angeles, California, USA
Site Master Planning
Planning and Urban Design Dates: 2013–2015
Site Area: 45 school campuses
Program: Facilities master planning for high schools, middle schools, and elementary schools
Client: Los Angeles Unified School District

REGION

Jinjiang River Corridor
Chengdu, Sichuan, China

- AIA California Council, Urban Design Award
- AIA Los Angeles, Next LA Awards
- Architectural Record, China Awards

Conceptual Master Plan and Land Use Policy Recommendations
Planning and Urban Design Date: 2007
Site Area: 69,000 acres
Program: Low-impact urban development, river watershed protection, historic town redevelopment, agricultural and forest preservation
Client: Shuangliu District Municipal Planning Bureau

Long Quan Yi District
Chengdu, Sichuan, China

- First Place, International Design Competition

Regional Urban and Rural Planning
International Design Competition Date: 2005
Site Area: 138,000 acres
Program: New urban business district, automobile manufacturing expansion, research and development, university, commercial office, retail, cultural and civic, financial, residential, agricultural, tourism, and nature preservation
Client: Long Quan Yi Municipal Government

Chinese Whiskey Valley
Gulin (Luzhou), Sichuan, China
Strategic Master Plan
Planning and Urban Design Dates: 2011–2013
Site Area: 787,000 acres
Program: Watershed and water resources protection, forest resources protection, town and village centers, and mixed-use development
Client: Gulin District Municipal Government

Tianjin Ancient Wetland Restoration
Tianjin, China
Regional Sustainable Development Planning
Planning and Urban Design Date: 2008
Site Area: 83,000 acres
Program: Historic wetland restoration, urban agriculture, residential communities, and two mixed-use urban centers
Client: Tianjin Real Estate Development & Management Group Co., Ltd.

Guangzhou Economic Development District
Guangzhou, Guangdong, China

- First Place, International Design Competition

Redevelopment Plan and Urban Design
International Design Competition Date: 2003
Site Area: 53,000 acres
Program: Mixed-use redevelopment within a manufacturing district
Client: The International Design Competition Committee for Guangzhou Development District Development Master Planning and Urban Design

LA Greenways
Los Angeles, California, USA

- AIA Los Angeles, Urban Design Award
- Progressive Architecture, Award for Urban Design
- MOCA Exhibition, "Urban Revisions"

Regional Open Space and Development Planning
Planning and Urban Design Dates: 1993–1994
Site Area: Los Angeles County, over 3 million acres
Program: Greenways and land use recommendations for 400 miles of abandoned rail rights of way, river and flood control channels, and infrastructure rights of way throughout Los Angeles County
Client: Pacific Earth Resources, Ltd.

IMAGE CREDITS

Page 20–21: The 111th
Page 22: Google Earth (image spread to page 23)
Page. 24: Google Earth (top and bottom)
Page 26–27: The 111th
Page 30: Johnson Fain (top and bottom)
Page 31: Johnson Fain
Page 33: Mark Lohman
Page 34–35: Johnson Fain (purchased from iStock)
Page 36–37: weknowsf.com
Page 38: Karl Nielsen Photography (image spread to page 39)
Page 39: The OLIN Studio (top), Justin Yap (bottom)
Page 40–41: Karl Nielsen Photography
Page 42: Google Earth (Image spread to page 43)
Page 46–47: Johnson Fain (purchased from Getty Image)
Page 50: Google Earth (image spread to page 51)
Page 52: Qingyan Zhu (image spread to Page 53)
Page 56–57: Qingyan Zhu
Page 58–59: Qingyan Zhu
Page 60–61: Qingyan Zhu
Page 62: Google Earth (image spread to page 63)
Page 70: Google Earth (image spread to page 71)
Page 78: Google Earth (image spread to page 79)
Page 80–81: Chengdu Wide Horizon Investment Co., Ltd
Page 82: Chengdu Wide Horizon Investment Co., Ltd (bottom)
Page 84–85: Chengdu Wide Horizon Investment Co., Ltd
Page 86: Google Earth (image spread to page 87)
Page 88: John Messer (image spread to page 89)
Page 90: John Messer (top and bottom)
Page 92: John Messer (top and bottom)
Page 93: John Messer (top and bottom)
Page 94: Google Earth (image spread to page 9)
Page 96: Ian Espinoza (image spread to page 97)
Page 100: Ian Espinoza (top and bottom)
Page 101: Ian Espinoza (top and bottom)
Page 102–103: Ian Espinoza
Page 104: Google Earth (image spread to page 105)
Page 108: Johnson Fain (all six images)
Page 109: Johnson Fain
Page 112: HemisFair (all three images)
Page 113: HemisFair (top and bottom)
Page 114: Google Earth (image spread to page 115)
Page 116–117: Alfred Twu, Wikimedia
Page 118: Jim Simmons
Page 120: Johnson Fain
Page 121: Johnson Fain
Page 122–123: Juan Tallo
Page 124: Google Earth (image spread to page 125)
Page 132: Google Earth (image spread to page 133)
Page 138: Johnson Fain (all four images)
Page 139: Johnson Fain
Page 140: Google Earth (image spread to page 141)
Page 142–143: Johnson Fain
Page 144: Norm Kondy (bottom)
Page 145: Norm Kondy (bottom)
Page 147: Norm Kondy (top)
Page 148: Norm Kondy (top)
Page 149: Norm Kondy (top)
Page 150–151: Mel Willis Photography
Page 152: Google Earth (image spread to page 153)
Page 156–157: Mel Willis Photography
Page 159: Mark Lohman (top and bottom)
Page 160: Larry Perron (all three images)
Page 161: Johnson Fain (three bottom images)
Page 162: Kansas Historical Society (top), Oklahoma Historical Society (bottom left), Seth Eastman (bottom right)
Page 163: Oklahoma Historical Society (top left), Unknown, Wikimedia “Eagle Dance” (top right), Dorothy Sarah Lee, Wikimedia (bottom)
Page 164: Johnson Fain (all six images)
Page 165: Johnson Fain
Page 166: Mel Willis Photography (image spread to page 167)
Page 167: Jim Pepper Henry (all three images)
Page 168: Johnson Fain
Page 169: Johnson Fain
Page 170–171: Scott McDonald
Page 172–173: Scott McDonald
Page 174–175: Scott McDonald
Page 176: Google Earth (image spread to page 177)
Page 178: Google Earth (top)
Page 180: Piatt Associates (top), Johnson Fain (bottom)
Page 181: Piatt Associates (top), Johnson Fain (bottom two images)
Page 182: Google Earth (image spread to page 183)
Page 188: John Messer (top and bottom)
Page 189: John Messer
Page 190: Google Earth (image spread to page 191)
Page 192–193: Al Forster
Page 194: Al Forster (top)
Page 195: Al Forster (top)
Page 196: Google Earth (image spread to page 197)
Page 198: Johnson Fain (top and bottom)
Page 199: Mark Lohman
Page 200: Johnson Fain (bottom)
Page 201: Johnson Fain (all three images)
Page 202–203: Mark Lohman
Page 204–205: Mark Defeo
Page 206: Google Earth (image spread to page 207)
Page 208: Google Earth (top and bottom)
Page 212–213: Mark Defeo
Page 214: Johnson Fain
Page 215: Johnson Fain (top), Benny Chant/ Fotoworks (bottom)
Page 216: Benny Chan/Fotoworks (image spread to page 217)
Page 217: Benny Chant/ Fotoworks
Page 218: Benny Chan/Fotoworks (image spread to page 219)
Page 219: Benny Chant/ Fotoworks
Page 220: Google Earth (image spread to page 221)
Page 222: Google Earth (left)
Page 225: Herb Lingl
Page 226: Google Earth (image spread to page 227)
Page 228: Larry Perron (top and bottom)
Page 232: NASA/JPL-Caltech
Page 233: NASA
Page 234: Google Earth (image spread to page 235)
Page 241: Hargreaves Jones (bottom two)
Page 246: Google Earth (image spread to page 247)
Page 248: Tim Griffith
Page 250: Photo courtesy of http://philip.greenspun.com
Page 252: Google Earth (image spread to page 253)
Page 258: Mark Lohman (bottom two)
Page 260: Google Earth (image spread to page 261)
Page 262: Chadwick School (image spread to page 263)
Page 268: Google Earth (image spread to page 269)
Page 274–275: Ian Espinoza
Page 276: Google Earth (image spread to page 277)
Page 280–281: Ian Espinoza
Page 282: Johnson Fain (bottom)
Page 283: Johnson Fain (bottom)
Page 284: Google Earth (image spread to page 285)
Page 289: Jason_she, Wikimedia (bottom)
Page 290: Google Earth (image spread to page 291)
Page 293: Johnson Fain
Page 302: Google Earth (image spread to page 303)
Page 310: Google Earth (image spread to page 311)
Page 316: Zhonghui Bao (bottom)
Page 318: Google Earth (image spread to page 319)
Page 323: Paula Goldman (bottom left)
Page 324: Johnson Fain

ORO Editions
Publishers of Architecture, Art, and Design
Gordon Goff: Publisher

www.oroeditions.com
info@oroeditions.com

Published by ORO Editions

Library of Congress Control Number: 2022923666

Author: William H. Fain, Jr.
Book Design: Kurt Hauser
Pre-press assitance: CircularStudio
Project Manager: Jake Anderson
10 9 8 7 6 5 4 3 2 1 First Edition

ISBN: 978-1-957183-97-8

Color Separations and Printing: ORO Editions Inc.
Printed in China

ORO Editions makes a continuous effort to minimize the overall carbon footprint of its publications. As part of this goal, ORO, in association with Global ReLeaf, arranges to plant trees to replace those used in the manufacturing of the paper produced for its books. Global ReLeaf is an international campaign run by American Forests, one of the world's oldest nonprofit conservation organizations. Global ReLeaf is American Forests' education and action program that helps individuals, organizations, agencies, and corporations improve the local and global environment by planting and caring for trees.